Once you decide on your occupation
you must immerse yourself in your work.
You have to fall in love with your work…
dedicate your life to mastering your skill.
That's the secret of success…
And it is the key to being regarded honorably.

Jiro Ono, Japanese sushi chef

TO THE INTERVIEWEES

Thank you for telling your stories, including success and failure, insight and confusion, lessons learned, and for thoughtfully answering follow up questions and finally for taking the time to review the draft of your interview for intent and errors. To a person, I enjoyed meeting and spending with you and I wish you all the very best.

BUILDER

Builders & Tradesmen Tell Their Stories

MARK Q. KERSON

Copyright © 2021 by Mark Q. Kerson

BUILDER, Builders & Tradesmen Tell Their Stories, all rights reserved. No part of this book may be used or reproduced in any manner without the written permission from the author, except in the case of brief quotations in articles and reviews.

For information, write to 514 Americas Way, #3180, Box Elder, SD 57719 or email, eob@dplus.net

Printed in the United States of America.

First Edition, 2021

ISBN: 978-0-9913277-1-3

Book layout & design by Deb Tremper,
Six Penny Graphics: www.sixpennygraphics.com

Editing by Michael & Pam Rosenthal, P&M Editorial Services:
https://pmeditorial.com

Sean Hepburn, mason/photographer, Dorset England, did the beautiful cover and title page photograph which he graciously gave me permission to use.
www.seanhepburn.co.uk
foto.synthesis.com@gmail.com

CONTENTS

Preface xi

Acknowledgements xiii

PLEASE READ THESE NOTES xv

David Lorber, *General Contractor* 1

Jim Fleming, *Cabinetmaker, Carpenter, General Contractor* 17

Gail Grycel, *Retired Cabinetmaker* 31

Dan Kolbert, *General Contractor* 41

Jesper Kruse, *General Contractor* 59

Pat Reardon, *General Contractor* 77

Heather Thompson, *General Contractor* 89

David Stuart Bull, *Chimney Sweep* 107

Sal Alfano, *General Contractor* 113

Chris Fralick, *Cabinetmaker* 137

Stephen Uhle, *Automotive Machinist* 141

Morgan Reiter, *Retired Yurt Builder* 147

Nick Nott, *Fixer-Upper / General Contractor* 153

Matt Risinger, *Home Builder, Blogger* 161

Bernie Calcote, *General Contractor* 171

Jarod Teichmer, *Carpenter / General Contractor* 179

René McIntosh, *Office Work* 187

Deva Rajan, *Retired General Contractor* 191

Otis Miller, *Home Repairs* 209

Desiree Bolman, *Remodeling Contractor* 215

Stephen (Steve) Nicholls, *Remodeler, Cabinet Maker, GC* 229

Paul Eldrenkamp, *General Contractor* 243

Iris Harrell, *Retired General Contractor* 271

David Gerstel, *Retired General Contractor* 287

Bill M. Fink, *Retired General Contractor* 303

Michael McVey, *Remodeling/Restoration Contractor* 317

Steve Ferguson, *Cabinetmaker* 327

Chris Clark, *Electrician* 333

APPENDIX 345

NINE KEYS TO SUCCESS IN THE BUILDING BUSINESS 347

GROSS PROFIT vs MARKUP,
David Lorber 348

INSURANCE NOTES,
David Lorber 349

CREATE A HOMETOWN SPLINTER GROUP,
David Gerstel 352

THE JOURNAL OF LIGHT CONSTRUCTION (JLC),
Mike Reitz 353

PROCESS OF LEARNING TO ESTIMATE,
Sal Alfano 355

THE PERFECT WALL,
Sal Alfano 357

IT'S A MYTH THAT THE LOW BID ALWAYS WINS,
Sal Alfano 358

ANONYMOUS 361

TERMS & DEFINITIONS 363

PREFACE

The idea for *BUILDER* arose from *WORKING*, Studs Terkel's wonderful book of interviews with blue-collar and no-collar workers in America.[1] In the introduction Studs quotes one of his interviewees, Nora Watson, "Most of us, like the assembly line worker, have jobs that are too small for our spirit." But for many builders construction is a calling, offering freedom and creativity and, if one persists, a fundamental value in the process and the result.

If *The Elements of Building*,[2] my first book, is a textbook about the business of contracting, *BUILDER* is a gathering of insights and the telling of tales. It offers guiding principles, lessons learned, and a glimpse into why we take up a trade and why so many of us are passionate about what we do. Its purpose, apart from telling these wonderful stories, is to help you navigate the process of opening and growing a company, by listening in as builders explain what they wish they'd known, how they learned, and what they would have done differently. Take the time to understand what is said, implement what you learn, and the process of creating and running a construction company will be significantly easier.

Throughout *BUILDER*, we are reminded that the best of us value honesty, quality, and relationships first, that we never stop learning, and that everyone, without exception, has made too many mistakes to count. It is also clear—despite the bone-deep difficulty of being a good builder—that many of us hold sacred beliefs about what we do and that the work provides ample room for our spirit.

1   WORKING, People Talk About What They Do All Day And How They Feel About What They Do, Studs Terkel, The New Press, 1997.
2   The Elements of Building, A Business Handbook for Residential Builders & Tradesman, Mark Q. Kerson, From The Ground Up Publishing, 2014.

ACKNOWLEDGEMENTS

While working on *BUILDER*, each time I struggled I asked one or all of you for help, and solutions were found. As indispensable as your knowledge and ideas were, your interest and ongoing encouragement is what I'm most grateful for. The rotating people in the writers' group in Borrego Springs, and the Zoom group, as we switched to online meetings, helped shape the idea. Bill Smith, an anthropology professor before retiring and a sometime neighbor, for reading the early interviews and offering useful insights. Isaac Kerson, my son, whose ideas are seen throughout and about whom, once again, I was reminded how damn smart he is. Sam & Katah, my brother and his wife, both artists, with useful insights about the first round of interviews and design issues, as was Earl Sepella, a friend and one-time builder. Robin Halford a friend who I often imagined saying to herself, Again, we have to talk about this *AGAIN!*, but her unerring common sense was an ideal sounding board. Marc Estrin, a book publisher in Vermont and old friend, graciously offered ideas and suggestions. David Gerstel, for our years-long discussions around this topic. David told me he wished he'd thought of the idea for *BUILDER*. I suspect he was encouraging me rather than stating a fact, but whatever his reason, it helped. Ezra Tishman, a dear friend, and rare book seller, for help with the title and an occasional insight. Sophia Kerson, my niece, while visiting for part of the winter 2020, graciously rough-edited several of the longer transcripts. Thank you, beautiful Sophia! Mike Reitz for his always useful thoughts on writing and publishing and his wonderful story about *The Journal of Light Construction,* which will be found in the appendix. And Steve Getlein, a retired newspaper editor who patiently suffered through my musings and questions in phone calls and emails as I struggled to learn how to stay true to people's voice and ideas while compressing the text.

As with every human endeavor, it was more fun and rewarding to work on this book with the help and support of people I admire and love. I am deeply grateful to you all and a few who are not mentioned. Thank you.

PLEASE READ THESE NOTES

- ∞ Within each interview will be found footnotes for terms specific to that interview. Terms with a caret (^) next them indicate the term will be found in the Terms & Definitions at the back of the book. If you find an unfamiliar term without a caret, look in the Terms & Definitions, you might find a definition there anyway.
- ∞ You will find helpful notes in the Appendix, including how to work with insurance companies, ideas on learning to estimate, a story by the founder of The Journal of Light Construction, and several other pieces.
- ∞ The initials EOB, which will be found throughout this book, refer to *The Elements of Building*.[1]
- ∞ Contact information is provided for the people interested in readers visiting their website or contacting them. By extension, no contact information indicates that they have chosen not to be contacted: please respect their wishes.
- ∞ The opinions expressed in this book are those of the interviewees or author. If you choose to follow one, some, or all of them, be thoughtful in how you use the information. The interviewees and author disclaim responsibility for any adverse effects resulting directly or indirectly from how you use anything in this book.

---

1 *The Elements of Building, A Business Handbook for Residential Builders & Tradesman*, Mark Q. Kerson, From The Ground Up Publishing, 2014.

Be impressed by kindness, generosity, warmth, intelligence, humility, creativity, integrity, and hard work. Don't be impressed by money, flash, degrees, looks, titles.

David Lorber,
General Contractor

dleelorber@gmail.com

David is sixty-five at the time of this interview and he looks and talks like a contractor. If you were in the business, you could tell from a hundred paces what he does for a living. He works in the Bay Area, around San Francisco. He matter-of-factly refers to himself as a contractor's contractor, and in his case, the idea strikes me as exactly right. His father was a contractor and his formal training was in junior high school shop classes, the unions, and his dad's business.

> *I woke up one morning and realized that building houses was the coolest thing in the world* ■ *In construction—unlike the tech industry—there's never going to be a sugar daddy who thinks you're a unicorn* ■ *A good tradesman, in addition to having integrity, loves working with his hands* ■ *Business is about relationships* ■ *I do consultative selling* ■ *If you don't know what you are estimating, you've got no business doing it* ■ *You've got to be extremely sensitive to overhead* ■ *It ain't about how much volume you do, it's about how much money you put in your pocket* ■ *My dad said, "Better to go broke because you are too expensive, rather than too cheap."* ■ *There are two types of guys: the guy who loves the craft, like me, and the guy who loves the business*

The business I own now, belonged to my father. I've worked in it since I was twelve, when my dad took me to work on Saturdays and I began sweeping up the shop. At sixteen, on summer vacation, I started driving to pick up materials and working on jobs. When I graduated high school, I went to junior college three days a week and worked in the field the other days. In junior high and high school, shop class was compulsory and there were tests and the teachers were strict. My father's business was a union shop, so I got formal training doing a union apprenticeship program. I took carpentry classes, theory, math, and related trades. We had great instructors.

I was living with my parents and I got a job with a guy who was building a new house across the street. It was 1974, I was making around six bucks an hour as an apprentice carpenter. After we finished, a friend wanted to take a trip to Alaska, so we went. It was the beginning of the pipeline boom and the money was really good. I got a job as mason tender and then as a carpenter for a general contractor. I was twenty-three, and all of a sudden, I'm running his projects. I learned about doing material take-offs and how to work with people. The subs were much more experienced than me. One explained how important it is to give capable people autonomy, another said, "Ask ten questions before you make one mistake." Now I tell my guys, "If you're not sure, don't fake it, ask as many questions as you want." and "Here's the job, this is how I think it can be done, and here's the materials you will need." I check in, but I leave them alone. Working for that general contractor was an incredible experience for a young man and I worked for him for several years.

What is a contractor's contractor and what is most rewarding about what you do?

You've heard of a doctor's doctor; the guy doctors go to when they get sick? If a guy can't do the work and the customer needs somebody to get it done, I'd be the guy they want to hire. It is the reason people hire me in the first place and why we get so much repeat business. It's never because we're cheap.

In business, there's an initial meeting with a customer, a concept meeting, and the project evolves through conversation. You spend months building it, you get everything done, they write the last check, you say, "Thank you very much." They call you back a month or year later on some occasion, the family has moved into the space, it's their home, you are surrounded by this thing that started as a concept. That's extremely rewarding.

How did you transition to working full time in your dad's business?

In '79, the pipeline work was tapering off and new construction collapsed. Besides, I was tired of those winters. The Bay Area was booming, and my dad said he needed help, so I moved back. My first project was a big deck, and then kitchens and baths. We had three lead carpenters, a couple of laborers, a tile setter, and three girls in the office. I worked with my tools for maybe a year—my dad's superintendents never lasted more than a year—so he asked me to do it. I begin running all the jobs so he could focus on sales. *I absolutely hated it.* Most of his guys had been in the company for fifteen or twenty years—they were my dad's contemporaries—and they didn't like taking orders from me. Subcontractors, same thing. I was trying to keep promises that the salesmen made—they set the customers' expectations so high it was difficult to meet them—so I was the one the customer and salesmen were pissed off at. The job documents were not remotely as detailed as they are today and the customer would say, "That's not what so-and-so said it was going to look like." I'd call so-and-so, he was onto the next job and not interested in this one.

While you had the superintendent's job, were you learning about business?

I was learning through osmosis. My dad began sharing profit and loss statements with me. He showed me how a 38 percent gross profit, versus 42 percent, versus 30 percent, changed the bottom line. We estimated with a 40 percent or more gross profit. If something cost you a $1000, you've got to sell it for $1700.[1] The sales commission came out of the gross profit. I learned quickly that 10 percent overhead and 10 percent profit is nonsense. I have no idea where that started, but the insurance companies still use it. It may work on commercial jobs, because on a $100 million dollar project, 10 and 10 is a hell of a lot of money. But residential and commercial numbers are totally different. Companies that survive in this industry are figuring *at least* a 30 percent gross profit if they are running a legitimate business, and if they aren't charging that much, they don't survive.

---

1 David's math: "$1000 (hard cost) X .70 = $1700. Take the $1700, deduct $1000 (hard costs), and divide the remaining $700.00 (gross profit) by $1700.00, that gives you a 40 percent gross profit (rounded)."

Around 1979–80 the country went into a deep recession. Our company got real small, real fast. We still had a few jobs, and because we ran a tight ship and didn't have a lot of overhead, we were making money and we survived, and after the bloodletting we came back. Later on, I decided I wanted to run a big company with a bunch of people—at some point we all seem to aspire to be a big-time builder— but I learned fast that you have to pay for all of that stuff and to do that you've got to keep the cash register ringing and that is hard to do. I finally learned—it took me years—it's not about volume, because when things go bad, you can lose three-hundred grand in a month and then you're looking at bankruptcy. I've chosen to go completely in the other direction. In the last twenty years or so, I've kept it small.

That was a big lesson for me. For the uninitiated, it seems reasonable that the bigger the volume, the bigger the profit and salary. But from what I've seen and lived, this ain't necessarily so. I have seen businesses with gross revenue in the low eight figures [$10 million] 'whose principals were pulling five-figure salaries [$99,000] or less, and the risk is far too great for the return. There are large companies doing better, but I believe these are anomalies. I have also seen excellent, well-managed large companies that did well for years but were unable to survive one of the nasty recessions that are as much a part of this business as lumber and concrete.

How did you transition to owning your dad's business?

My dad was a three-pack-a-day smoker, he got lung cancer in '83 and had a lung removed. He was ready to get out. I was comfortable with what was required to run the business but needed help. I had a friend who was a smart guy and a good salesman and marketer, so I asked if he wanted to buy the business with me. We paid my dad $200,000 and we bought a building that was around $350,000, and we had to renovate it. We got a small business loan; it was a lot of debt for young guys. We worked our asses off. I was putting in twelve-hour days, six days a week, and we were doing well. We paid off that loan in four or five years.

I said to my partner, "These are the rules. We are no longer a sales-driven company. Don't promise when we can do the work, how long it will take, or how much it will cost, until you check with me, and don't you dare tell them they will get something that is not written in the contract." We used checklists and drawings, so we knew exactly what it was going to take to produce a job. Once a project was sold, I went over every detail and got it in writing or on the drawings. We were 99 percent design/build and we had about fifteen employees.

What advice have you given most often to builders and tradesmen?

I don't think you should do this! [*Laughter.*] I have young guys say, "I've got an opportunity to do this project. What do you think?" I ask, "Do you own a house? Do you have assets? If you don't, do it, because you are not exposed." I tell them, "If you can, keep things out of your name to limit liability and don't take a job with a big foundation repair or a second-story addition—that will get you in trouble." I tell them to keep it small and make friends with designers and architects to get business and don't do design/build, at least at first.

What don't you like about building now?

There is so much not to like these days: building departments, guys working under the table, insurance (for each of my guys over sixty I write a check every month for over $1000 for medical insurance). The number of homeowners who deliberately work without permits and hire "contractors" who use undocumented illegals and cheap labor, paying under the table—no payroll taxes, social security, liability insurance, worker's compensation, or medical leave—is astonishing. Fortunately, we have been able to find people who value our approach to business: honesty, quality, fairness, and playing by the rules. I don't like walking into a building department where it takes six months to get a permit to build a deck and—while I'm doing my damnedest to run a tight ship—they treat me like a criminal. I really don't like that. The coding system is the reason houses are so absurdly complicated, and therefore impossibly expensive, and in part, why we don't have enough housing.

When you took over the business, did you have long-term goals?

Yes. To establish the business so it became a household name for remodeling and construction in the Oakland area, to set up systems to run it, and then to step back from the business. The idea came from the book, *The E-Myth*.[2] The author uses McDonald's as an example. I believed it for a while, but it's baloney. There is an enormous difference between serving

---

2   Michael E Gerber, E-Myth, Why Most Small Businesses Don't Work & What To Do About It, Harper Collins Publishers, 1986

food and stepping into someone's "castle," tearing things apart, and building their dream kitchen. I've read about companies that claim to have figured it out, they might be out there, like UFOs, but I've never seen it done in this business.[3]

Did you have failures that set you up for later success?

Yeah, that first business failed. My partner and I were doing well, '86 through '89, and then the stock market collapsed; they called it Black Friday. At first, the East Coast got hit, and we were still riding a wave, and then everything collapsed. Then in '91 the Oakland fire burned three thousand houses in primo neighborhoods up in the hills. We rebuilt eight new homes between '91 and '94. We thought we'd have work for ten years, depression or no depression.

Up to that point, my experience with insurance companies was that they paid fifty cents on a dollar and guys were going broke doing insurance work. When the Oakland fires happened, I remembered a guy from a conference in Las Vegas who taught how to negotiate insurance settlements.[4] I hired him to help us work with the insurance companies. The way he showed us, we were getting a 40 percent gross profit. That was the best time I ever had in business. But because the entire country was in a recession, we had guys coming from everywhere to build houses and the work ended in three years, not ten, and then there was no work.

I bought my partner out in 1995. His heart was never in the business, we had almost no work, and he wanted out. I ended up closing that business and opening the company that I have now. I moved into a space with my electrical contractor, who was also suffering tremendously. I've been there for twenty-five years, running a small operation with three or four guys. We do around a million a year. It's a lot less pressure.

Is there a conflict for you between working in the field and running the business?

Working in the garden and doing woodworking, fulfills my desire to swing a hammer. At one point we had five to eight jobs going at once, so it was impossible for me to work in the field. Quite a bit later, when the

---

3   For what it's worth, neither have I.
4   See David's notes about how to work with insurance companies in the Appendix.

recession hit, I picked up my tools again, doing pickup work, because it was too expensive to send a guy back to a job for a few doorknobs.

How do you respond to this idea? If your goal is to be a tradesman, work for someone else. If your goal is to establish and build a significant company, put your tool belt aside and focus on business as soon as it is practical.

I think you can still have a business model of staying small and working for yourself. Around here, I don't think a guy can make enough working for someone else. If he is driven—ten- and twelve-hour days don't bother him—he's not going to be happy working for another guy anyway. The wages are low because of an inexhaustible pool of illegal immigrant labor, guys who work too cheap, and places like Home Depot. The competition is insane. If you had asked me thirty years ago, I might have given a different answer. The wages were better, and you could make a good living working for somebody else, eight hours a day, five days a week.

What advice do you give about money?

Money is the lifeblood of any business. Be careful with it, save it. Do not spend a dime you don't have to and put away every nickel you can. You can't always live like that, but if you do most of the time, you'll have enough to buy what you want. You don't need a new truck, and if you do, get one that's economical. Save money because you're going to need cash and assets. Think five times before you buy some fancy tool. Invest in things that make money. As a builder you can build sweat equity in real estate because you know how to build and you can get it done for a lot less than retail, maybe half of retail. Buy property, renovate it, and rent it.

Do you actively mentor your people?

Yes. Briefly, we did it formally, but these days it's me, on a job, showing people how to do things. I trained one of my guys to do sheet metal: cut, fit, template, and spot weld. I was on one job with a young guy—he's got a lot of experience at some things, but he did not know how to cut a jack rafter. I showed him how to lay it and gave some quick pointers. When I'm asking them to do something they are not familiar with, I'll take the time.

Thirty or forty years from now, I want somebody to look at something we've done and go, "Goddamn, these guys really knew what they were doing." Sometimes I stop my guys to point out some particularly well-done detail and say, "You see this? There's a guy that knew what he was doing. That's the kind of work I want you to do."

What would you tell someone to learn first as they were going into business?

Learn the difference between your cost and what to sell the job for. If you don't know that, you will go broke. You have to understand that every job has to make money. Have a pencil and notebook and write down how long every task takes. When somebody asks how much it will cost to do a job, you will have a point of reference.

One young guy who had worked for me—an aspiring contractor—was in over his head and asked me to look at 8-foot doors that were falling off the hinges in a big old house. The owners were supplying the doors and he told the people $1200 per opening for labor. It was going to be more like $7000 per opening. I told him, "Tell these people that it is going to cost five times more than you said." The first lesson: if you don't know what something will cost, work Time & Material. That's the sort of stuff I tell young guys.

How do you estimate, who does it, and do you ever look at a job and just "know" what it is going to cost?

No, I never know what a job will cost. I always do line-item estimates and give lump-sum pricing to the client. I will give some people a ballpark figure if it's the first meeting. I ask, "Have you thought about what this might cost?" About 80 percent of the time, they'll say no—which isn't true—and I'll say, "The least expensive kitchen I've done in the last four years is a hundred thousand dollars; what would you say to that?" They say, "It sounds pretty good," or "It's too high." Actually, we usually have that conversation on the phone.

I do our estimates. I use my own sheets of paper with tasks and how long each thing took, because I've tracked our costs for years. I've used Master Builder software since the mid-eighties[5] —we use a fraction of what the thing is capable of—but it tracks costs extremely well. The carpenter turns in a time card and my bookkeeper puts it in the system. If a job is complex, I'll

---

5 Master Builder software has become Sage 100 Contractor and focuses on small to midsized general contractors, specialty contractors, and home builders.

go to my CSI format^ checklist, which was generated when we started with computers. We took their list and cut out everything that wasn't pertinent and added what was relevant to us. Quite often I tell clients, "I will give you hard numbers on the things that I can, but I can't be sure about some things. On those I can't give you hard numbers."

How often do you miss with your estimates?

I have come up short on many estimates, for reasons too numerous to list, but carelessness and wishful thinking are at the top of that list. I can think of two times I sold jobs for less than it cost me to produce them. Those are hard lessons.

I remember my dad telling me—funny how the older I get the smarter he becomes—"When you bomb on a job, it is rarely because you screwed up on just one thing, it's because you were a little short on everything." I have found this to be true. Therefore, you need to be extremely careful when estimating your labor and getting accurate pricing from subs. And you need to be as clear as possible in defining the subs' scope-of-work and the expectations that you have for them. This takes hard work—site visits, careful communication, and often, long discussions— "Did you see the note, S2.1, on the plans?" or "How will you get those ducts (or pipes or wires) upstairs?" Also, these conversations help uncover things that you might have missed.

Do you bid work?

I can't remember a job I've bid in years. When I hear the word "bid," I ask people if they understand that a bid assumes a set of drawings and specifications—half the time they don't—and I explain that it has to be a level playing field; everybody's got to have insurance, pay prevailing wage, and workers' compensation. I'll pull out a project that is similar to theirs and go through the scope-of-work and explain this was a $70,000 job, then I'll describe another one, fancier, that cost $100,000. Eighty percent of the time, they'll say, "I thought I could get this done for twenty grand." I say, "We'd love to work with you, and I totally understand."

If you had a method of reaching every builder and tradesmen in the U.S., what would you say?

Be fair to yourself, your family, and your employees. Charge enough to make a decent living.

What makes a construction company successful?

Good sales staff, good reputation, which comes from doing good work and requires good employees. Good estimating and accounting procedures, without those you are not going to succeed.

How did you learn to sell?

It was over a period of time. Working with salespeople and going to sales seminars, although a lot of what they told me I ignored. Where does high-pressure sales even work anymore? There is no place for it. I do consultive selling. I listen to what the client wants and ask questions and make suggestions. I assume nobody knows anything about building and explain, "This is what goes into this and this is how the process works and if we are going to work together, you need to know this." I know what I'm talking about, and that comes through. I under-promise and don't make promises I can't keep. I don't ever want somebody to say, "You promised…"

What about your best and worst customer makes them that?

Trust and generosity. The best customers that we have are those we've worked for in the past, who trust us implicitly and we trust them. We know they're fair if we're fair. Nobody likes writing big checks, but they do it because they know that they've gotten their money's worth. There's a mutual respect. Those are my best customers.

The worst: I know that woman! [*Laughter.*] She hid who she was; she was sneaky and nasty and the worst customer I've ever had. The worst people don't trust you or your judgment. I don't get fooled often these days, but recently I had another one, and I knew I should not have taken the job. They were nice people, but they were indecisive, and indecision is a nightmare. I'd send a guy to set fifteen feet of baseboard and it took him all day because she was asking questions. I billed her for every frickin' dime. It was T&M and they paid every invoice.

Do you turn down customers, and if so, why?

It doesn't happen often now and when it does, it happens automatically. If I'm not getting along with somebody, they're not going to like me. And really bad customers go, "This guy's got too much experience, I'm not going to be able to manipulate him." They move on.

How do you respond to this quote by Richard Branson: "Clients do not come first. Employees come first. If you take care of your employees, they will take care of the clients."

I agree. Good employees automatically respect and take care of the people that we're working for.

What do you look for when you hire and what don't you expect from employees?

My best hire is somebody referred to me by someone whose opinion I respect. I don't hire out of the newspaper or off of Craigslist anymore. When I'm interviewing, I say, "Tell me what you've done and what you haven't done and where you've worked. If I put you on this kind of a job, how are you going to do?" Hopefully, he says, "I can do this and this, but I can't do that." Fortunately, now, I don't have to do it often.

I certainly don't expect them to take abuse from any customer. I say, "If somebody abuses you, be polite, call me, pack up your tools and leave. I'll deal with them." That's a conversation I've rarely had to have, but I have had it. I don't expect them to give me any time, they are paid for all the time they put in. I don't expect them to work on weekends unless the job calls for it and they've agreed in advance.

What's a bad tradesman and what makes a successful tradesman?

A guy that's not honest, doesn't give a day's work, and does sloppy work. They may be an excellent tradesman but they cheat on time. I've got no use for guys like that. It's not just tradesman, it's every possible job, some lawyers and doctors are deadbeats too.

Successful is a journeyman carpenter who can tackle 95 percent of the tasks that come his way and also, doesn't drink to excess, shows up on time—all the time—and earns the respect of the client and the people he works around.

How do you market your company and, if you have too much work, what do you do?

We have job signs and a website. We pay money for Diamond Certified.[6] I've been with them for a long time and I've gotten enough business that it

---

6   Diamond Certified is a rating agency for contactors and other services, in the Bay Area of California. Their web site: https://www.diamondcertified.org/

pays for itself. I do get some work from certain social things that I go to and a bicycle group I'm part of. We send out a newsletter from time to time to let people know we're still alive. My old customers keep me in business, so I keep in touch with them. Sometimes I call people.

When we have too much, I turn work away. I'm the project manager and superintendent, and I handle sales, so when we get too much work, I tell people, "I'd love to talk with you, but I can't get to it right now. I'll call when I have more time and, if you are still interested, we can talk." It is kind of self-regulating.

What would you tell a group of young tradesmen about getting an education apart from their trade?

Being well-rounded is *so* important. It is something that everybody should do. Education doesn't necessarily mean a classroom; you can learn by reading and listening to balanced programs.

Today, what is the best path to learning a trade?

Around here, figure out which trade you want and try to get involved in a union apprenticeship program. If you want a career as a tradesman, make up your mind to be the best at what you do (there will always be guys better than you, but that's the goal), and learn everything you possibly can about it. Union is the way to go. If you can't find a union, find a big, well-established company and work for them. You might want to get into the commercial end of things, because residential is so unprofessional these days. There are career opportunities in doing the big commercial stuff. Some states have non-union training programs. Find a good company, tell them what you want to do, show up every day and work hard. Try to make a deal with your employer to send you to night school in your trade. Most employers will say, "Hell yeah, we want to help you do that."

Word Association

Integrity: Doing what you say you're going to do.

Job safety: Very important, because we care about our employees.

Overhead: Be *very* sensitive to it.

Profit: Essential.

Marketing: Find somebody that's good at it because you probably ain't.

Sales: Critical to any business.

Estimating: Critical for success in the building business.

Employees: Choose them carefully. Take good care of them.

Company image: A no-nonsense company that delivers the goods.

Cut-Offs

There is a spirituality to this work. I think about the guys that are really good at what they do, the people that built the cathedrals. People like Michelangelo, that talent comes from somewhere.

I live in an area where the economy is strong and many people make a great deal of money, but we compete with trades who will commute three hours one way to work and who don't realize they are grossly undercharging.

On some jobs there are eleven inspections: under-floor, framing, electrical, plumbing, drywall, plywood nailing, and on and on. If you move a wall or a window in a remodel, the rule is that you can't make the building weaker, so you have to compensate. We have to call in a structural engineer who calls for hold-downs and plywood and there are inspections for all that.

When I was younger, I read in magazines about guys who were doing huge volume, and who were out on their yacht or flying their own plane. It was bullshit. But you don't know that when you are starting out.

I took over the business thinking, *There's gotta be a better way to do this. I am working too hard and not making enough money.*

Large volume requires large overhead, and overhead is the kryptonite of the full-service remodeling company. Using simple numbers, let's say you need to add $100,000 for overhead "to get to the next level"—in our area it would be double that—you now need to sell approximately $250,000 more at 40 percent gross profit or $303,000 at 33 percent. Not an easy task month after month, year after year, forever! And these figures are optimistic because with increased volume comes decreased efficiency, more client dissatisfaction, more warranty work, and greater stress on management.

I attended Business Networks^, and a couple of times a year we met around the country, seeing how other people ran their business. It was informative, we had a lot of fun, and it was *amazing* what some of these guys didn't know. I learned that our business was doing a lot correctly.

Stand in any building, on any street, in any town, and look around. Everything that you see, everything behind the walls, under the street, and over your head was put into place by a builder. Building is a science, requiring organization and engineering, and an art, requiring creativity and communication.

EOB

Jim Fleming,
Cabinetmaker, Carpenter, General Contractor

Jimmy is one of my oldest friends—we worked together at the start of our carpentry careers in the early '70s in Vermont—and among the best carpenters I've ever known. While visiting me in Virginia years later, while I was at work, Jimmy got bored and built a fireplace mantel from square stock material, entirely with a table saw, including cove molding, dentils, and fluted legs. He has a natural talent for the trade and remains—even after fifty years—fascinated by the process and the result. Jim turned seventy soon after we did this interview.

> *It's a whole lot easier to spread a bad reputation than a good one* ▪ *I've been working in the trades for fifty years* ▪ *Making money is not everything, money is a small part of life* ▪ *You have to pick your clients carefully and have faith in humanity* ▪ *I focused on what I was best at, finish work and cabinetry* ▪ *I might make more money if I bid, but we're talking about remodeling, you can't jack it up high enough to cover what you don't know* ▪ *I've built all kinds of things that were drawn on the back of a bar napkin* ▪ *Make sure your customers are satisfied; make sure you're making money; you can do both* ▪ *If you don't feel comfortable, there's a reason, go with your gut* ▪ *I've enjoyed my life and my career and my customers*

I went into the trades when I was thirteen with my father, who was an electrician. My old man wanted me to be an electrician, but I never liked the work, and eventually, we figured out that I was right, I was no electrician. [*Laughter.*] Working with my dad, I watched the guys building houses. It seemed like they should be having more fun, 'cause it looked cool. I wanted to be a builder. I still like the look of a stick-frame or post-and-beam building, seeing the bones, they just look right. In the beginning I was a laborer and apprentice framer, but I liked the finish end of things, and as soon as I could, I got into cabinetmaking and finish carpentry, which led to remodeling houses. I have two years of college, but it didn't help me much. I'd never been away from home, so it got me into trouble more than anything else. It was better to come home and go to work.

I was drawn to the trade because I've always liked wood. I can't tell you one tree from another but cut it into boards and I can tell you exactly what it is. When I was starting out, I met a woman with three kids, the next year we had twins, and you can't support five kids on the pay of an apprentice carpenter. I went into business so I could charge more. People asked me, "Can you do this?" I'd say, "Of course I can." They would give me the job and I'd go figure out how to do it. I have no formal training and most of the things I was taught, I found out were wrong.

What is most rewarding and most difficult about your trade?

The end product. On day one, as I talk to the client, I see the thing in my head. When it's finished and it looks like I thought it would, knowing I did that is extremely rewarding. I don't need anybody to tell me how great it is, I know already. What's difficult is getting too many things going at once and staying on task.

When you started, did you work for someone else and did it help in your career?

I had to start somewhere. You and I worked for one of the best builders in the area when we started. It helped. Somebody has to tell you to cover the X.[1] I liked listening to the older guys, they had great stories and I picked things up. When I work with young guys, I show them shortcuts. It's so obvious after you show them, they say, "Oh, jeez," but they don't see it until you show them.

---

1   When laying out top and bottom plates to frame a wall, they are marked with a line and an X at each point where a stud is to be placed. The line indicates were the stud goes, the X shows which side of the line the stud is nailed.

Talk about some mistakes you've made.

Oh, my God, do I have to? [*Laughter.*] I've made some terrible mistakes. One time we tied a new porch roof back into the main house, my guy did not flash the valley right. The roof leaked. I couldn't find it, couldn't find it, and finally I called a roofing company to find and fix the problem. It cost me a lot, but I took care of it. In 1988 I built a beautiful cabinet shop. It was much bigger than I would ever need and it was set up with the best equipment. I sold it. I wish I'd never done that.

My trade skills are quite good, my business skills are hippy dippy. I'm not a good bookkeeper or money manager. I just manage to keep running. I make mistakes all the time because I'm always correcting something I've done. I go a little too fast, I don't consider everything I should. I go slower now and plan things; being old makes it easier.

What's a good and a bad sub?

A good sub: above the building codes, on time, for a reasonable price. A bad sub: a guy that tells you he will be there and doesn't show up, also, it's in their attitude. You can tell when you talk to a guy if he knows what he's doing. If I come around and his butt's up and his head's down, he's working; if he's standing around talking to the electrician, how good is he?

What is the best path to learning a trade and what advice have you given most to tradesmen?

I don't know, nobody seems to want to learn a trade anymore. They're not interested because they are not going to learn it overnight. But apprenticeships are four years long for a reason. I'd tell them to go find a guy who is forty or fifty years old and go to work for him. Pay your dues. They say the absolute best way to teach a kid anything is one on one. If you go to work for a good tradesman and you're the only guy there, that's one on one. That's the best way to learn.

I heard this years ago and I still ask guys this: "Why is it that you don't have time to do it right the first time, but you have time to go back and fix it?" Take your time. Make it right the first time.

If you were to lecture to a class of aspiring tradesmen, what would you tell them to learn first?

Respect. Respect for the man who's telling you what you want to know. Pay attention and avoid showing up late. If you want a job, I guess it doesn't matter when you come to work, but if you want a career, it makes all the difference in the world. Learn all you can about everything! Read. Pay attention. Most of what I've learned is from watching and from people I've encountered and what occurs when I'm present. Find one thing and get nerdy about it, dig right into it. Keep your interests up and your mind open.

How would you describe a successful tradesman?

A guy with a big smile on his face. Life is good. He makes enough money, he's happy with what he does, he has a good reputation, and people respect him for what he does.

What about your best and worst customer makes them that?

I've got a husband and wife—he's a surgeon, but you wouldn't know it to talk to him—they are friendly and understand when someone does a good job and they appreciate it. The worst is the one that looks over your shoulder. I did a whole house remodel for a woman; I don't think she'd ever heard the word no. She was a nightmare. She would ask for things that were impossible and I'd have to say no, and she would storm off. That went on for a year and a half—it was a big job—and I was glad when it was done.

I turn people down, basically on first impression. I could be way off, but if I don't feel comfortable, I don't want to do it. When I meet a new client, I shake their hand and get a feeling if they are a happy or a grumpy person. If they're grumpy, they are not gonna be worth the aggravation. If I get along with them, I know I'll give them a good job, so everything's fine.

What do you look for when hiring?

I've made some terrible choices with employees. I've hired a lot of friends; that's seldom worked out. They took advantage of me because I let them get away with too much. At one point I had fourteen men trimming condominiums. I didn't make any more money than I made working by myself and I had all the headaches and the whining and crying. I don't like employees. [*Laughter.*]

What do you expect from employees?

I expect loyalty—not to bad-mouth me—or to steal from the job, and that they come to work when they should. If you're here to work, let's work, and if you're not, you don't have to work, but you can't stay here. I don't expect them to kill themselves, but they can't be on the phone or around the corner smoking cigarettes.

What advice would you give about hiring?

Be careful and thorough, and do not hire the first man you talk to. Thorough means taking half an hour, sitting down and asking what he's done, what he'd like to do, what he's most comfortable with, what he won't do, what he expects to get paid, and what he expects to get paid next year.

How do you let people go?

I hate that part of it! The people I work with become friends. When I have to say, "I gotta let you go," it hurts me as much as them. I feel I've let them down. I've fired people for stealing, being drunk, and one guy 'cause he was a goon. I had two guys who were friends, so I let them work together, they loaded thirty sheets of plywood from the job into their van and drove away. When I fired them, they were indignant.

What books have been most important to you?

Cabinetmaking and Millwork is a textbook, it helped me understand the machinery and the processes in a woodshop.[2] *Fine Woodworking* magazine—which you gave me my first subscription to—was really useful. It always seemed to come just before a job I had to do, but didn't know how to do, with an article explaining how to do it.

How do you market and sell?

I've never done marketing. I waited for word of mouth to get around. Because I don't advertise, somebody has to tell the customer about me. If they tell them something bad, they're not going to call me. If they call me, someone has done my marketing. In my career, the phone has always rung.

I learned to sell out of necessity. It's a little song and dance and we all have our own variety of it. We may start out with two left feet, but we work it out. I had to have work, so I convinced people that I knew what I was

---

2 Cabinetmaking and Millwork, fifth edition, John Louis Feirer, 1988.

doing, I won't gouge them, and I'd do what I said. I love the sales part. It's fun. I sell myself and I have answers because I know what I'm doing, and they feel confident in me and I'm confident I'm going to get paid. And they are glad to know I'll be doing the work—I'm not sending a crew—so it's a personal interaction, a little take and a little give. In the end they sign up and give me money! When I walk away, everybody's happy and they're glad to write the last check.

I would tell a new business owner to let the customer meet you, not your construction manager, because you are who they hire. I've always had a gut feeling about people—when it comes to picking women, I've been 100 percent off—but when it comes to customers, I've been 98 percent on. If I feel comfortable with you, we're good, if I don't, I'm never gonna. Also, regardless of my reputation, I'm not everybody's right guy.

How do you deal with nasty customers?

If you're into a job, committed, you can't allow yourself to break, but you gotta bend. You gotta keep it civil enough so that you get paid. If you're going to fight with them about everything, you're gonna fight to get your money. I always knew good from bad customers, but there's needing work too. If you're desperate, you don't care if the devil knocks on the door. Avoid him when you can, put up with him when you have to.

Is there a difference between how you sell now and how you sold twenty years ago?

I have a story for yeah. This guy calls me on a Saturday. He's right around the corner, and he asks me to come over to look at some work. I smoked a joint, so I was feeling good and I get there and he said, "Let me go over what I want done." He had this big stack of papers with all his jobs. I said, "I didn't come looking for a lot of work." He said, "Well, over here we have these sills...."[3] I said, "No, I don't do sills." He said, "Okay, my roof is..." I said, "No, no, I don't do roofs. Do you have anything waist-high?" At this point we started laughing. I fixed his deck; it was waist-high. [*Laughter.*] The

---

3   In New England, older wooden houses were built with an 8"x8" wood sill (or 10"x10", 12"x12", etc), usually laid on a stone foundation. A house floor and wall framing began on the sill.

difference between twenty years ago and now is that I don't care as much, I don't have a family to support.[4]

When you have too much work, what do you do?

I take them all on, get them started, and make them wait. And they do. I have two-bathroom remodels going on right now.

Did you have a conflict in running the business versus doing your trade?

I always let someone else do the paperwork and I had an accountant. I did the selling and billing, it's easy to figure out how much they owe me. That was the limit of it, the rest of the time I never left the field.

How did you learn to estimate?

By mistake. [*Laughter.*] In the beginning if somebody wants a price, you make mistakes and you eat those mistakes; when you don't know, you don't know. If you're smart, you only eat them once. Estimating is an entirely different thing from doing the trade and from running the business. It's a trade unto itself and you will save yourself a lot of headaches if you learn to do it well. At this point, I don't charge for material. The customer buys those materials that need to be selected, like a tub and tile, so it is always right, and I have the customer give the lumber yard a credit card, and every time I charge something, they get an email and know exactly what was spent. They feel they're getting a good deal—which they are—and I don't get lumber bills anymore.

How do you feel about bidding?

I don't bid. If they're talking to somebody else—if they are shopping around—I don't want to do it, they've pissed me off. [*Laughter.*] I won't work for less, and there is always somebody that comes in for less. If they are coming to me because they want me, mostly, I'll do it.

A lot of people will only bid. They think not adding a fee to materials is foolish, it doesn't fit them, but it fits me. I do T&M^, forty-five an hour, and every minute I spend concerning you, I'm charging you for. Customers understand they are better off by the hour. If you want me to do your job, I'll give you a round number that you can never hold me to. I say, "This is

---

4   Jimmy texted me after reading his interview: "You know that waist-high story is no way to treat a potential client." "I know," I wrote back, "but it makes me laugh every time I read it."

going to be a $10,000 job. If it comes out to nine, it's a $10,000 job, if it ends up at eleven, it's an $11,000 job." That's Jimmy math.

Do you have absolute principles that you follow in business?

You gotta do a good job. You gotta give them more than they pay for, so you're proud of it, and you're not ripping anybody off. I guess people sleep fine that rip people off, but I don't.

How did you learn about business?

Trial and error. I listened to people, but most of them were wrong. In the end, business boils down to honesty. If you are an honest person—you may not be a millionaire—but you won't have a lot of trouble.

Have you made memorable mistakes in your business?

I got involved with two lawyers, a husband and wife, it was a big remodeling job and they never planned on holding up their end of things. They were New York lawyers, taking on a country bumpkin—who do you think's gonna win? The lesson: "Never, ever, EVER, work for two lawyers." The biggest problem is that I never get anything on paper, I didn't have a contract or plans.

Did you ever write a business plan?

No, nothing. I knew the reputation I wanted and realized what it took to get it. I wanted people to say, "If you want it done right, call him." If I got a do-over, I'd hang on to that cabinet shop. If I hadn't had to keep the money coming in, if I had given the cabinet shop a year or two, I'd have been happier. If you fix sills and roofs, you are not known as a cabinetmaker.

What did you dislike about being in business?

Having to be a hard-ass. That's not me. But when it's my job and I need something done my way; I have to be. It doesn't happen often. And I dislike what the work does to my body. I'm in good shape for 70—I was hanging sheet rock last week and framing this morning—but I don't get around as fast or up and down as well as I used to. But I'm better off with a few aches and pains then sitting behind a desk. I couldn't do that.

Talk about working with designers and architects.

I like it, and I don't like it. In general, I like designers' ideas because, without them, I don't have the imagination to build some of the things I've built. But they don't understand or appreciate the sweat and blood required to build those ideas. They should have some experience working in the field, it would make them better at what they do. I worked with a young guy years ago, he was really good, and we collaborated on a lot of cool things. Everything I needed was on his plans and he made me more tuned in to detail and structure. I learned a lot from him. I do like having a set of plans, I just don't get them much.

Respond to this idea: If your goal is to be a tradesman, work for someone else. If your goal is to establish and build a company, put your tool belt aside and focus on business as soon as it is practical.

It depends on what you want in life. You don't have to succeed at business, to be a success. Why would you want to hang your tool belt up? If you want to be a carpenter, if you love what you do, why would you trade it for a stack of paper? If you want to be a businessman, be a businessman. Also, my business is so small, I can't fuck it up that bad. When I had all those guys working—it went on for a couple of years and all I was doing was running the roads and checking on the guys—it was the most unhappy I've ever been in my life.

What is your advice about money?

I never learned to manage money, and I can't do it to this day. My advice, "Don't do what I did." I'm happy with my life, but I wish I'd paid attention, run it better, been a better businessman. I'd have more money today. I could use it.

What does someone starting a business need to know first?

Do you really want to do this? You can lose everything. You can think you're growing, doing great, and somebody pulls a contract or doesn't pay. If it happens a couple times, you're in bankruptcy court. Your business is a living breathing thing; it grows, it gets fat, it gets thin, it has pains. When it gets fat, put money away; when it gets thin, pick up the pace or raise your prices. The worst business advice I got was "Don't worry about it, it'll all work out." For the most part, these are the guys who used to have a business.

If you had a method of reaching every tradesman in the U.S., what would you say?

You're only as good as your word. Deliver what you say you will. Don't promise things you can't deliver.

What is a successful business- and tradesman?

I don't know, it depends on how much money you want to make. If you want to be comfortable, you can be small. If you want to be big, get ready for the headaches that come with it; there's a lot of them. You're successful if you've made enough money to not worry, I guess. A successful tradesman is working thirty years and glad you did, glad you showed up, glad you were able to contribute.

Word Association

Integrity: You can't run a business without integrity. Not in the same state for long anyway.

Job Safety: Safety is no accident. You gotta pay attention to it. You gotta follow the rules.

Community: Community is everything. Your business won't survive if you're not a vibrant member of your community. Be part of things, you'll be glad you did.

Communication: If you can't tell the people working for you what you want, you're not going to get it. If you don't understand what the customer wants, they're not going to get it, and you're not going to get your money. Although I hate the goddamn cell phone, when people want to talk to you, they want to talk to you. Communication is the key to everything.

Quality: You have nothing if you don't provide a quality product. You have to get quality out of employees and subs, and you have to use quality products.

Company image: Doing good work, in a timely manner, for a reasonable price. Having a good reputation.

Gratitude: You've gotta have it. If you don't, how do you realize when something's good?

Fear: Fear is good. Fear keeps you in the moment. It doesn't let you ignore shit. It makes you attuned to your surroundings and able to deal with everything that is going on. I like fear. I don't get it much anymore, but I enjoy it when it shows up.

Overhead: Something I've never understood, but it's there. Looming like a sword waiting to come down. If you don't know about it, it'll bite you in the ass. Also, keep your overhead small.

Profit: The elusive profit. It's supposed to be there. You've put it in the price. But did you do the job well enough so it's still there? You never know until the end.

Marketing: I guess it's necessary in some places and if you have employees. If you're a small fish in a small pond like me, you don't need to worry about it.

Sales: Clinching the deal.

Estimating: It'll be what makes you or breaks you.

Bidding: Unnecessary. If you are bidding competitively, you're going to cut your price, if you're going to cut your price, you're not going to make money, if you don't make money, what are you doin'?

Cut-Offs

I don't take direction well. [*Laughter.*] I'd rather stumble around and make a couple of mistakes and figure it out myself instead of having somebody telling me what to do.

She came to me and said, "This job is costing a lot of money. What can we do to be more efficient?" I said, "You can leave my men alone and stop having them empty your wastepaper basket and jump into the dumpster to find your cell phone. Let my men do their job." She said, "Okay." *The very next day*, she has one of my guys carving toes for a coffee table. What could I do? If we don't make the toes, I'm going to have trouble at the end.

Most people try to pigeonhole you into giving them a number: "Just give me an idea of what it will cost." Because I don't advertise, I don't have to worry about these people. People come to me because they want me, not because they saw an ad in the paper. If you want me, what do you care what it costs?

When you start out as a carpenter, you take whatever work comes along. The first thing that comes along is what nobody else wants. Like replacing rotten sills. If you do that, you won't get known as a cabinetmaker, you are a sill repair man. Whatever job you want to do, pick that and do it.

I hear stories about how so and so didn't get the last payment from a job. Well, you picked the wrong people, or you didn't do a good job, one or the other.

People will be happy to pay you what you want to get paid, provided you do what you said you would do.

Don't think that because something is new on the market it will solve everything; nothing solves everything. Do your research and make sure it is a good product and it will stand the test of time. Sometimes the materials that have stood the test of time are the only thing that will.

I try to get the customer as involved in the job as I can. A lot of them want nothing better than to grab a sledgehammer, so I let 'em make a big mess and I let 'em clean it up, so they realize how hard it is.

Be the best, it's the only market that's not crowded.
George Whalin

Gail Grycel,
Retired Cabinetmaker

www.Gailstravel.weebly.com

www.Twinbirchwoodworking.com

Gail is a sixty-two-year-old cabinetmaker and a trained classical musician. Oboe was the instrument with which she earned her performance degree. She is relaxed and friendly, and like nearly every other woodworker, she has scarred fingers, witness to a lost argument with a table saw. Gail was a cabinetmaker for thirty-four years. She is currently (March 2019) traveling around the U.S. in her truck. The day after this interview she was headed to Austin, Texas for a country dance.

> *Everything I do is very much out of the creative spirit ■ A teacher friend said that I made cabinetmaking accessible and that women would love to learn woodworking from a woman, so I began teaching woodworking classes to women ■ I would not go back to the client and say, I made a mistake, the job is going to cost more; if I can't do an estimate it's my fault ■ I learned that I didn't have to be the best cabinetmaker, I had to be the best communicator ■ Perfection is never perfect—strive for it, but be okay that you will never achieve it ■ My best marketing was every job I did well*

Was getting a music degree the right choice?

Yes and no. I have a four-year degree in musical performance. In some ways it is a silly degree because either I can play or I can't, and a piece of paper isn't going to convince anyone. What it did do, later on, was to open different doors. Not in woodworking, but in continuing my music career and in teaching.

What drew you to cabinetmaking?

I picked up a book called *The Woman's Carpentry Book*, by Jeanne Tetrault, and thought, *What's this about?* I bought the book and read it cover to cover. It was stories about women who wanted to build something and did. I was astounded; *What would it feel like to build something with my own hands and have it be there the next day and the next?* That book entered the dream of building into my thinking process. Another couple of years went by as I shifted my music to teaching and playing gigs where I had more creative control, and I looked for different work. But I didn't reach out and say, *Oh I want to do that.* I just thought, *That's kind of cool, what would it feel like?* In the meantime I had moved to a town in central Massachusetts, and in the local paper I found an ad, a cabinet shop was looking for part-time help. They hired me, to my surprise. It went from part time—low pay, no benefits, lots of sanding—to full time. I spent ten years working with these two men learning this trade and I remember feeling; *This is my destiny.*

They taught me practical stuff: this is a table saw, this is a router, this is how you make a cabinet box. I did the less-skilled work at first, but they always included me in the installations, and as time went on, as they realized I had aptitude and the desire to learn, they would stay after hours and show me things. They would feed me small projects and I would do them from start to finish, with them overseeing the work.

It was amazing to realize that I could build something that could withstand time. With my music performance, I'd do it and it's gone. So now I had something that was tangible. There was the smell of the wood, the sound of the machines, the sound of a hand plane over a piece of wood. All of those things became very rich for me and I felt empowered and capable to be able to do this work.

These two guys had limitations. I came in one time and said, "I want to make a rocking chair. Will you show me?" It took me awhile to realize that they didn't do chairs. They did some woodturning and woodcarving, but they weren't turners or carvers. They were cabinetmakers. I learned to take what I could from them.

At this point, you've been working in the shop for ten years, how and why did you transition to owning a business?

Times changed. The speculative house building boom of the '80s and '90s shifted and the work wasn't there like it was. They didn't want to lose me, but they didn't have the work. So they allowed me to use the shop for my own clients. They'd been showing me different aspects of the business: quality work, attention to detail, not to cut corners, good communication. We were working within our little system and we did not talk about bookkeeping or employees or marketing. Once I started to use the shop for my own work, they were a resource. I would ask, "How do you estimate a job; how do you bill for work?"

You have one foot out the door, how did you feel about it?

I'm feeling ready. Confident. I'm getting people interested by word of mouth. Work is coming to me. I thought, *This is the way to start.* On my first kitchen job, the woman said, "I don't have a lot of money, but I'd like you to build the cabinets." I said, "I'll do it, but I'm going to take a bit of a loss and you're going to rethink some of the bells and whistles to get down to the budget. And you're going to tell everybody you know about me and you're never going to mention price." It was a win-win. The first person she told was an architect. I ended up doing quite a bit of work through him over the years.

How did you feel about working for yourself, in your own business?

There were pros and cons. I left those guys' shop at three-thirty in the afternoon, nothing was my problem. I didn't wake up in the middle of the night thinking about design issues. I didn't have to work with clients directly. But I didn't have ultimate control over how to do something. I needed to go on my own, but now I'm waking up at three a.m., going, *How do I invent that wheel?*

How did you learn about business?

I saw an ad for a weekly business networking group. I knew I lacked in certain business areas. There I met a guy who had been a contractor but left to become a small business consultant. So we bartered. I built him a piece of furniture and he sat me down and said, "Let's talk about profit margin and overhead costs—not just sandpaper, but insurance and wear and tear on your vehicles." And we went through my overhead checklist and he added still more line items. [*Chuckles*] We talked about what percentage to tack onto a job for overhead. We came up with 40 percent and my reaction was, *Wow, that's almost half again*. I decided I would not charge a markup on material, but I added 40 percent on my labor.

The consultant said, "You can't spend two days making a set of elevation plans on a kitchen you may not get. You've got to get that time down to a couple of hours." That's where the price-range idea came in. I said to people, "Depending on how your job goes—I can't see what's behind the walls or know what I'm going to run into in an old house—but I estimate it's going to fall within this price range, and I will guarantee that it won't go over the high end of the estimate."

I did my own bookkeeping. I used Excel and plugged in my numbers at the end of the year. I'd go through receipts to see how much I spent on supplies, tools, advertising, and so on. I did my own taxes and took deductions. I had a simple process because it was just me, but I was pretty loosey-goosey about business. It was more important to be the craftsperson than to grow a big business. But it was a tricky line, and I purposely kept pulling myself back from that line over and over to stay small.

What did you do for contracts?

My proposals were broad-brush, and they covered the basics of what the customer and I had talked about. My bid included a price range, what was included, a payment schedule, and maybe some quick sketches. The proposal was also the contract. We'd all sign and date it, and anything added afterward cost extra. My proposal was one page—it's a small thing—with little legalese. There's no recourse. There's no, "*I'm taking you to court if you don't pay.*" This gets into the conversation we had earlier—I approach the world in good faith. I may get burned, but if you've come to me, you've seen my work and you feel like you can trust me, I'm going to trust you back. I did give a thorough invoice at the end of the job, too.

Was there a conflict, working at your trade versus running the business?

Yes, it's about making the wage. My craft side wanted to do a good job no matter how long it took. The business part is asking, *What is cost-effective?* The craftsperson was asking, *What is important to me?*

Your Money or Your Life,[1] a book by Joe Dominguez, is one of the best books I ever read. Before the book, money was always scarce. The book asked me to track expenditures and examine the value of these expenditures. I started to look at money as a resource. If I wanted to buy a new machine, I'd ask, *Is it a better value to buy it used, to pay someone to perform the task, or use their machine for a fee?* I was asking, *What is the best value for the money at hand?* With this mindset and ongoing examination, I learned to keep my accounts in the black.

Did you have long-term goals or ambitions?

I didn't. I knew that teaching music and woodworking were important to me. I knew my evolution as a craftsperson and stepping into the gender questions were important: *Can women do this? Can I do this?* I had to find my own way. In 1996 I bought property in Vermont and started to build my home. If I've had any goal, it was to build that house. It took twenty years. I finished in 2014, and when I finished, I thought, *I'm ready to reinvent myself and do something new*. I rented my house and started traveling.

What about your trade interests you now?

Teaching. Not that I know everything, or have learned or practiced everything, but I've learned a lot, and I can bring that to a class and give it away. That excites me. My body doesn't want to do the grunt work anymore, but I'm happy watching other people figure it out.

Have you ever not taken a customer and what was that decision based on?

Yes, but it was the odd case. If I could tell it was going to be a pain-in-the-ass job. If a couple sat on either side of me in their home and talked over me, I thought, *They're not going to agree on anything and I'm going to play mediator in their marriage*. If they wanted glossy computer-aided-design (CAD) drawings or a hard-baked cabinet finish or period work like Queen Anne, I'd say I was not set up to do that. Or when they nitpicked every penny, I knew they were going to be high maintenance. Instead of saying no to some of these jobs, I would tack on an aggravation fee—like the guys I used to work for—so I did not get sideswiped. I'd double my fee because of the constant phone calls, nitpicking, and second-guessing. I'd overprice it and hope someone else came in with a lower bid.

1   Your Money or Your Life, Joe Dominguez, Viking/Penguin Press, 1992

Who were your best and worst customers?

The best were the ones who had seen my work, they knew about me from a neighbor or friend. They knew what to expect, they trusted me, and appreciated my work. They were the customers who—like the architect I talked about—came to me and said, "You're the expert, help us do our vision and we're going to leave you alone to do your work." They are reasonable about what can be done with their wedge-shaped doors because their funky old farmhouse had settled.

The worst ones don't trust me. They have some knowledge or experience and micro-manage everything I do, they look over my shoulder saying, "What's that? What's that?" At the end, when the invoice comes, they question every penny. Those are the worst. Or, if it's a couple, it's the ones who are constantly at odds with each other. With difficult clients I often overrode my gut feeling because I wanted to help them out. Change orders are tedious, especially with someone who's changing their mind every day. But doing them would have helped me a lot.

Did you have absolute rules in your business?

Yeah, my integrity is set in stone. It is trickier when my client says to cut corners. If someone asks me to do a job where there's a lot of corner cutting, I have to really weigh that. Integrity makes sure I do good work. I don't care how tired I am, I call that person back, because I said I would. I clean up the job. It's part of who I am. It's too easy to cut corners. It's too easy not to take responsibility for what we do. The cheap way out is, *They'll never see it.* But I'm like, *Maybe they will, and I'll know, so I'm not leaving it like that.*

What is your sales process?

Most of my work comes by word of mouth, so 50 percent of the sales work is done. Then I listen well. I'll ask what doesn't work in their current kitchen and what they'd like in the new one, and I'll let them talk about it. From that process I glean what their vision is. During the next go-round, I get back to them with general thoughts and ideas about their job and we have a little banter. When people feel heard, they like that. That becomes a piece of why people buy from me: "I've heard about her and seen her work, she called back, and she listens."

In 1998 I got myself juried onto an open studio craft tour in my area, with twenty to twenty-five artisans of different media, to market my work. It was right after Thanksgiving and we would open our studio doors for three days so people could drive around, meet the artists, and maybe buy something. That became my yearly marketing and I could make anywhere from two to twelve thousand dollars. It was well worth being part of that creative community and having a market that I wasn't reaching through word of mouth.

If you were to lecture to a class of aspiring tradesman, what would you tell them?

I would say to apprentice yourself to someone in the trade that you want. You can do all the education and book learning you want, but there are so many things you can't learn except through experience. Ask questions and learn; that's the key. If you can get yourself attached to someone who's been doing it a long time, shut your mouth and be a sponge.

I would tell them to learn processes and language first. When I teach a women's shop class, they need to understand the processes: what is joinery, how is a box made, how do things go together. And they need to understand the language of the trade: board feet, linear feet, and so on. This is the foundation of any trade. Education is really important; I need to know my craft, I need to know my business, I need to know who I want to be. I need to choose all of these things and not just fly by the seat of my pants.

When they wanted to open a business, I would say—although I never did it, and that's a regret—take a business course. Figure out what your niche is. I filled a certain niche as a custom cabinetmaker, and I recognized where my weaknesses and strengths were. So figure out what is needed and where your passion is.

Cut-Offs

In the '80s when I came on job sites, men were asking, "What are you doing here?" At first my fists went up and I said, "How dare you?" Years later I realized it wasn't so much that they didn't want me there, they were asking, "Can she do this work?" So I took the fists down, both inside and outside myself, and thought, "If I show up and do my work, they'll see that I can do this."

I wanted to believe that there was something about me that the customer wanted. Whether it was my personality, my ability to listen, the fact that I returned phone calls right away, whatever it was.

I decided that there's two ways to make more money: make a better wage or not need as much.

My company image is marketing; are people happy with what they got? Are the neighbors going to say, "Wow, who was your cabinetmaker?" That's my image and my marketing.

Communication is tricky; even though we have a common language we have so many biases and filters it's hard to hear what someone says, so I only get a percentage of what someone is telling me, and I have to fish for the rest. But I have no chance if I'm not listening closely.

There are some jobs I just stopped tracking my hours on because I was going to lose money and I didn't want to know what my final hourly wage was.

...the idea that a four-year degree is the only path to worthwhile knowledge is insane.

Mike Rowe

Dan Kolbert,
General Contractor

www.kolbertbuilding.com
dan@kolbertbuilding.com

Dan was fifty-five at the time of this interview and has lived in Portland, Maine since 1988. He has been working in the industry since just before moving there. He took a break from contracting to teach construction to at-risk youth in the mid-'90s, and he returned to it in 1998. The interview was done in his fifty- by sixty-foot wood shop.

> *If you want to make a living you have to work for well-off people* ■ *"Sustainability" gets thrown around a lot—I think it is bullshit—building single-family detached houses is never going to do the world a favor* ■ *I still do too much project and day-to-day management* ■ *A successful tradesman is somebody who is aware of what came before them and what will come after them* ■ *I am reactive instead of planning well; it is because of my inability, or refusal, to be rigorous about business* ■ *I hire people with skills, you can't set someone unskilled loose on renovation, because nothing is unimportant* ■ *I don't do enough marketing to know if I like it, but I have a native ability for it because our company does have an identity* ■ *I'm sure there are times when I'm bidding but don't know it; but if I know, I won't bid, because competitive bidding doesn't get anybody what they think they're getting* ■ *When I was still in the field, the business stuff was totally half-assed* ■ *I may work more Time & Material into my life, but my instinct is that I'm gonna hate it*

I had summer jobs, but I didn't know what I wanted to do. After I graduated from college in the mid-'80s, I considered academia, but the idea of going back into the classroom was more than I could bear. I stumbled into a construction job, it appealed to me and I was good at it. I was fortunate because my parents sent me to college and I had no debt, so I was free, and that allowed me to take risks. I was living in the middle of Connecticut, so I traveled for a while, did some political work, and decided Portland, Maine was a nice place to live. The economy was terrible when I moved here—it was the depth of a recession—but I was young, didn't need much money, and managed to find jobs as a carpenter. Four or five years later, I had skills I'd learned by slow accretion. Sometimes people were willing to teach me, but I knew I had to teach myself too, so I subscribed to *Fine Homebuilding*^ and I read carpentry books. I'm an okay carpenter, but I never worked for anybody great and I regret that. At a certain point I realized, *I can't be a carpenter, I've got to run the business if anything's gonna happen.* Being a carpenter is a minuscule part of my life now.

What is most rewarding and most difficult about being a builder?

The most difficult part is the business, because I don't have great systems. At a certain point I was doing kitchens and dinky renovations and contracting got boring. Then I got interested in building science^, which has social utility and is rewarding, and that was a second wind, because now we build better homes with healthier materials that are less harmful environmentally.

The most rewarding part of business is the relationships. I have clients I've worked twenty years for, and they have incredible houses that I'm lucky to steward. I like having a crew, I like figuring shit out together, even though it's often difficult. I've got subs I've worked with for years; they are colleagues and friends and we commiserate. We get to do beautiful work that will outlive us—that's rewarding—and not everyone gets to leave a physical legacy.

Several years ago I had a stable crew; we had some great years, and then it went to hell. I had two talented leads with different skill sets and temperaments and a longtime office manager. The first lead left in 2014. He worked for me for a long time—his relationship with the other guy is what made him leave—but he also had things he wanted to do. The other lead was the stereotypical grumpy old-timer who'd done a great job training people over the years, but they'd left, and he lost interest, and after that he drove away hire after hire. I made two fantastic hires, but he was being an even bigger jerk than usual, and I was faced with the choice of losing them or getting rid of someone I was close to and who had been loyal. It was tough on me, but not a difficult call to make. That was summer 2016.

In between the other two losses I fired my office manager. She was in her mid-'60s, a friend I'd hired because she'd been unemployed, and I knew she wouldn't find a job that paid as well. Also, I'd never had an office manager before her, and thought, *This could be great, she is type A, and she will get the business together.* She was not great—she was nasty and a bully—and I let it go on for years. One day she stormed out, saying, "I don't appreciate you telling me how to do my job." But that was the definition of *my* job, and I spent the weekend arranging for her departure. It finally clicked how fucked-up it had gotten. It was such a relief to have her gone.

After I lost them, I made a string of the best hires of my career—I now have a fantastic and stable crew—but I went from three long-term employees to two new guys and I lost all that institutional memory. It was both good and bad; having new people forced me to get better at setting up production, but it took me a year and a half to put it back together.

What academic education do you have, did it help in your business?

I have a degree in Latin American history, and because of my education I am a good writer and I present information well. That helps with sales. Also, being bourgeois is helpful, because my clients and I speak the same language and I understand their cultural references. At a purely mercenary level, that is part of the process.

Were there memorable mistakes while you were learning your trade?

Early on, the first addition I did, I put a terrible estimate together, not realizing until I bought them how much more expensive shakes were than shingles—they cost a fortune. It was one of those "I don't know what I don't know" moments, and I realized I'd better learn how to estimate.

When you began your business, did you have goals or ambitions?

None. I wanted to build and be a carpenter. I focused on that. I never took the money part seriously and I don't remember reading business books until fifteen years ago. Even then, I wouldn't implement what I learned. At this point it's biting me in the ass. I had good years in business, but I read a book recently that made me realize the good years were accidental and the bad ones entirely predictable.

If you were to start over, what would you do differently?

The trades were a good choice for me—for anyone who gets bored easily—because you deal with different people, there is always something to learn, and you can reinvent what you are doing. If I were starting over, I'd find a fantastic carpenter or a well-run company to work for, and I'd focus on learning about business. I'd do that instead of thinking, *I'll learn some shit and go out on my own,* which is what a lot of us do. [*Laughter.*]

Talk about plying a trade versus developing management skills.

The problem with being a carpenter and then a contractor, is that the pull is always toward carpentry. It is much more fun to talk about how to trim a house than to stare at a spreadsheet for three hours. But I realized I needed to find competent people who could replace me in the field because it was too hard to do both the field and the office. It could be cultural, because it is hard to convince myself there is the same intrinsic value in a well-put-together estimate as there is in a well-put-together house.

What is a good and a bad sub?

A good sub I can trust to point out problems in the estimate and during the job. A bad sub does mediocre work and leaves me in the lurch.

What curious thing do you enjoy?

I drop everything to go pond skating between when it first freezes and when it snows. I love floating on oceans and lakes, it is relaxing. I enjoy music. I just got my stereo turntable set up so I can listen to my old vinyl records. And cigars.

What advice have you given most to tradesmen?

Learn from good people and develop good judgment. Although I can't tell you how to develop good judgment, some people seem to have it, and some don't. Maybe, you think about what you are doing and be critical of it? Maybe it's not assuming anything and learning when your confidence is justified and when you are making assumptions?

What is the best path to learning a trade today?

It's a terrible time and a great time. It is a great time if you are young, want to work in a trade, and show up eager to learn. Because there is a shortage of people like you, it will be easy to find someone good who is willing to teach you. And it's terrible because our attitude toward training has been debased over the past few decades and contractors expect people to show up and be useful immediately. Maybe it's because of the decline of unions or the increase in specialization, but there are no standards or traditions of training, and because of that, there are too many people making it up.

What would you tell a class of aspiring tradesmen?

Be good with numbers: fractions, geometry, trigonometry, angles, triangles, and working with numbers in your head. And learn to frame first. I would rather teach somebody with framing experience to trim, than teach a trim carpenter to frame, because the framer knows how a house goes together. Also, if it's available, a vocational education is valuable, and, although I'm not sure it's part of a trade, building science is fascinating and important to the industry. Also, avoid specialization too early. Get exposure to many different things and learn about other trades. I'd tell them that people with intellectual interests apart from their work are more interesting and probably more successful.

What is the best investment you've ever made?

Everything I've ever done with NESEA^. Hands down. It's the people. Everyone brings their A-game to the yearly conference and hanging around people you think the world of is an amazing experience. For the people that present and the people in the audience, we know something magical is gonna happen every year. Also when I had two guys working and I was my own lead carpenter, I bought my first laptop. I left at lunchtime to go to do office work at a coffee shop and I thought, *Shit, this is game-changing!*

What about your best and worst customer makes them that, and when do you turn down customers?

Seeing and acknowledging that we care a lot is the best that I can ask for in a client. The worst is taking us for granted or being a perfectionist in a way that is demeaning. I turn down most calls because we don't do small jobs and we are a small volume company—around a million a year—and because of that we do a few big jobs and don't need a lot of work. Also, a lot of the calls are for things we don't do, like shingling. We have a small, really good, really smart team and it is a waste of our time to shingle a house.

You have a fictitious sister in Kansas, what advice do you give her about hiring a contractor?

I'd tell her to get referrals from people she trusts. Then meet with a few of them—don't ask for pricing—and talk about your project. Are they listening, do they understand, do they have suggestions, do they talk about other projects with similar issues? Pick the one with the most integrity and work on pricing with that person. I'd tell her not to get multiple prices because, even though you are my sister in Kansas and I love you dearly, you have no idea how to meaningfully compare pricing.

What advice would you give new contractors about hiring?

Know what it costs to put a person in the field, otherwise you don't know if you are making enough to cover them. The only way to know is to track your workers' time and turn that information into square/linear-foot rates. When you have these numbers, remember: you're not as productive as you think you are and you are making up for it by working too many hours; a hire's productivity never matches the bosses (take this into account when estimating); and your productivity will drop as you spend time supervising. I'd tell them that the difference between no employees and one employee is much more than between one employee and three employees, because now you have to keep them busy, which requires increased sales and workers compensation, and you're now responsible for their safety and livelihood. Oh yeah, and don't make them do the shit you're not willing to do.

What do you look for when you hire?

It is hard to hire well, it's always a crapshoot, and I don't know of a realistic test. What I look for has changed over the years. At one point, I was just looking for skilled carpenters. But Paul Eldrenkamp[1] says something like this: "We can teach skills and provide experience, but good judgment is what they bring with them; so hire good judgment." Now I hire people for their qualities as human beings, even though those qualities are ineffable. Also, I'm a small company, so part of the hiring process is, *Are my current employees gonna like this person?*

---

1   Paul is also interviewed in this book.

What is a good and a bad employee, and what don't you expect from employees?

A good employee thinks about the company and they are aware of everything on the job: how the pieces go together, how the client is feeling, if the subs need anything and if they are doing their job. They bring problems to me beforehand and they have an interest in bettering themselves. I don't expect employees to spend their off-hours thinking about work, or to pay for their mistakes, or to supply more than basic tools. A bad employee doesn't clean up after themselves, literally and metaphorically.

Do you have an educational program in your company?

It is not a formal program, but I believe in helping people improve, so I've sent people to nearby conferences and workshops. A guy who works for me is turning into a big deal in the education circuit for sealing penetrations and air sealing—he has presented a couple of times at *JLC^*—so I give him time off to do that and it is gratifying and exciting to have someone who is associated with the company doing cool stuff. A few months ago I taught my crew what markup is, why we mark up, and I explained why I bug them for time cards and what I do with that information. I'm trying to do more things like that.

What books have been most important in your life?

Catch-22 and *Companies We Keep*.[2] The last one really helped my business.

How do you define marketing and sales and what is the difference between them?

They are completely different things. Marketing is how you present your company to the public and what people on the outside think about your company. Sales is how you convince a client that you are the right person to do that job. I do a little advertising, with the Audubon Society and a magazine called *Green and Healthy Homes of Maine*[3]—I write a column for them and I'm on their advisory committee—and there's a monthly paper that does muckrake reporting, and although I don't know that I get any work out of them, I advertise with them because they provide a good service.

2   *Catch-22*, 50th Edition, Joseph Heller, Simon & Schuster Publisher, 2011; Companies We Keep: Employee Ownership and the Business of Community and Place, 2nd edition, John Abrams, Chelsea Green Publishing Company, 2008.
3   Website: *HTTPS://GREENMAINEHOMES.COM/*

The building science discussion group that I moderate is good marketing, even though it's for the trades. It's gotten me a reputation as a leader in building science in Greater Portland and I know people have come to me because of it. When I write articles for trade publications, I'll put them on our website. I do community engagement because it's important to me, but there is some marketing aspect to it too. I don't letter my truck and I describe my web presence as "search engine minimization," because someone who found me while searching Google for bids is not going to be a good customer for us. Although I do occasionally get good leads from my website.

What would you tell a new business owner about marketing and sales?

Past clients are the best source of new work and staying in touch with them is absolutely the most important thing. Now marketing is so internet-driven—and it is overwhelming for young contractors—I tell them to avoid sites like Angie's List, Yelp, and Home Advisor, because they are not good for contractors. I ask my clients not to review me on these sites, because I don't want these companies involved in my business, my marketing, or my online presence, and because I don't want people calling to sell me stuff. If you are doing a high-volume business, like window replacements or specialty services, they might work.

How did you learn to sell and what form does it take now?

Most of our business is repeat and referrals, some from vendors and subs, the standard routes, but little from marketing. I get aggravated when the phone rings [*laughter*] so I've structured the business to fit my personality—not surprisingly—and we rarely bid competitively. I send new clients an article I wrote for *JLC* that explains why I don't bid.[4] People find it persuasive, or at least they know not to ask me to bid. I don't charge for estimates because my close rate is so high that I am not wasting time doing proposals. And, during this process, I'm deciding if I want to work with the client. Typically if we don't get a job, it is because they can't afford the work. When I sell, I let people know I'll be thoughtful about how I approach their job, and that I either have, or know where to find, the expertise to get it done. Part of my process is explaining similar situations and how we

---

4 *Four Alternatives to the Competitive Bidding Process*, Dan Kolbert, *JLC*, April 2011. Search for the article on *JLC*'s website.

handled them and what we learned. I'm also open about my limitations. I'll say, "I don't know how to do this." or "We screwed this up and this is what we learned from it."

When work slows, or when you have too much work, what do you do?

We always have work and mostly it hasn't been a problem. In 2008 when the bottom fell out, my biggest job ever was just starting, so we had sixteen months of work and it got us through. After that we were slow—the recession caught up with us—and I lost a couple of guys, but we weren't slow for long. When we have too much work I don't respond well. My weakness is keeping the ball rolling and jobs running smoothly.

What has most improved your business recently?

I've done something called a process map. It's a flowchart, broken into phases; I do it for the entire job, from the first phone call on. It will always be a work in progress, but it is helpful to break down what we do and learn how to do it better. I've shown it to people in my crew and in my NESEA group. It has helped.

What principles do you follow in business?

I don't paper over or hide problems and I'm open with my clients. For existing clients we'll do anything they ask, even small jobs.

Why did you open a business?

Right, good question. I have a joke on my Facebook page, I describe myself as the founder of *Socialist Business Owners of America*. [*Laughter.*] It was not a natural choice for me, but I enjoy the work. I often describe contractors as being like Hollywood directors, because we've got six million parts to fit together—I like that—and one of the variables is how much money we have to do it with, and how that constrains a project and focuses people's attention. I like that too. Part of it was out of necessity because I thought, *I can't stand working for these people anymore.* It was a long time ago, but I was working on a big island off the coast of Maine and we'd catch a boat Monday morning, sleep on site, and come home Thursday night. It was fun, but we had few plans or specs^ and had to figure things out on our own. The owner or boss would show up and be pissed off or surprised at what we were doing; I had the aggravation with none of the control. Then I was running a job as a subcontractor and there were things he did that were unethical, which ate away at me, and I'd make suggestions to lessen the chaos only to be met with "It's the nature of the beast." I decided I needed to get my own work and figure it out for myself.

Talk about specifications^ and contracts.

I write our specs, even when I work with architects. Their specs are usually weak because they write them early on and never update them. I do stick to their plans religiously though. Specs are critical and most clients don't read them, so I go through them line by line with the client. Still, by the middle of the job most have forgotten what they are, so I've been toying with the idea of reviewing the specs at every new phase, saying, "We're entering this phase of work, these are the specs. Do you want to change anything?" In some ways, I like working for lawyers because they know how to read construction documents and they ask questions.

I use a standard contract of five pages. My lawyer tweaked a couple of things and I said to him, "If I handed this contract to one of your clients, I want it to be such that you would tell them to go ahead and sign it." Typically I write a proposal earlier on and put the budget price at the top. When we're all set, I'll retype it and call it the Scope-of-Work^ and it gets incorporated by reference into the contract. I don't break the final price into line items or break out the overhead and profit, but I think if they wanted it, I'd give it to them.

Talk about estimating.

I learned to estimate by breaking the job into its parts. I've always used Excel—I've looked into estimating programs but I'm not crazy about them—and I have a long and idiosyncratic spreadsheet that is not CSI^, which is intimidating to the outsider. Doing a $900,000 estimate takes me a hundred hours or more, but I'm always underbidding labor, partly because I'm not disciplined and partly because I don't keep great job cost^ records.

As you were transitioning from trade to business, how did you learn what you needed to know?

Only a few of us are smart enough to realize how difficult contracting is, and it took me a long time to realize it was a skill set I needed and even longer to do anything about it. I read accounting and building books and magazines and I absorbed some of it and started doing my own accounting early on—using QuickBooks—so at least I had that data. Now I would tell young builders, "Your business skills have to be as good as your trade skills."

How would you respond to this idea: If your goal is to be a tradesman work for someone else. If your goal is to establish and build a significant company, put your tool belt aside and focus on business as soon as it is practical.

I absolutely agree with it—I might quibble with the brightness of the line dividing the two—because being a part-time carpenter isn't a great idea, unless you're *really well organized*, but even then, it won't work long term. They don't call it contracting for nothing, you're writing and selling contracts, that's the job. The irony is, to be successful in contracting, you have to give up the thing that attracted you to it in the first place.

Do you have any memorable mistakes in business?

There's that sinking feeling when you realize you've left something out of the estimate, those are always memorable moments. [*Laughter.*]

Do you use change orders^?

I do what everybody else does. I don't want to deliver bad news, so I let it pile up and dump it on the client all at once and they eat some of it and I eat some of it, and everybody's pissed off. I don't have any brilliant wisdom other than we all make the same mistake and none of us should be doing it that way and it is at the top of my list of things to be more disciplined about.

Which do you prefer, Time & Material^ or fixed price^ contracts?

Whenever possible I do fixed price because I hate Time & Material (T&M),[5] but I know people who do T&M successfully. Fixed price forces you to figure out the job details and front-load the administrative work. Although part of the reason I'm in rough shape now is because for two years in a row I had huge renovations that I seriously underbid. I told myself after the second one that if I get into another one, it's got to be T&M because I can't subsidize other people's jobs.

---

5   For more information on contracts, see Types of Contracts, page 204 in *The Elements of Building.*

As a contractor, sometimes you need to be a hard-ass.

I fire people and I tell subs when their work sucks. But being a hard-ass does not come naturally to me, I don't do it often enough, and that has cost me a lot of money over the years. Also, sometimes it is hard to know who I'm advocating for; I want to protect my crew, subs, and client, and in each situation, I've got to decide who's the victim. That's not my favorite thing.

What do you like and dislike about having a business?

I like having a good team and good subs and that clients come to me to get shit done. I like that a lot. I dislike the anxiety and the solitude. The roadside is littered with failed partnerships, but I think it would've been fun to spend the last twenty years doing this with somebody else. The fact that I'm not in jail or bankrupt means that I'm doing some things right. There is plenty of good stuff in my business, and I need some objectivity to pick out what is working and to build on that.

How do feel about working with designers and architects?

Many in the trades think designers are overeducated sissies who don't understand the real world. I've gone up and down. At first it was awesome, until I learned the quickest way to lose money is to work with an indecisive architect. Now, having worked with good designers, I have more respect for them. Early on I had a renovation where the architect was a little crazy, but smart, and the clients were great, but they had a terrible visual sense and I had to run interference between them and the architect. I did not understand his design up front, but I loved the final product and later I thought, *Oh, that's what he was trying to do.* That was a big moment for me because I realized designers can bring something important to the table.

How did you learn to manage money?

I'm naturally and temperamentally frugal and I don't have many desires that money can solve. That's made life easier. I'm not broke, but I don't manage money especially well. My advice is to budget your whole life.

Do you actively mentor people, and if so, how?

Yes. I share my business experience with a guy that used to work for me. Some of it is basic, like how much to mark up. Some of it is about how to sell a job and things to say to clients. One client wanted to supply the kitchen cabinets and I told my guy to charge his full overhead anyway, as if he were buying the cabinets. When the customer asks why, tell them, "My overhead doesn't change because you supply the cabinets, I still need to make a certain amount every week, I'm assuming liability for working with the cabinets, and the only way you will get the cabinet order right is if I prepare it for you. I can't do any of that without my markup."

You are standing in front of a group of skilled tradesmen thinking of going into business, what do you tell them?

If you like being a tradesman and you make enough money, keep doing it. If you are interested in business, learn from somebody instead of learning on your own, because it is a dark and lonely place learning how to run a business by yourself. One of my biggest regrets was deciding there was no one better than the &%#*%#& guys I was working for. Now I'm sure that was not the case.

What would you tell someone going into business to learn first and what to avoid?

Know your overhead. It is *the* critical thing. Know what your cost of being in business is, avoid buying a fancy truck, renting an expensive shop, and spending money you don't have to. A common mistake is that because you got paid twenty dollars per hour working for someone, you charge twenty an hour when you work for yourself. But now you're paying for tools, truck, insurance, and for the mistakes that your boss used to pay for.

If you had a way to reach every builder and tradesman in the United States, what would you say?

There are a lot of idiot builders; I'd tell them to work on their integrity.

Do you have an exit strategy from your business?

No, other than a heart attack. [*Laughter.*]

Word Association

Integrity: Truth.

Gratitude: Humility is critical, because you realize how dependent you are on everyone and everything.

Job safety: Group support. Mutually supportive.

Company image: Competence. To me, "competent" is a huge compliment.

Fear: Fear is tough and I'm afraid of change and I'm gripped by fear often; but fear is not all bad. In the trades it is healthy, because if something seems dangerous, it probably is, so it can save your life.

Overhead: It is like medicine: you need it, but you don't want too much of it, because too much of it is poison. But it is critical to your business, so the first question should be, *Do we need this?* If the answer is yes, then listen to that.

Profit: I spent twenty years avoiding understanding its importance. I didn't appreciate what not having profit was doing to my business, or its effect on my family, or my retirement. Now I know that predictable profit allows you to run a healthy, successful business.

Marketing: You need to know why you are marketing and what you want from it; otherwise it can be seductive in bad ways. The point is, when a client thinks about a contractor, your name comes up. So you need to keep the company name out there somehow: ads, newsletter, or public service—and you need to know if they are working.

Sales: Sales needs to be fully integrated into the production cycle so you know when you need work and how long the sales and estimating process will take.

Estimating: Estimating is the core of everything; it determines if you make money and it is where you collect all the job information. A good estimate builds the job on paper, setting you up to build the actual job well.

Bidding: Bidding is stupid. The client, the architect, and the builder don't get anything out of it and often the high bidder gets the job anyway, so—if cost isn't the most important factor—why go through the bidding process to begin with? When it is done, the two or more contractors who didn't get the job have wasted a lot of time. Unfortunately, when you are starting out, often you can't avoid bidding.

Community: There are levels of community and your relationships within each level are critical and they need to be nurtured.

Communication: Open, not concealing. If you are not constantly thinking how, what, and why you're communicating, you're not doing it right.

Quality: That's huge. You and your team need to know what it looks like, although I don't know how to define it. There are objective standards, but you'd need a million of them for a house. Maybe it is like communication, you constantly need to be thinking about it. You can also obsess about quality and never learn to say, "It's good enough," and never finish anything or make a dime. So when an applicant says, "I'm a perfectionist," that is not a good thing.

Success: Success is sustainability and putting out a product that you're proud of.

Cut-Offs

If you want to make a decent living, unless you're going to specialize in one thing, stay away from anything you can put a square/lineal-foot cost on—roofing, siding, and gutters for example—because you're competing against the other guy's unit cost^.

I have an endless list of fake company mottos: "Making the lives of the bourgeoisie slightly more comfortable, one kitchen at a time," and "There's a little bit of quality in everything we do!" and "We rip off the next guy and pass the savings on to you!" [Laughter.]

We're about to start a large new house, and when it is underway, I'm going to hire a rookie because it's a great opportunity to train someone.

Being competent is what convinces people that you are competent, and the sales process is about highlighting that competence.

One of the good things that comes from fear is a better culture of safety in the trades. I tell young people, "You take incredible risks without being aware of it—to your body and to your finances—and you assume liability all the time, for little reward."

We've had this woodworking shop for about a year, but 90 percent of our time is in the field. The rent was so cheap it was crazy not to have the shop, but now I'm trying to figure out how to work it into our lives, because it is nice to have inside work when the weather is bad, and it's fun.

When I hire, I don't do a trial period because Maine is an "at will" state, which means you can fire anybody, anytime, for any reason. So a trial period is unnecessary.

Cheap is the last refuge for the [builder] who can't figure out how to be better. The alternative is to choose to be worth it, remarkable, reliable, a good neighbor, a worthy citizen, comfortable, trusted, funny, easy, cutting edge.

Seth Godin

Jesper Kruse,
General Contractor

info@mainepassivehouse.com
www.mainepassivehouse.com

Jesper is Danish and has been in the United States for many years. We met at his office, which I imagined would fit perfectly in his home country, because it seemed not to contain a single thing without a practical use. His company's name is Maine Passive House and he lives and works in Bethel, Maine. After the interview, looking at his company's website, I was impressed by the crispness of his projects and the glowing references of his customers.

> *If you have a successful company, you owe it to your employees to treat them well* ■ *You're much better off managing the customers' expectations by being clear from the beginning* ■ *Don't base your hourly rate or markup on what everybody else is doing; they could be wrong* ■ *I don't expect employees to give up their life for my company, they have a life outside of work* ■ *I show the client category totals so they don't see how much the windows are, how much the labor is, or how much we markup* ■

I came to this area of Maine originally by working for Outward Bound, and I came to work for them through training sled dogs in Alaska. I have no formal building training. When I came to the U.S. I was looking for a job and some friends were building a house and offered me six bucks an hour. That was 1997. I worked for them and quickly realized I really liked, at the end of the day, seeing what I had done. In Denmark I was a social worker, and at the end of the day I couldn't see a damn thing. There was nothing tangible. My dad was a cabinetmaker—I looked over his shoulder a bit—and that made me somewhat interested, although I never thought about it as a career. Denmark has a strong tradition of trades, so if you're in the trades you have self-respect and take what you are doing seriously, and that might have affected how I ended up running my business.

What was most rewarding and most difficult about plying your trade?

Most rewarding is learning the trade, seeing the work, taking pride in creating something. Most frustrating is the repetition and being told what to do when you're starting out and feeling boxed in and being outside when it's nasty weather or being in a crawl space.

What academic training do you have, and has it affected your life?

I have a bachelor's degree in social work. It is helpful when interacting with people and working at Outward Bound in stressful situations. I'd think, *Okay, you can do this.* And reading, writing, and math—which seemed stupid at the time—definitely the math.

Talk about when you started and what your goals and ambitions were.

When I first came here, it seemed like everyone was building their own house, and my wife and I liked that idea. I never thought I would run my own business, but I became good at what I did, and I remember thinking, *Maybe I want to be a cabinetmaker and do really intricate stuff.* Then it was becoming a really good carpenter and then making money to provide for my family.

Given that Demark has strong trade programs, have you ever wished you trained there instead of learning on your own in the United States?

No, I liked learning here. I was motivated and sought out people that I knew were really good. I worked for three builders with good reputations and what I learned was beneficial. The first guy, I was learning how to use tools and basic carpentry skills. I worked for him for about a year, and then I worked for another guy who was younger than me and he had three or four guys building four homes a year. He was a slave driver, but it was awesome to work for somebody and go from "I can do this much in a day" to suddenly "Holy shit, man, I can do three times as much work in a day if I hustle and get good systems going." That's what I learned from the second guy. The third guy was a timber framer and I had to be precise and not cut corners. Speed was way less an issue and I went from this guy who gets a bunch done, to this guy who said, "We're going to do this right, and we use slicks and drill out for mortise-tenon joints." We took coffee breaks and went out to lunch together on Fridays. It was totally different. I remember him saying, "Hey, let's make this fun." That was mind-blowing because I thought work was supposed to be miserable. [*Laughter.*]

Do you have memorable mistakes you made while learning the trade?

I was carrying a ladder through a garage door that we had just trimmed, and the ladder clipped the trim and I had to redo it. And definitely the mistakes everybody makes, like cutting the same piece of wood wrong three times in a row.

If you were to start your business over, what would you do differently?

I think I did pretty well and I've gotten out of it what I wanted. In some ways I wish I had realized earlier that this is what I wanted to do. I graduated high school and traveled for five years and then I went to college for four years, so it was almost ten years from when I left high school till I started the business.

Talk about trade versus business skills.

In a trade I'm thinking precision, streamlining processes, planning stuff out, and cleaning up after myself. In business I'm thinking about being tidy and precise—I guess they are similar—and being sure everything gets invoiced and I didn't leave money on the table. Making sure my customers are always happy and that nobody is disgruntled.

What do you love?

Skiing as often as I can. I ski at Sunday River, which is ten minutes from here.

What advice have you given most to field employees and do you have educational programs in the business?

I say, "Tell me what you need, and if you need help, come to me. Ask questions. Let's make it smooth and make it work well." We are trying to set up more formal programs, and every once in a while we'll do a training session.

If you were to lecture to a group of aspiring tradesmen, what would you tell them to learn first and what to avoid?

Precision. Give a shit. Pay attention. Somebody told me once, "You are doing the job anyway, you might as well do it well." Avoid working for hacks and picking up bad habits—being sloppy and not caring—and cutting corners. You are going to cut the board anyway, do it right.

What would you tell them about getting an education apart from their trade?

I don't think college is necessary. It's good to be able to read, write, do math, and speak well—it's always good to have general knowledge—but in terms of "Everybody should go to college," I think that is hogwash. It doesn't make sense because it's so expensive. Since you don't need a bachelor's degree to become a plumber, is it worth spending $100,000 or more on college? In Denmark you go to carpentry school for four years. I wish there were better trainings for the trades in the U.S.

What's the most worthwhile investment you've made?

Getting into passive house and taking the time, energy, and money to do the training to become certified as a passive house consultant.[1] It set our business apart from everybody else in this area. Also, joining the Building Energy Bottom Lines Network (BLN)^ helped my business. BLN is a peer-to-peer group that helps companies improve their business. I'm part of a group of ten companies that meet twice a year—spring and fall—and every meeting has one facilitator and is hosted by one of the member companies. The first day of the meeting everybody gets fifteen minutes to talk about their company and then fifteen minutes of feedback from the other members. The second day is all about the host company's business. People sharing their business documents at these meetings has been huge for me. I thought I was doing a good job and running a successful business—in a lot of ways I was—but joining them made the business so much clearer. As a trade person, not a businessperson, it's been super helpful. Also hiring Vermont Helm Construction Solutions,[2] a consulting company, helped with

---

1   Passive house (originated by Passivhaus Institut in Germany) is a certified building standard for energy efficiency that reduces a building's ecological footprint, resulting in structures that require little energy for heating or cooling.
2   *HTTPS://WWW.BUILDHELM.COM/*

contracts and markups. Businesswise, they have been an even bigger help than BLN.

What about your best and worst customer makes them that?

Some are easier to work with than others. The good ones are pleasant, fair, and understanding. They know stuff goes wrong and say, "Alright, cool, I understand." The best thing is good chemistry between you and the customer and being on the same page. The worst is being in an adversarial relationship because the customer thinks you're out to screw them and they are constantly looking over your shoulder. Also, lack of communication. I had one guy who would show up on the job, look around the site and at the drywall seams with a flashlight, but never complain or ask questions. He never said, "It looks great, guys" or "Good job." That was super stressful.

How do you influence a potential customer's expectations?

I'm honest with people—to a fault, I think. I tell them, "Yes, it is going to be overwhelming sometimes and stuff's going to happen, but we do it all the time and we're going to communicate about it, and we're going to guide you through it." I've gotten better at that. Now it's about being clear what it's going to cost. If they don't have the money or if they don't want to pay for it, I weed them out quickly.

Do you turn down customers and if so, why?

All the time. Distance, because we don't travel more than forty-five minutes, and if someone is really flaky—if it feels loosey-goosey—that turns me off. I haven't had anybody who was a jerk, but if somebody were rude to the employees, I would back out as soon as possible. I've never left a job, but I've been close. And I've had clients that asked us to do more work, but I won't work for them again. I tell them I'm too busy or give them a high price, so they won't hire me.

We just turned down a huge job because we looked at the plans and they were standard, not energy efficient, and we said, "It doesn't have to be a passive house, but it can't be a just-to-code house." They did not want to do that. Surely, if you're spending a million dollars, you can spend another hundred thousand to make the house healthier, safer, and better for the planet. It sucked because it was right next door, but also, in this day and age, you can't build like that and be responsible.

How would you tell someone to choose a contractor?

Do it the way I hire subs; I go with whoever I know is good. Ultimately, I'd rather pay more so I don't have to deal with problems down the road. If someone has the money and wants to build a passive house, they should look for somebody who builds sustainable, energy-efficient buildings, who knows what they are doing and has high integrity. I would tell them to interview the builder's clients too. If they were pressed for money, I would tell them to look for somebody young, intelligent, just starting out, and with a good reputation, because they will work harder and charge less. The other thing about hiring someone young; they are more willing to try something new, like a passive house.

What do you look for when you hire and what do you expect from your employees?

I hire based more on personality then skill. I want somebody I can rely on and who I get along with. You can be a really good carpenter or plumber, but if you're a mess to work with, that's bad. I might call references, but I do it more on instinct, and we've got a really good group. If they are highly skilled, I expect them to care about what they are doing, to take initiative and ownership of their work, and to really crank it out. If they are new; being willing to learn is important. I hired a woman with no experience, but she shows up, pays attention, does exactly what you say, and she takes initiative.

I've never fired anybody. I've been close a couple of times, but they knew it was coming and left on their own. I'd fire for not showing up or being repeatedly late and having stupid excuses or creating tension on the job. If someone is not working out, I try to work with them to fix things.

Do you have company activities that you do with employees?

We do. We floated down a river together two weeks ago. We've done that a couple of times. Last year we went whitewater rafting and sometimes we go skiing together. It creates comradery and company culture. We do this so that we're not just working together. Outward Bound had corporate programs where companies would pay big bucks to develop teamwork. This is the same, but less deliberate and much cheaper.

Have you had a mentor or a teacher that influenced your career?

Tom Wentworth, the timber framer I worked for, he took my skill to a whole other level. He taught me to be precise when I lay out, to cut so it fits nicely, and that "give a shit" thing. Timber framers and cabinetmakers are at a whole other level anyway. I had another mentor, my brother-in-law, who works in a Fortune 500 company, and being able to call him with my questions was really helpful. I was thinking of giving one of my guys parts of the company and my brother-in-law said, "As hard as you have worked, you can't give away that asset. If you bring someone in, they have to pay for what it's worth."

Why did you open your business and what were the first three things you did?

By chance. I quit my job so I could be home and take care of my young daughter and work on building an apartment on our property. And then I had the idea of being my own boss, because I would be able to call the shots and not have somebody tell me what to do. That was attractive to me. In the beginning it was just me and I liked that. First three things? I registered with the state, did the paperwork that came with that, and opened a bank account and a credit card for the business.

How would you define marketing and sales?

Marketing is getting the word out, sales is pulling the customer in and getting them to sign on the dotted line. In the beginning, sales was going out there and selling on face value; now we are starting to get systems in place. The most important thing in sales is convincing the customer that they can trust you, that you have their best interest at heart, and that they are making the right choice in selecting you. But the most effective thing is word-of-mouth and personal connections. Also, passive house connected me with a bunch of architects, and that was really big. I joined the Chamber of Commerce and being on their website does seem to help.

At first, I didn't have any money for marketing, so it was about getting in the paper and doing presentations about energy efficiency and open houses for passive house. All free stuff. It was to promote our company and raise awareness about efficiency and better homes. Because of the consulting company I hired, we now have a marketing plan, but it's often something that gets done when I can fit it in.

Now I spend a relatively small amount for ads in a local magazine and movie theater. The magazine costs about $2000 a year, it is free to the public, and it ends up in all the rental homes in this area. I don't know if we get any jobs from the magazine, but the theater is a no-brainer; people see beautiful photographs and the company logo. We do Facebook and Instagram and other social media, and I get a kick out of making a video and putting it on Instagram. Marketing is kind of fun. I don't track how effective our advertising is, but when someone calls, I try to ask where they found out about us.

What would you tell a new business owner about marketing and sales?

Don't have any unhappy customers. Do whatever it takes to make sure they are happy, because word-of-mouth is *the most effective thing*. In terms of sales, it's obviously helpful if you have your stuff together and have a package of sales material and a good contract.

If you have too much work, or if work slows, what do you do?

I don't really know. It's changed, because it used to be just me, and if work was slow, I did my own projects and worked on passive house training. Now that we have ten people, if work slows, I don't know, I'd find something on my house, I guess. I'd try to keep everybody, but if there's no work, I'd have to let somebody go. If we have too much, I turn work down. I try to see what is coming and be vague about timing for a while and see if I can get some clarity. It is just riding it out man, the ups and the downs.

In the past few years, what behavior has most improved your business?

Having a plan, getting organized, getting systems in place, having better documents, and being more deliberate about how we do business. Our accounting books are really good because of our new office manager. Before she started, I was doing the books with the help of the consultant. We are working on budgets and we cost code everything and I get reports. I drive more on instinct, but looking at the numbers helps. It's easy now because business is really good and there's money in the company, so we don't have to worry as much about what we are spending.

It's not going to get better than it is now, so I'm doing things for my employees. Everybody gets sick of working for the same person eventually, so if I treat people well and have good benefits, it will be hard for them to quit. Few people switch jobs if it means getting paid less.

As you transitioned from tradesman to business owner, was there a conflict between doing the trade and running the business?

It was definitely a conflict in the beginning because I had to work in the field and I did the business at night and weekends. I learned how to be a good carpenter, but I like it when there's something new and interesting going on, so I was pulled to the business because it was exciting. Last week I worked in the field for two days and I think the guys like it when I'm out there and everybody appreciates when you pay attention to what they're doing. It also reminds me that it is hard work. It is good to remember that.

I did my business based on what I thought was right. The whole integrity and honesty thing. Bookkeeping, estimating, sales, I learned by the school of hard knocks. I built my own house early on. That was a good lesson in cost and paperwork, and I understood I had to track the money and make sure the paperwork was done correctly. But I didn't have a system and it was a big fat mess. Somehow I managed it.

Do you have absolute principles in your business?

Definitely. Number one is, "Make sure the customer is happy." To treat people with respect and help each other. When subs come on a job, introducing everybody and telling them, "If you need anything, let us know." I want to create a work environment where people are comfortable and know they are appreciated.

How did you learn about contracts?

On bigger projects with more money in them, people are used to reading and signing contracts and wanting stuff a certain way. That made me realize I needed to understand my contract and put more work into it. At first I used Maine's general construction contract. But that contract was biased toward the client, so an attorney friend helped me figure out a couple issues and then I hired an attorney to write a contract that was more balanced. Our current contract is good, but it could use some work.

Did you have goals and write a business plan when you started?

I tried to, but I didn't understand what it was supposed to do for me. In some ways it did make me think about what I wanted to do, but it was not something I'd take out and look at.

If you were to start over, would you do anything differently?

I would have spent more time getting better systems in place, especially when it was small and I had more time. But then it did not seem that important, and I really needed to work in the field. I would have carved out the time because, in reality, it's just as important as what I was doing in the field.

How do you feel about needing to be a hard-ass?

Normally, that is not me, it is not my personality. I can have difficult conversations with employees—be a hard-ass—without being an asshole. With subs I can say, "Dude, this is what you need to do. This is what I'm paying you to do and I'm not gonna take the loss because you screwed up." I can be clear without being a jerk. With customers I stand my ground. And I'm good at—I don't want to say manipulating—but getting what I want without making people lose face.

What do you like and dislike about having your own business?

I love the satisfaction of running a company that's successful, having employees that are happy—knowing they can provide for their families—and having customers that are happy. The enjoyment of being on the cutting edge of the building industry and educating the people that are coming up and making money while we do it.

When it was just me, I'd think, *There is nothing coming up, I'm going to take six months off.* What I don't like now is that I can't do that. I went away for three weeks last summer, but the business is a ball and chain and I'm tied to it. But, when I weigh it against other options, I haven't found a better one.

What did it look like as you began to focus on passive homes?

I was building a house and somebody said, "Maybe you could be the guy who carves out a green niche in this area." I remember thinking, *From a business perspective, maybe that would be a good idea.* I started reading and trying to understand what LEED-certified^ and ENERGY STAR^ rating meant. Then I was at a bachelor party in Denmark, late at night, and somebody mentioned how Passive House had a 90 percent savings in heating cost. I knew there were these little, incremental things you could do, but this was a leap, and it was way better than anything else that was being built. Building using so much less energy seemed like the most important thing to me.

How did you learn to estimate?

Sitting down and counting every damn piece of wood that went into the building and trying to figure it out on my own. I went through the job and wrote everything on an Excel spread sheet and added it up. I've taught my office manager to do area take-offs and now we use Construction Suite, which integrates into our accounting software to track job costs.[3] Our estimates are accurate within 5 percent.

Mostly we do Time & Material jobs. We use Construction Specifications Institute's (CSI)^ format. We don't bid because I know we're not the cheapest ones and I don't want to do estimates for free because it is a ton of work; a new house takes us a hundred or more hours to estimate. Our consultants are trying to get us to bid jobs. They say you make more money bidding, because in the estimate you assume the worst case and, if the estimate is done well and things go well, you pocket that contingency.

When we started, I used a flat rate for all of my employees, but customers would call and ask for my best guys—they get the most money of course—but I was charging an average rate, so I was losing money. Now I add 85 percent—this figure includes overhead and profit—to each trade's hourly rate and 15 percent on material and subs. In theory that gives us 10 percent profit on labor and 15 percent on subs and materials. In reality we end up eating some sub and material costs, but if things go well, we end up with 10 to 15 percent profit.

What advice would you give about doing estimates?

The biggest thing is making sure you have included all the materials and labor and to include a contingency, 'cause something is going to go wrong. You are going to get scared by the final number—*Oh my God, I can't believe it is this much*—and the tendency is to cut the number down to get the job. Don't. Give the customer your best shot and be ready with solutions to bring the number down if they think it is too high.

When I started, I thought, *Time & Material, great, I don't have to worry about what it is going to cost*. But it doesn't change anything for the client—it is just as stressful—and if it is stressful for them, it is stressful for me when I have to say, "Sorry, it is not going to be sixty thousand, it is going to be

---

3   HTTP://WWW.UNITEDDESIGN.COM/CS_OVERVIEW.HTML

ninety thousand." It is almost more important to do good estimating if you are doing Time & Material jobs.

Do you have memorable business mistakes?

Underestimating jobs is a big one. We do mostly Time & Material, but I still get a sick feeling when I've told the client it's now gonna be X price, when I told them it would be Y and they are too far along to back out. I've also done a few bid jobs that I lost money on; *that just sucks*. And not anticipating things has been a problem, so I've learned to spend more time on estimates and to be super thorough. Now I realize that sometimes you can't build what people want for the amount of money they want to spend and that I'm better off pursuing other jobs than working for free.

Why don't you bid?

That's not how I'm running my business. If somebody wants a bid, they're looking for the lowest price. I run my business on people knowing that we're going to take care of everything and that we're going to treat you right. If there's an issue, we're going to deal with it. You hire us because you want something built well and you don't want it to be a headache. If you're looking for the lowest price I'm thinking you're going to be a pain in the ass to deal with and you're going to be a penny-pincher and that's just not what I'm interested in.

Talk about working with designers and architects.

I like it. It can be really cool when I'm working with somebody good, who understands how things are put together—I learn neat stuff—but it is not cool working with someone who designs things that can't be built. It is satisfying to work with someone who knows what they are doing. I want the architect to be happy too, because if they love my work, they refer jobs to me. I do have to be able to push back sometimes though and stand my ground.

How would you respond to this idea: If your goal is to be a tradesman work for someone else. If your goal is to establish and build a significant company, put your tool belt aside and focus on business as soon as it is practical.

Roughly speaking, I agree with it. But if you want to be in the trades and have your own company, if you are working on your own, I guess it could work and you would get better pay and have a flexible schedule. But if you don't like doing books and paperwork, that is a problem and you should probably work for someone else. Putting your tool belt aside as soon as practical, in general, overall, I'd say it's pretty damn true.

How did you learn to manage money?

Growing up, living on my own, traveling around the world with limited funds. I've always seen through that thing about getting a large check and thinking it is mine. I'm not going to buy a new truck because I got a big check, I know it is more important to have a bit of a buffer in case things slow down. I always try to pay for everything that I buy and not borrow money. For a long, long time I've kept my overhead as low as I possibly could. I only buy a tool if I really need it. I have a piece-of-shit truck. I just don't spend any money that I don't absolutely have to. Now we have a ton of money, so I tell my guys if they need a tool we'll buy it.

Do you actively mentor your people and what does that look like?

I try to, in daily conversations. I've always done it, but I don't necessarily have a plan for it. Now we are doing employee reviews—that's a horrible word—but trying to set goals and figure out how they can become more valuable to the company and how they can feel fulfilled and happy here. We are trying to do more trainings and to give them opportunities to pursue things they find interesting. Everybody in the company is really bright and go-getters, so I'm trying to make sure they don't get bored.

What would you tell a tradesman—in any trade—about going into business for themselves?

Do it by the book. Do your research, use SCORE,[4] get everything set up right, so it's legit. Don't pay people under the table, keep your overhead really low, and don't spend any money that you don't have. I would tell them to learn financial literacy first. To understand overhead and what the bottom line is in business. To get their head around that.

I learned that on a $400,000 house when I'm charging 10 percent overhead—$40,000 seems like a lot, but it's not. So I would tell them to learn

---

4   SCORE is a network of experienced business mentors in the United States with more than 10,000 volunteers in 300 chapters. For over 50 years SCORE has served as a source of free business education and mentoring. *HTTPS://WWW.SCORE.ORG/*

about overhead. As you grow there are more and more things you have to pay for—tools, advertising, vacation time, office space, owner's pay, office staff, insurance—that is not included in what the customer pays. These things are overhead and somehow those costs have to be included in what you charge. Whether you're marking everything up or charging a flat fee for overhead, you have to know what you need to get.

I would tell them, "Don't try to be the cheapest guy, and avoid bidding." There is always somebody who's going with a lower number because they don't do their research and they are going to kill themselves to make money. But they're not going to make any money, because their price is too low.

If you had a way to reach every builder and tradesmen in America, what would you say?

Don't frickin' build a house like you did thirty years go. Build a passive house or a net zero house. Get with the program.

What is success in business?

Happy employees and happy customers.

What is success in a tradesman's and builder's career?

Doing quality work, enjoying it, and still having a life. I have a sub who does really nice work and is successful in business, but he works all the time, and his life looks horrible to me.

Do you have an exit strategy?

I don't really have one except to put as much money as I can in my retirement fund and do something with the business like selling it to one of the employees or making it an employee-owned company.

Word Association

Fear: Failure. Injuries. Having to lay somebody off.

Company image: Green. Sustainable. Non-polluting. Energy-saving.

Job safety: Super important. But there are rules that get broken all the time. One is height and not being tied in or having railings in place. It scares the shit out of me. We don't do safety training, except when they're using a new machine, then we train them on it.

Gratitude: I'm grateful to my employees.

Overhead: Expenses.

Profit: What I have in my pocket. What's left over after all the bills are paid.

Marketing: Word of mouth.

Sales: Honesty.

Estimating: Hard work.

Bidding: I don't do that.

Community: Giving back.

Communicate: Be clear. Reply to everybody.

Quality: What it's all about.

Cut-Offs

I had a client recently who was questioning our markup. I said it is based on our expenses and if it is a good year we get a 5 to 10 percent profit and we use it to grow the business. This is a good way to justify how much we are charging.

Whatever the person I was working for was doing, that's what I did, so if somebody is working for a bad builder they end up with bad habits.

I've been in business for about fifteen years. In the beginning it was just me and another guy, and then for eight years it was me and a crew. In the last few years it has been ten guys with multiple job sites and this office.

Then I found that you can build a passive house with crappy materials—lots of spray foam and stuff[5]—and the life span of that house is actually worse than a code-built home because there are so many greenhouse gases in the spray foam. So we use dense-packed cellulose instead and foam in the ground and rock wool in some places. Hopefully in the next five years there will be foam-free products.

We missed a $6,000 exterior door on a $420,000 job we bid—the profit dropped quickly on that one—but we were lucky to make it up it up in other areas.

---

5   I asked Jesper what "…and stuff" was. His response: "Basically any kind of foam is bad, but especially XPS foam (blue board) is a horrible material in terms of the carbon released during fabrication. Spray foam is a little better. We only use expanded polystyrene (EPS) foam underground. In our walls we use cellulose insulation because it sequesters carbon, it's a renewable material, and it has a low carbon footprint. It works really well."

Any work when you kneel down—it's a kind of worship.
It's part of the holiness of things…
Just like drawing a breath is. It's necessary.
Nick Lindsay

Pat Reardon,
General Contractor

Pat was sixty-nine at the time of this interview, which we began at low tide, on a private boat dock on Bustins Island off the coast of Maine. The planks were deeply weathered and covered with boat paraphernalia and it was a perfect Maine day—a cool light breeze off the calm water, blue sky, high white clouds, and a slowly rising tide. We discussed doing the interview on his work vehicle—a converted lobster boat, which Pat used as a shore-bound contractor would his truck—but there was no comfortable place to sit for two hours. His company name is Island Crew.

> *Pretty much I do work that's fun. If it's not—I'll always finish my obligation—but I'll go do something else* ■ *I really enjoy working because I've got a great crew and we have great clients* ■ *I treat my customers the way I want to be treated, it's kind of a mantra with us* ■ *Every one of my crew know, if they're doing something, do it like it's their own house* ■ *We have days where everything goes wrong and we don't get anything done, I still pay my men* ■ *I got one guy who gets hurt every other day, he's either going to change or I'm going to cut him free* ■ *Like every contractor, some people I just can't make happy* ■ *I keep my overhead as low as I can* ■ *A good tradesman is confident and he's willing to work with people, every bad one I've ever seen has a bad attitude*

I got into the trades 'cause it's something I naturally picked up and I was bored with just getting up and going to work, doing the same thing every day. My father was a master electrician, he was handy, and he taught me a lot. When I was fifteen I found a summer job working for a residential contractor. I had a natural aptitude and before the summer was out I was running his crew, I was the only guy who could read blueprints, I picked that up from my father. I did one year of college, it was boring, but I took a lot of math classes and that's been helpful.

Now our work is on remote islands. I don't want the business to get bigger and I struggle every week to keep it small. At one point I had twenty guys, now I've got five and I did that on purpose. I don't need the income or the headaches of trying to keep all those people straight. My crew works with me primarily on Saturdays and we get a pile of work done. They all have regular jobs and they don't have to work for me, but they like to. When I take a project I tell the customer, "This is where you fit in my schedule." Right now I can't see the light of day until next summer. Now that I'm retired from all my other jobs, I work two to three days during the week and Saturday. I have a separate crew that does roofing, because we're too busy to bother with it, and we renovate whole houses and build new ones and we do support work for a solar subcontractor. We do soup to nuts.

What is the most rewarding and the most difficult part of contracting?

The most rewarding is coming back ten or twenty years later and seeing that what we did stood up over time. The most difficult is doing a job the very best you can and the customer is not satisfied. That happens infrequently, but people are people, and when it does, I do everything I can to make it right.

I didn't have any goals when I started, just to keep my head above water. It was survival, that's how it started anyway. I've done everything wrong in business and the hard way at one time or another and I learned what I know about business from other people. When I was younger I did a lot of different things. I've always thought I might do something else: an airplane pilot, a train engineer—I love trains—or get my Coast Guard papers and run a tugboat. Whatever came in front of me I was like, "That looks like fun, let's try that." Then I worked seasonally for eighteen years as a ranger in the Allagash Wilderness Waterway—we worked ten days on and four days off, six months a year we were on layoff—and that whole time I worked part time for contractors, because the state doesn't pay anything. I had a commercial electrical business for a while. I worked for a union as a business agent and then went back to work for the state as a human resource manager. But I had this side business going all the time. For the past twenty years I've been almost exclusively working on remote islands, because it's not boring.

Do you have any mistakes that you made while you were learning business?

I've done everything the hard way at least once. I don't know if they were mistakes, but there's certainly things that I would do differently. I kept a guy on the crew too long. He had personal issues and I was trying to turn him around. It didn't work. I should have cut him loose, but I did what was right at the time. Also, I would have forced myself to do more formal education—not that I would give up working with my hands—but I enjoy learning and there is always more to learn.

Talk about trade versus business skills.

I've never been a good businessman. The paperwork drives me nuts and I put it off until a rainy day. I had a great customer years ago who said, "I haven't gotten a bill in a month and you've been working steady. You're not much of a businessman, Pat." I go, "Did you hire a businessman or a contractor? Which do you want?" He goes, "Okay, you're right, send me a bill when you have a chance." I like physical challenges and making the customer's vision happen and making things work.

How do you pass along information on working with new material or construction methods to your men?

If the material is something they haven't worked with before, we'll sit right down and talk it through. I'll say, "This is what we're doing and this is how we're doing it." For some of the younger guys, if it's a skill thing, I actually show them how to do it. Yesterday, I sent a guy who I thought knew how to do the work, and we ended up taking it apart and redoing it together. I let him finish the job after he learned how to do it right. Because we do so many different things, there's always something that somebody in the crew hasn't done. Chris, and now Jake, have become experts at a lot of different things, so I try to rotate people with each of them, to give them a taste of different stuff.

When you talk with customers on a job, how do you track what was agreed to?

I keep notes during the day and every night when I get to the office I'll pull out the job binder and write it down. I never do change orders. Mostly I do Time & Material. Some customers want a fixed price up front, but my regular customers know that if I do that, it is going to cost more. Most of my regular customers say, "Are we talking $20,000 or $50,000?"

What unusual thing do you enjoy?

Being out on the water. I worked in the Allagash on boats every day for eighteen years, so I was drawn to working on the islands and getting to work in a boat.

What advice have you given most to tradesmen and what is the best path to learning a trade today?

Treat your crew the way you want to be treated and don't ask them to do stuff that you wouldn't do. You can have all the best equipment in the world, but it won't matter if you don't have the right people. My lead guy—he's been with me for twenty-plus years—will tell you, "The most valuable part of your business is your people." There are so many different ways to learn the trade today, but if you can find a company that's doing what you want to do, see if you can get a job with them. They'll teach you how to do it.

If you were to lecture to a class of aspiring tradesmen what would you tell them to learn first?

There's so much to learn. Guys that come to work for me without the necessary skills, I tell them, "There are people here that know what they're doing, when they tell you to do something pay attention, if you don't understand, ask questions, and learn everything you can from them." and, "Avoid loudmouths and people that know everything." Loudmouths don't last on my crew but a week anyway.

What good investments have you made?

The first piece of equipment I bought was a little track-backhoe-loader. It is still running and has made the difference between what I can do and what other contractors can do. Since then I've bought two more, so I have three on different islands right now. And this boat. I was working out of smaller boats before. This one has given me the ability to travel further, to other jobs, and carry a full complement of tools.

What about your best and worst customer makes them that?

The best ones communicate well, and because of that they're happy and appreciative of the work when it's done, because they got what they wanted. And that makes me feel good, and every one of my crew responds to this too. The worst ones, you just can't make them happy.

Do you turn down customers and if so, why?

I send more work away than I take. I have a good client base and I take care of them and they take care of me, so I'm taking on almost no new customers. But sometimes, somebody comes along with realistic expectations and saying all the right things, so I read that and say, "Okay, I'll take this project on."

When something doesn't smell right, I turn them down. A guy called and he needed a roof put on, but the roof was all chopped up and it was a nightmare of a job. In the middle of the conversation he says, "My brother and I did this twenty years ago in one day." But it was easily a two-week job for two guys! That's a good one to run from. Another one called and I said, "Okay, we'll do this." He wanted an idea of the cost and I said I'd get back to him in a couple of weeks. He called a week later and said, "I talked to you a couple of months ago and you were going to get me a price." I did not call him back because I knew I was never gonna make this guy happy.

How would you advise someone to find a good contractor?

I would tell them to check with their friends to see if they had a contractor they trust. I would tell them to go look at some of the contractor's work to see if the quality meets their expectations. And I tell people they can always find a cheaper contractor than me, but I'll stake my crew that you can't find the quality of work for a better price.

What do you charge?

If it's a T&M job, I charge fifty dollars an hour per crew member and I mark materials up 10 percent. I do charge for hauling freight, but at a 10 percent markup, I probably lose money on materials because of the time involved in getting them to the islands.

Do you charge for planning jobs, that is, writing specs^ and making drawings?

If we need them, I write the specs and do the drawings. I don't have CAD^, just a small portable drafting board. It's paperwork, I don't like it, but I sit down and visualize the job in my head and draw it out, just like I'm building the place. I charge my hourly rate for doing it. If somebody doesn't think my time is worth it, I don't have a problem if they cut me loose. I certainly want to come them loose.

What do you look for when hiring?

There are so many things to look for. The very first is, do they get along with the rest of the crew and the customers? I can teach almost anyone how to do something, but I can't teach attitude. If they know everything and they're going to set the world on fire—if they're all ego—they are not going to work on my crew, no matter how good they are. If they know there's no shame in asking, "What's the best way to do this?" that's good. I look for people who are confident in who they are, competent, and don't mind sharing what they know. And somebody who, at the beginning and end of the day, looks forward to showing up to work and going home and leaving it behind for a few hours.

What do you expect from employees and what don't you expect?

I expect the people that work with me to treat wherever we're working with respect, like it was their own. Just as important, is to look out for each other's safety. I don't expect them to stand around—I'm not gonna say we don't waste time here and there—but I want people to work hard when we're working. And I expect them not to walk past something that needs to be done.

When do you let people go?

Fortunately, it happens naturally. If somebody doesn't fit well with the crew, they usually figure out it isn't for them. I've had people who, if they weren't right next to their truck, it bothered them. I had one guy that had a drug problem and I was afraid to let him work because of the power tools. I've got this kid now who keeps getting hurt and it's hard—I don't want to fire him—and don't want him to think I'm firing him because he got hurt, but I don't want him to get hurt anymore. He needs to think about how he works if he's going to work in the trades, because it's dangerous.

Talk about job safety.

If there's anything that is really high risk, I do it personally. I make sure if they see something that is not safe, they say so. I buy the strongest ladders and the best tools that I can and everything we do, we ask, "How can we do this safely?" I've got two people on the crew that piss me off because they baby me, they say, "Okay, I'll do that because somebody might fall." [Q. Do they call you old man yet?] Naw, they don't dare, they've got to keep up with the old man before they can call me that. [*Laughter.*]

Have you had a mentor or a teacher that influenced your career?

I think everybody you meet does, and everyone you get to know. There are so many people I've met and respected over the years. I can't think of any one specifically.

How do you define marketing and sales?

I try not to do either one. When I think of marketing, I think of mass marketing, like radio ads. I've never done that. I'm terrible at sales and I don't try to sell jobs. My work speaks for itself and once I've communicated with somebody, and we get down to what they want, the sale becomes, "Okay, let's do it that way."

What would you tell a new business owner about marketing and sales?

I would say the most important thing in getting work is happy customers. At the end of the day, they got what they wanted, at what they expected to pay, and they get to enjoy it every day. Your customers are your best salesmen.

If your work slows, what do you do?

In the '80s, when we had that depression, work was slow. I don't borrow more money than I can pay off in a month, so I don't end up with a pile of debt when things go south. I borrow when I buy a boat or a tractor or for a major equipment repair. I could wait for the phone to ring because I had no debt—and I had money put aside—so I put the crew to work on my house and my sister needed some work done too. For a couple of months I went to work for another company running a framing crew. I told them, "This isn't a permanent job for me." They were okay with that and I did what I had to do until things broke free.

When you have too much work, what do you do?

Besides pulling my hair out? I try like hell not to have too much, by being realistic about time expectations. I used to get in that bind a lot. This summer I got a little more than I wanted because of some issues that took me away from work for a while.

What behavior has most improved your business?

Mostly, accepting people for who they are rather than who I want them to be.

Q, Has there been a conflict between working in your trade versus running the business?

No. Working my trade, that's what I do. I don't know, I do have to balance them back and forth though.

Do you have absolute principles that you follow in business?

The overriding ones: "Treat people the way I want to be treated" and "I will not build something that I can't stand back from and go, 'That's done right.'"

What do you do for contracts and estimates?

Right now I have a septic system and I told the owner, "We're talking twenty to twenty-two thousand dollars." There is nothing in writing but I'm careful who I have for customers. If it's new construction, that's pretty easy, you're much more in control. If it's a remodel without a hard number, I'll say,—"This is what I think it's going to be."—and we'll have the conversation: "I don't know what's behind the walls and if it's ugly, I'll send you pictures, and we'll talk about it and figure out what to do." If they need a hard number for the bank, I'll develop an estimate like I'm building the place, and I add a certain amount for what I can't see. If I give a hard number and I run into something unknown—it's off-season so the customer is not here—they will never know about it because if I go back to people every time I run into something, it hurts my reputation. With hard numbers, I'll send a proposal with a scope-of-work^ and that's my contract. I hate giving hard numbers because I have to be fair to myself and the customer and trying to find that point is really hard. The fear point is between covering my butt and the right price for the customer.

What memorable mistakes have you made in business and what would you have done differently?

When I was younger, it was money. Credit was easy to come by and I used it unintelligently. I learned to manage money through trial and error, mostly error. I would have invested more in equipment and I would have worked smarter. Now I tell guys to throw out every credit card they have because it will chew up too much money. I tell them not to borrow expensive money and to be realistic about expenses, to learn what their expenses are—material, equipment, crew—and then figure out what your time is worth. I tell them to avoid people with an attitude. For me it's "What do I want my life to be?" If you have people that go through life the hard way, they are not the ones to surround yourself with. If you work for good people and have good people on your crew, you're okay.

Talk about working with a designer or architect.

I've never had a great experience working with an architect. Inevitably I end up redrawing their work so that it will stand up or so the cost is reasonable. I had one where they had a stair going right through a support beam—we changed the direction of the stair—and another where the architect had spec'd $100,000 worth of galvanized steel, every piece handmade, and we changed that too.

Talk about profit and overhead.

You've got to have profit or else the first thing that goes wrong, you'll be out of business. In my company, I treat myself as another employee. Actually, I pay my lead guy more than I pay myself. Profit is the money that, after everything else, it goes into the bank, and when an engine blows or we need a piece of equipment, that's what it's for. Do I always have that? No, because I pull out of the same pile for material, so it's a slush fund. But you've got to have profit or you won't be in business.

What is a successful business and a successful career?

In my business, it is being happy at the end of the day and being able to look back at what I've done and say, "That's good, my customers are happy, and a lot of them have become friends." My exit strategy is for one of my guys to take over the business when I can't do it anymore.

Word Association

Integrity: There's a person that comes to mind, a fellow I worked for years ago, he had the highest integrity of anyone I've ever known. In the face of a lot of adversity he still said, "No, this is the right way."

Communication: You can spend all day busting your butt doing what you think is right, but if it hasn't been communicated properly, you wasted the day.

Job safety: Number one. If I see something that's unsafe, I tell them we're not doing it that way.

Fear: It's gonna sound stupid, but research, because I need to find out why I'm afraid. I've had things in my life that scared the pants off me, and I would say, "Okay, what's going on here? What am I afraid of? What's the worst that can happen, let's go to the back of that closet."

Company image: People. How people see you, how your people look.

Gratitude: Nice to have and it's a gauge of success. Real gratitude comes when I return to a job twenty years later and it's just as good as the day we left.

Overhead: Minimum.

Profit: Necessary.

Marketing: I don't do it.

Sales: I try not to do it.

Estimating: I hate doing it, but I do it when I have to.

Bidding: I won't bid.

Community: Very important. It's people knowing people.

Quality: Quality is what keeps your customers. If I can't do it right, I'm not going to do it and I won't stumble through something, instead I'll call in an expert to either do the job or train my crew how to do it.

Cut-Offs

When the word "bid" comes out of someone's mouth, I tell them, "If you're looking for bids, it isn't worth my time because you're always gonna find somebody cheaper."

The question is, "Did the customer tell me what they want to the degree that we can give them that? Are they happy with the end product?"

Be realistic with your client and don't create expectations that are unrealistic—you're not going to build the Taj Mahal for ten thousand dollars—follow through with what you said you would do and be realistic about your schedule. Don't say, we'll jump on this next month, when really, it's gonna be four months down the road.

I've seen people that weren't terribly competent, but their attitude overcame that and they were willing to do whatever needed to be done.

I had a subcontractor who told me he got people to work for a lot less money than I was paying and that I didn't need to treat my people as well as I do. That's bad advice. Stupid advice.

I only schedule work part time and I have a client base that keeps us busy, so we don't look for new customers, which means I don't have to break in new customers.

Now people come to me and tell me what they are looking for, and I'll say, "Okay. Your project interests me, I'll take it on."

I still swing a hammer, and it gets a little frustrating when I can't because I'm running everybody else around.

Recently I looked up a material online, found a local distributor and went there and asked them to show me the stuff and asked what people's experience with it had been.

Stopping advertising to save money
is like stopping your watch to save time.
Henry Ford

Heather Thompson,
General Contractor

www.tjwhome.com
heather@tjwhome.com

Heather and I met one summer evening at a friend's woodworking shop in Portland, Maine—amid tools, sawdust, electric cords, and air hoses—and talked about her journey to owning a construction company, Thompson Johnson Woodworks, on Peaks Island off the coast of Maine. Heather is forty-eight, thoughtful, and she laughs easily.

Business is about self-confidence and basic things like being honest and treating people well and paying attention to the details ■ Our best customers are collaborative and they understand it is a creative process that evolves and changes ■ We used to watch This Old House and that was our formal training (you can't tell anyone) ■ The salesperson should not be the estimator, but that is the situation in my company ■ We are paid for estimating because we are helping to define a realistic scope-of-work^ during the design phase ■ The worst customer is indecisive and blind to their contribution to the shit show it causes ■ My job is getting customers and doing estimates and managing the projects and running the business ■ I don't know if my estimating is getting better or if I'm getting more comfortable giving people a high number ■ I'm always willing to forgo comfort, money, and stability for the payoff that may happen down the road ■ I like the creative aspect of marketing, but it's the easiest thing not to do because it does not seem to be critical ■ In an apples-to-apples comparison, we will be better and faster, but it's never apples to apples ■

Out of college, my husband and I started a furniture company in South Portland, Maine. It was not impressive craftsmanship, but we were building furniture for a guy who was on the recycled wood bandwagon—it was big in the late '90s—and he was our one customer. We built display tables for Timberland shoes and then Timberland tried to renegotiate the price, but the guy we worked for wouldn't negotiate and they easily found someone to do it for a lot less money. I don't like furniture making. It's boring and I hate finishing. I liked sales, working with customers, and coming up with new ideas and getting someone to buy it. I liked the business side.

My husband and I moved to Peaks Island in Maine—our son was one year old—where it was easy to get construction projects, and my husband and my dad worked together doing construction. Neither of them was good at business, and my dad pulled out about a year later and went back to being a school principal, and my husband and I started working together again. There was enough momentum through word of mouth that we had tons of work, so we hired a guy as our project manager. We wanted him to partner with us, but he didn't because he knew it was risky. It's good that he didn't, it did not work out. We dodged a bullet. My husband and I ran the company together until 2008 when we split up. I went to work for a landscape architect as an office manager and I was terribly bored and unhappy and so desperate to make a change that it gave me the courage to approach my ex and say, "Okay, I'll take over the business." For years he had wanted to stop doing construction, so I bought the tools and the name, and the crew agreed to keep working for me. I paid him $10,000 over three years and he didn't have to pay me alimony anymore. I did it because no one was going to hire me to do anything that met my potential. I'm terrible at selling myself, but I knew I could run the business. I've owned the business for about eight years.

What do you do if you are unsure of a decision or lose direction?

If there is a big decision or something that I have to overcome, I get depressed for a day—I'll talk to people—and then I get over it and know that I can do it. It happens every time.

What academic education do you have, and did it help your career?

I graduated from South Portland high school and went to MassArt in Boston for two years where I studied sculpture.[1] I'd done well in high school and decided I wanted to do something more academic, so I went for a trimester of pre-med at the University of California, Santa Cruz. I was like, "Yeah, no thank you." Then I did anthropology and then I was hanging out in the ceramic studio and ended up majoring in sculpture. I learned to think creatively about problems—to think outside the box—and I learned a sense of aesthetics. When I worked for the landscape architect, I learned that I didn't want to be an office manager and that I didn't know as much about bookkeeping as I thought I did.

When you and your husband started the business, what were your goals?

This was a trade we could do that we liked, but we slid into it, neither of us intended to become carpenters. We wanted to do green building. We wanted to hire people and do it right—workers compensation and liability insurance—and not hire people under the table. It is exciting to grow something and I always wanted to hire more people. At that point I was doing the books and I would start the sales process, but I wasn't involved with estimating. In 2006 we had fifteen people on the crew, but it was a shit show. Now we have nine people in the field and two in the office.

What do you love?

I love to sing. I did theater in high school and I did some jazz singing with a guy on Peaks a couple years ago.

What is the best path to learning a trade and what advice have you given most to tradesmen?

I don't think there are many training programs for carpenters, so working in the field is the way to learn, but I also think going to college and getting a degree is important, it helps you learn how to learn. I tell them to slow down and take their time and avoid hack carpenters who get it done as fast as possible; it's not about being fast, it's about doing it right so that we're not redoing it. I tell them to learn how to install a continuous air barrier.

---

1   Massachusetts College of Art and Design, branded as MassArt, is a public college of visual and applied art.

Ninety percent of building a house is obvious to a carpenter, but the last 10 percent takes time, patience, and attention to detail.

How would you describe a successful tradesman?

Someone who is organized and doesn't give up. A lot of people will do something, it'll get complicated, and instead of figuring out how to fix it, they get stuck in a loop or they throw up their hands and move forward anyway. Someone who can figure out problems and complete a task is successful.

What is a good sub?

Someone who will prioritize getting our work done. Also people who tell us, "I can't do it this week, but I can do it at this time next week" and then actually show up. A good sub is organized enough to have their schedule under control. Generally we have really great long-term relationships with subs.

What good investment have you made and what recent purchase has helped your business?

My children were my best investment, then buying the business. I just bought a really good truck for $6,000 and we bought a dump trailer, that was a smart investment.[2]

What about your best customer makes them that?

The best customer is good at making decisions quickly and understanding that their decisions impact the final price. This brings the stress level of the project down and the job goes better. Also, they aren't going to freak out when we give them their final bill. We tend to work with incredible, collaborative, reasonable, decisive customers. They are smart and good-looking too! [*Laughter.*]

What about your worst customers makes them that?

The worst customer is indecisive and unwilling to accept that things cost what they cost. They will go through multiple rounds of pricing and design changes to bring the cost down, but when they can't get rid of the $7,500 shower surround and $12,000 countertop package but need to cut $150,000 out of the budget, there is a problem. We do a pre-construction contract and

---

2   Later Heather laughed at having told me the truck was a great investment because she ended up paying $5000 to repair it.

charge $65.00 per hour for estimating, so it's not wasted time to do multiple estimates—actually it is part of a good preconstruction process—but the estimate gets too lean because of the compounding effect of scope and cost reduction, times optimism, times number of estimates: when the customer, the builder, and the architect are working toward reducing cost, it is hard not to get overly optimistic. We end up with a poor final scope and a poor estimate which often results in conflict.

Also, the indecisive perfectionist bogs the job down by requiring attention from the lead carpenter, nitpicking details before something is complete, and asking, "Can we move that door over six inches?". They change their mind after a task is complete or ask for multiple iterations of change orders^ or reintroduce scope that was removed during the estimating process. If the person acknowledges their indecision adds to the cost of the project, it's fine, but if they push the blame onto others and won't take responsibility for their behavior, they end up disputing the final cost and often not paying. The other worst customer is someone who, from the start, has only their own best interest in mind. They are aggressive and combative and talk about how they are related to lawyers—as if they are the only people with access to legal counsel—and they take advantage of mistakes instead of accepting that there was a mistake and working together to figure it out.

Do you use Time & Material^ or fixed price^ contracts?

We do Time & Material (T&M), ninety-nine percent of the time, and we do change orders^ for unseen scope^—rot repair for example—and customer-driven scope changes, and unanticipated material and labor overages. We carefully track actual cost for labor and material against estimated cost. In the past, when we got to the end of a project, it was not unusual for me to give a discount because I felt bad about going over the estimated cost. This is a bad business practice and we've stopped doing it. I would consider going to a fixed price; it might be easier and less stressful than going back to customers at the end of a job to say we went over. Overages are painful.

We do a preconstruction phase^ for jobs that have design/drawings and we work in partnership with the customer and designer. We consult on systems, buildability, insulation methods, and building science^ during preconstruction. We are hired from the beginning to do a series of estimates, usually three to four during the design phase. These estimates ensure that the proposed design is on target for meeting the customer's stated budget, and they get progressively more detailed. The final estimate/scope is the contract document for construction. We also have an optional "hold-your-place" fee which puts the customer in our queue. It is non-refundable and it's typically 5 percent of the budget the customer has in mind when they come to us. We move into the construction phase after design and estimating, and the hold-your-place fee is applied to the first construction invoice.

I heard about the hold-your-place fee in my builder peer group. A builder was offering it as an option on their pre-construction contracts. We typically have one to one and a half years of booked work and people like the idea of getting in line. We do lose some customers because of the long wait, even though it takes that long to get drawings and permits. The hold your place fee is unusual in the industry.

How do you shape a new client's expectations and what do you want them to know about the planning and construction process?

People who understand that excellent work takes time and money are the people we want to work with. New customers will tell us their budget—they want a $100,000 renovation, I let them know it is more likely $200,000—and I'll give them that news early on, before we've become invested in each other. That is what I do up front.

Do you turn down customers and if so, why?

We've been doing the preconstruction phase for a while, and we usually work with the same designer. When people call me, I'll say, "Okay, if you want more than new appliances, you need to hire a designer because we need permit drawings, and this is the one to work with." When I do the estimate and they freak out or don't pay, it weeds out the bad customers upfront. I haven't had to fire a customer.

How would you tell someone to pick a contractor?

Ask friends for recommendations, check references, and look at previous work, but hire the person you like, because you're going to work well together. If you approach a relationship with integrity and trust, then it'll be a successful project.

Have you failed at something that set you up for later success?

If I hadn't gotten divorced, I would never have taken over the business. I was afraid of estimating and afraid of running the business myself. I didn't think I could ever do it. Getting divorced and having that terrible job gave me the kick in the pants I needed to go ahead and run the business.

What do you look for when you hire, and what advice would you give about hiring?

Hiring is hard for me because I believe everyone. Before, if they said, "I'm a great carpenter, I have ten years' experience." I'd hire them. Now I do a couple of phone interviews or meet with them initially and then have the leads interview them with me. Now we all have to agree on hiring. We're having a hard time finding people with experience. We get a lot of twenty-something college graduates who are super excited to work for us, but we really need people who have more experience. When I advertise a job, a woman will apply and say, "I don't know anything about carpentry and I'm willing to work for free as an intern." Guys are like, "I've been building and working with wood my whole life." They are twenty-two and they know everything! [*Laughs.*] It's crazy. I'd tell people to be honest, and not to oversell or undersell themselves. I'd say, hire brains and integrity and someone you like, who will work well with your group, and then skill.

What makes a good and a bad employee?

Someone who is collaborative and listens and does what I ask them to do or figures out a better solution with me. I would never scream—I don't do that—but I'm persistent and if I need to be more direct, I will be. A good employee will own the task they're on and make sure it happens, and even if they don't know the next task, they stay busy anyway. Bad employees oversell their experience, they don't show up on time, and they don't get along with the crew. We've fired people because they were doing drugs at work. I don't do drug testing because I trust people and because our culture is absolutely no drugs or drinking at work. I'm letting people go much quicker than I used to—I used to "passive-aggressive" people out of the company—now I fire bad hires within a month, unless they're really bad; then I fire them immediately

What do you and don't you expect from employees?

I expect them to work hard, to listen to their leads, to ask questions and to be curious about the process so they learn. I push people to do more than they might be comfortable with because they're going to figure it out and that is how you learn. I don't expect them to give people bad news. I do that.

Do you have educational programs within your company?

We are part of the BLN^, through NESEA^. I've started having my lead carpenter Mark come to those meetings with me, and that is helping him think about the business in a larger way. If someone wanted to go to a class I'd pay for the class, although I couldn't pay them to go. We don't have a formal training program, but the leads are in charge of training and they are intentional about it. Once in a while I will get nervous and we'll have a safety meeting.

How do you relay information on new material or a method of construction to your crew?

I have to figure out how to estimate it and the leads have to figure out how to install it, so we sit down together and work out what it's going to take. They do the research and read the paperwork.

Do you have employee benefits?

We have *very good* benefits. We pay 100 percent of their health insurance premium. We have a high deductible with a health reimbursement account (HRA) and the company pays the first $1500 of medical expenses. They get one week of vacation after a year, two weeks after three years, and three weeks after seven years. We have forty hours of paid time off, which covers doctors' appointments, or if it snows and they can't work. It is personal time, but it is not extended to vacations. We have a tool allowance of $350 a year. We have a simple IRA with a 3 percent match.

We hire new carpenters at $17 an hour. Someone with five-plus years of experience starts around $20—$22. We pay leads between $27—$35. Our billing rates are $52.50 for carpenters, $60 for leads, and $65 for project managers. We markup materials and subs 20 percent. After factoring in our labor burden^ rate and benefits—taxes, workers compensation, vacation, health insurance, retirement, tool allowance, forty hours sick/weather/personal time—and our overhead costs (typically around 13 percent) our net profit is, theoretically, 10 percent.

What books have been important in your life?

I loved J.R.R. Tolkien's books, *The Hobbit* and others. I was a voracious reader and I'd walk to school reading. Now I buy business books and never read one page. I don't have the capacity to read anymore, I'm too busy.

Have you had a mentor or teacher who influenced your career?

I haven't had a single mentor, but I am part of a business peer group, BLN^, and working with that group of people—they all own businesses of a similar size with similar problems—was incredibly helpful when I took over the business. Having them as a sounding board, working together to figure out problems like "Are you billing enough?" or "Do you have to fire that person?"—it is like having a corporate board of directors.

How do you define marketing and sales? What would you tell a new business owner about them?

Marketing and sales are intuition. For clients, hiring a contractor and doing a project is a huge and scary process and most people have no idea how to start, so getting a recommendation from people you know, who had someone do a good job for them, is still the best. Being honest, treating people with respect, and spending a lot of time on your estimates, is what matters. The strongest marketing is a good reputation. You need a website; it needs to look good and you need to update it often. Social media matters. Maintain Facebook and Instagram pages, get five stars on Google and Yelp. We have a captive audience on Peaks and although we have yard signs, we forget to put them up because everyone knows who we are. If we were in Portland, I would do a better job of signage. Here is what doesn't work: an ad in a magazine with all the other ads that look exactly the same.

Sales is meeting with people—the face-to-face interaction—it is being friendly and listening. Be a listener! In sales you have to be able to tell people, "What you want isn't achievable, but we can figure something out." I generally like everyone I meet and that's huge because people know that I like them, and they are more willing to work with me. You want to work with someone who likes you, right?

We're developing relationships that bring us work and I would rather be considered a highly skilled expert and have the people I work with bring us work, than to get random calls from social media. Those are generally not the customers we want. Joining NESEA and focusing on promoting high-performance building has done more to increase our exposure than anything else.

When work slows or when you have to much work, what do you do?

We haven't had work slow much. Last spring, we were working on a project and the customer added three times our original estimate to the scope. That was fine, but it pushed our schedule up. I thought I could take the lead off the big project so he could go do a kitchen and still oversee the first project. That was a mistake. It didn't help the schedule and it made two customers irritated because we weren't giving them the attention they needed. Now when we have too much work, I push people off.

How did you learn to estimate?

When I took over the company, I was nervous about estimating, and our lead carpenter, Mark Pollard, was going to customer meetings with me and doing our big estimates. I started out doing small estimates and Mark would review them with me. Eventually, I gained confidence and I took over all of the estimating/scope writing. Now, I have the lead on each job review the estimate with me before I send it to the customer.

Eventually we transitioned from Excel spreadsheet estimates to using Construction Suite.[3] In an estimate the materials are clearly defined, and we get numbers from subs, so it is only labor that is a guess. We use CSI^ codes to break the project into its parts and then it's a lot of "It's going to take about this much time to frame that wall." I calculate square footage with PlanSwift—which is an awesome program—and it gives me how much of each thing is required.[4] I haven't taken the time to learn it fully—it can do a lot more than I use it for—and I never write that information down so whoever's doing the time crunching has to go back and look at the project all over again. There is a lot of redundant bullshit that we do because I don't feel like setting it up properly. I've never hired an estimator because we do stuff that isn't typical, and what am I gonna do if I don't do the estimates?

3   HTTP://CONSTRUCTIONSUITE.COM/
4   HTTPS://WWW.PLANSWIFT.COM/

Talk about your contract and how it has evolved.

Our contract is a page and a half, it's Maine's general construction contract and it hasn't changed much. It describes the type of contract as Time & Material, and our rates, and that our figures are an estimate, not a fixed price. There's a dispute resolution paragraph required by the state—mediation, arbitration, or binding arbitration—and we break payment into four or five chunks and work off of that money.[5]

What were the first three things you did when you bought the business?

Once I finally owned it—my ex owned it for about year and I worked with him during the transition (he made the process easy)—the business grew quickly, the crew got larger, I started charging more, but the most impactful thing was joining BLN.

How did you learn about business and did you write a business plan?

I haven't taken business classes or read business books. It just makes sense; it's relationships and good business decisions. I did not write a business plan, but I think it's important. I'm good at big picture stuff and for a while, especially in the BLN group, I resisted the impulse to write a plan because people spend too much time naming and quantifying what they are doing. It is busy work. But it is important to sit down and think about what you want to do. I work on maintaining the idea that we do really good work and we have really good people. Our website statement—which I wrote—says what I want our company to be.

Do you have memorable mistakes that you made in business?

Poor hires and not firing when it needed to happen. I repeatedly make the same mistake and it is mostly around not giving bad news. I'll procrastinate—being over budget, firing, overtime—but it is always better to give bad news up front, in dribs and drabs, than it is to give it as a tsunami at the end of a project. We had a customer who, once the project started, added back every change they'd stripped out to lower the cost during preconstruction. They ended up not paying us $35,000 because our project manager did not write change orders as the customer added these items back in.

---

5   Some months after our interview, Heather had a lawyer make her preconstruction and construction contracts more robust because she had problems when a project fell through in the preconstruction phase.

What do you like and dislike about having your business?

I like owning a business that's successful. I like having a great crew and I try not to think of them as my children [*laughs*]. I've gotten over this, but it's kind of lonely. There's no one patting me on the back saying, "Wow, this is great." I've thought about having a partner in the business, but I'd have to find a person who complements what I bring to the table, and partnerships are fraught with problems. Also, there are many things that I should do that I don't, and if I were working for someone, I would do them. And the stress when things are not going well is really hard.

Talk about change orders.

I write detailed scopes and, in theory, review them with the customer as part of the contract signing. We run our Time & Material jobs like a quoted fixed price contract; when we run into something that we didn't put in the scope—besides the customer wanting extras, which is an obvious change order—we write a change order and we have biweekly customer meetings to talk about those changes. I try to get fixed prices from subs, but if they say, "I forgot to include something," I pay them because people should be paid for their work.

Do you bid jobs?

Not much. My policy is that we don't bid competitively, but I will sometimes. We are going to be expensive because we employ "best practice building standards". These details are not usually specified in the job documents and we are meticulous, which means, when we are in a bid situation, we are going to be more expensive. The most successful projects are when the relationship is centered on trust and mutual problem solving with a customer who understands we will deliver the *very best* product possible within the time frame and cost allowed. Competitive bidding runs inherently against these ideas. Also, we get a lean drawing set from the designer and that doesn't work to get bids because with scant details, the bids will be all over the place. With T&M, theoretically, if we bill everything, we're reimbursed for everything, even if the job runs over. If I've done a good proposal on a T&M project, there aren't any big surprises at the end and it is potentially less expensive for the customer because we have not built in a large contingency, like you do in a bid situation.

Have you ever had a job come in under the estimate?

Yes, significantly. We just had a kitchen project come in $10,000 under. They are friends of mine, and they were not as excited as I thought they would be. At the same time, I have a project that's $30,000 over. We are usually within 10 percent.

What advice would you give to a group of new business owners about estimating?

I don't know that they need to spend money on an expensive monthly estimating service because they're only going to use one eighth of its capacity anyway. And estimating software has a long way to go before it is user-friendly.[6] If you have a complete work category list with subcategories and your base rate and markups in an Excel spreadsheet, you can do a good estimate and it doesn't have to be complicated. But you do have to write a detailed scope-of-work separately and job cost reports^ aren't as easy to create as they are with a packaged program.

Talk about working with designers and architects.

Most of our projects have been done with one designer who used to work for my ex and I in-house when we were running the company together. There are not a ton of details on her drawings because we don't need them. She knows what we are going to do, and we know her intention. We worked with one architect when we had our first terrible customer experience, in part because he threw us under the bus with the customer. Which is why I believe in the design/build^ philosophy where everyone has an equal part in this three-pronged team—customer, designer, builder—and you're working together from the beginning to make it a success.

How would you respond to this idea: If your goal is to be a tradesman work for someone else. If your goal is to establish and build a significant company, put your tool belt aside and focus on business as soon as it is practical.

I agree with that. Any famous artist is an excellent self-promoter. If you want to think about building all the time and do the best job you can,

---

6 Author: This made me laugh. Many, many years ago I used these exact words about our then computer estimating program and again, every time a new estimating program replaced an old one.

there isn't time to then run a business successfully. Usually you are good at one thing or the other. It's not that you can't do both—you can if you work eighty hour a week—but that sucks.

If you were giving advice to new contractors about money, what do you tell them?

Figure out what you need to charge to be profitable. If you're not profitable, you're not in business and it doesn't matter what you want to do, you can't. You have to make money to live and you have to be able to pay your employees well. Potential customers whining about what something should cost, doesn't matter. You have to make money. And don't use new customer deposits to pay for previous jobs. And start putting money away for retirement every month when you're twenty years old!

What would you tell a tradesman about opening a business?

If you create a culture you're comfortable with, your whole business runs that way. Don't think that people are out to get you. Don't be divisive. Don't badmouth competitors. Be part of a team. Be friendly. Treat people with respect. Spend the time required to do good estimates, know what your billing rate needs to be, and don't be influenced by what people think something should cost and don't feel guilty for what you need to charge. I would tell them to understand their accounting books and chart of accounts in an intimate way—they need to get the *what* and *why* of them—so they can calculate their billing rate. Learn what a budget is and make one.

What is success in business?

Success is a happy crew, the right people wanting to work for you, doing interesting projects, and having happy customers. It boils down to creating a company that is a good place to work.

What is success in one's career?

Building a company that doesn't go away when you're ready to quit. That would be success. I'm starting to think about an exit strategy, and I talked to a consultant about employee ownership. Giving them ownership in the company will make it stronger, they'll start to think in a bigger picture way, and it is fair. It would, potentially, allow me to draw some income after I've retired too. In five years, I want to either transition to that, or have a plan to do it.

Word Association

Communication: Giving bad news early and often is the most important thing, and the hardest. With anything where there is going to be a disappointed response from the customer, it is the right thing to say it up front.

Job safety: We hire people who are not reckless. Hopefully, that's contributing to a culture of safety. We need to be more intentional about it.

Fear: A recession, or work drying up, and the personal stuff.

Company image: People know we do excellent work and they think we're expensive. Which is great. So, we meet their expectations every time.

Gratitude: I have gratitude for our customers working with us and being supportive and I have huge gratitude to the crew because they're amazing and they work their asses off.

Estimating: Take time to understand the project, write detailed scopes so the information is there when people need it.

Bidding: In bidding, you give the customer a scope-of-work and a price and tell them what your structure is, and they compare it to the other peoples' bid and they hire the cheapest one. But the cheapest one left out one half of the things that I included.

Overhead: The cost of the people in the office, my salary, the cost of the office. It's any costs associated with running the business.

Profit: Profit is on top of overhead and it is what I theoretically take home.

Marketing: The best marketing is word of mouth, but most people don't talk to more than a few people and that is why it is important to have a website and Facebook and Instagram. The way to become respected in your field is to do good work.

Community: You spend more time with the people you work with than with your family and your friends, so you better like them. The culture of the company—people supporting each other and working together as a team—is everything.

Cut-Offs

Going to school doesn't have to be a four-year degree, but learning is important.

I have a love-hate relationship with luxury finishes that are going to be passé in five years. But I get it. When I have to make that decision, I want all the same shit.

We do between $1.8 and $2.3 million in volume. My fiancé and I are renovating a building for ourselves and that has lowered our gross for this year.

We have a number of subs we work with all the time. Part of it is being on Peaks Island there are a limited number of people working here, so when I find someone who will work with us and their price is reasonable, we will go with them. I don't like to negotiate; it makes me uncomfortable.

We want to do more work in Greater Portland because I want to do more high-performance building. We do quite a bit on Peaks, but I want an opportunity to build super-efficient green houses.

I'm always doing things like this big project that my fiancé and I are doing—a building with four apartments and our offices—where it's a big leap and big commitment, that in the future is going to be awesome! But right now is a slog.

You can have an innate ability—and not need fifteen years of experience—but you do need experience.

The bad customer does not understand that the best projects are always the ones where everyone works together to make a project successful.

We have to work outside in the winter because Peaks is a summer place and people want their houses ready for the summer, so our volume of work is slower in the summer than is in the winter. It doesn't matter how hard I try to schedule inside work during the winter, the crew is always working outside.

If anything goes bad, I did it.
If anything goes semi-good, we did it.
If anything goes really good, you did it.
That's all it takes to get people to
win football games for you.

Bear Bryant

David Stuart Bull,
Chimney Sweep

David is a seventy-nine-year-old good-natured chimney sweep with a slight English accent which he turns on for effect when selling his services and he has a flair for the dramatic, as evidenced by his amateur acting career. We are sitting for this interview in a mutual friend's field under a canopy in Eugene Oregon, enjoying perfect summer weather.

Back in the old country, people would think that ghosts and goblins and witches were in the chimneys, and the chimney sweeps would come along and sweep them out, and they became associated with good luck ■ Having a coal fire was one of my earliest memories, and included in that is the blizzard that happened when the chimney sweep showed up on his bicycle with poles and brushes and a gunny sack

I was driving south in an old junker of a car in December—cold, foggy—with my wife and kids. I could hardly see anything. We stopped in Eugene because we liked it here. Then I started. I had wanted to do something on my own for quite a while. For a few months I planted trees, which a lot of people do when they first come to Eugene. At the same time, I was looking into starting a chimney sweeping business. I was somewhat inspired by my experiences in England, where I was born and lived in a house warmed by a several coal fireplaces, but also by the fact that this is a big wood-burning area. And there weren't any chimney sweeps. So that, coupled with my investigation, I decided I'd give it a crack.

I liked the fact that chimney sweeping has such a history of folklore behind it. That appealed to me. You dress up. You put a top hat on, put on tails, and that was very attractive to me, because everybody, even now, says, "Oh, there's Mary Poppins."

The long and the short of it, I hated the suit-and-tie corporate trip. Basically, I don't like people telling me what to do. That might be a common theme among the people you interview. [*Laughter.*] I like being my own boss. As I see it, it's me and the customer, that's very simple. I like the physicality of chimney sweeping. You're around a new roof every day and a new view every day. It beats sitting behind a desk with a rubber plant in a corner. You get to see people in their homes, and their dogs and kids. It's just a very cool situation.

Within a couple of years I was doing enough that I could make it just about a full-time business, although during the spring and summer months I did rototilling as well, because chimney sweeping drops off. I dressed up like Robin Hood for my rototilling, and I was a jolly good rototiller in the spring and summer, and a jolly good chimney sweep in the fall and winter. So, you know, those kinds of things attract people.

I give customers an education so they don't burn down their house. And then human relations are one of the bonuses of it. You get to know a lot of people, and they're always glad to see you. And it's fun. I still enjoy it, even after all these years. Forty-plus years. It's a bit of a workout though, you get dirty. I've taken a couple of bad falls. So the most serious that you have is a torn rotator cuff, which heals more or less by itself.

People call you up on the phone and ask for service. Fortunately, I have a very well-educated and conversant wife—we've been married fifty-four years—and it's that initial contact that makes the sale. They don't know me from Adam, but she's so good on the phone and gives them so much good information. I'll ask, "Why did you choose us?" and they say, "Well, your wife is so pleasant, so nice, we did not call anyone else." Yeah, she charms people. And she has this delightful message on the voice machine. So it's the same old service business, isn't it? It's that first impression, which is usually on the telephone.

When I started my business, I think in the back of my mind, I had visions of grander things. I mean, a whole covey of chimney sweeps. I think my idea of having a lot of people working was a lot of bullshit. So it was an easy idea to give up. I'm with those guys who say small is beautiful.

I do think education is important, though. I went to boarding school, and prep school, and college, and it helped me. Well, it makes you a more complete human being, doesn't it? And it makes you more accessible to more people. I relate well to people. It's surprising to them, they can have an educated discussion with a chimney sweep. [*Laughter.*]

My advice to any tradesman is to anticipate, preventing problems before they happen. If you see something wrong with the chimney, then be sure, as much as you can, to tell the homeowner. If you make a mistake, own up to it, give them their money back, and give compensation somehow, as quickly as possible.

Well, you know, you work a little bit harder when you do it all yourself. And you spend a fair amount of time generating new business. I've tried to make my business as simple as possible, so paperwork is minimal. It is a very simple process because I don't have employees, and it's basically checkbook accounting. But my job has given me flexibility to do a lot of stuff I really like to do.

The way I try to stay away from bad customers is that my wife has a very sensitive ear. If she thinks there's a problem, she'll say, "I suggest you call somebody else." People who are overly cautious about what's going to happen to their house we avoid. And it's a gut feeling you get. Some people just make problems, it's their nature. The bad customers are the ones that won't pay you. Well, in forty years I've had maybe five people who haven't paid me. And when something like that happens, especially when it's the normal amount, after six months I just let it go.

I left a few jobs, only two or three times though, if they were rude to me. I don't appreciate that. Most of my customers are good people. They're there when they say they will be. If there is any preparation work to be done, they've done it. If they've got a dog that is bothersome, it's locked up.

If I were talking to a group of young people about what they should do, well, if you love to do something, hey, that's a good place to start. If you like woodworking, if you like working with metal, landscaping, those are great places to start. And then you put your foot in the water and go for it. Having a trade is satisfying, and I get satisfaction from physical labor.

That's a big one right there. When you've finished the day, you're tired, you clean up, you have your dinner, and you enjoy the evening and your family. A lot of those guys who work in offices, you know, never get that feeling of satisfaction. Working like that gets to be a real rat race; you try to keep up with your colleagues and business. Having a trade is not like that.

I think being in business for yourself is a great experience. If you're wanting to work hard, keep an open mind, and know that things aren't going to go right always. But you can largely determine that they go right a huge percentage of the time; 95 percent maybe. You do that by good communication skills, by doing good quality work, by checking in with people, and making sure they're happy. I would tell new guys not to go in it half-assed. You know, it's about not letting the work run you to the point where you're working all the time. You have to take account for yourself and your family. And you've got to feel good about what you're doing every day. People need to understand, it's not enough to make the sale once, you've got to keep the sale sold. And that basically means to check back with people, and just making sure your reputation is reinforced every day by the good work you do and the way you treat people.

People ask me, "Why do you wear your top hat?" I'll tell them that back in the old days, rich folks in the manors would put their old clothes in the bin to be thrown away, and the chimney sweeps would come by and wear it like a costume, a uniform. Sometimes they'll ask me, "Do you dance?" "That's extra," I say. [*Laughter.*]

The purpose of life is not to be happy. It is to be useful, to be honorable, to be compassionate, to have it make some difference that you have lived and lived well.

Ralph Waldo Emerson

Sal Alfano,
General Contractor

sal.alfano@gmail.com

Sal was a carpenter/remodeler/custom home contractor in Vermont for almost twenty years before he began writing for and eventually became the editor of *The Journal of Light Construction (JLC)*^. He spent 14 years as editorial director of the Remodeling Group of magazines at Hanley Wood, and retired as executive editor of *Professional Remodeler* (PR) magazine at the beginning of 2019. Sal was sixty-nine at the time of this interview and he and his wife had moved from downtown Washington, D.C. back to Vermont in the fall of 2017, when he began renovation of the 1925 colonial that is now his home and where this interview took place. Of this project, Sal said, "I think we're finally done... though in my experience, you never really stop remodeling."

The Japanese start work with group exercise; it's not a crazy idea ■ *Contracting is a local business, even slight variations in the local economy make a big difference* ■ *Life will be a lot easier if you take care of your body when you are young* ■ *Saying, "I don't know" is hard, it takes a lifetime to do it easily* ■ *No contractor is a hundred percent, there are always going to be some issues* ■ *In remodeling you need a plan B because plan A almost never works* ■ *It's a myth of bidding that the low bid always wins[1]* ■ *The average client doesn't have a clue what a two-dimensional blueprint says or what the final product will look like* ■ *I was always around for the excavation of the foundation, to be certain we got that right* ■ *Not marketing*

---

1 In the Appendix see Sal's *It's a Myth That the Low Bid Always Wins.*

> *is a disease in the remodeling industry* ■ *The natural progression is to go from production to business* ■ *A lot of people are struggling to run their own business who would be much better off working for somebody else* ■ *The fun part was getting the job going, the excruciating part was getting it finished* ■ *Marketing takes time, money, and faith, because it's hard to understand why it works.*

I started in carpentry because I needed a job in 1971. I fell in with a couple of guys studying architecture and design/build^ at Goddard College in Vermont—design/build was unusual at the time—who were building a new house. I was labor and I knew zero about construction. I'd never even used a hammer. I was fortunate that those guys took time to answer my questions.

In 1976 I decided to go to grad school in philosophy of religion at Emory University in Atlanta, Georgia. I always thought I had an academic future, and carpentry remained a stopgap when I needed income between semesters. I was working with a remodeler in Atlanta when I realized how much more I enjoyed construction than academics. My graduate studies were interesting but less tangible, and the prospects for a vocation as a professor were not good in the late '70s. One summer my wife and I went to visit friends in Vermont between semesters, and when we got back, I resigned from school. I had a full ride for a PhD, so I signed a document giving the school the money back. We moved back to Vermont and I took a job as a carpenter with one of the first design/build companies that I know of. It was 1977, the company was Circus Studios, and it was three architects and a contractor as partners. The contractor ran the production arm. I was good with people and paperwork was not an obstacle for me, so I became a project manager quickly. I worked for them for almost three years, but my intention was always to run my own business, and in 1979 I went out on my own.

My first job on my own was a custom home, and the next substantial project I got was in Waitsfield on a giant remodel. I turned the job down four times because there were too many red flags. Money was no object and the owners kept making offers, so I finally agreed to do it at an hourly rate as project manager. In today's dollars it was a four-million-dollar project and I packed in ten years of experience in those eighteen months. Not just with architects, carpenters, and subcontractors, but with a client who was a one-of-a-kind meddler who complained and picked and changed her mind all the time. It was impossible in some ways, but I learned a lot about managing customers and employees.

There weren't a lot of resources for learning about the business of remodeling back then, and the first thing I became aware of was *New England Builder*,[2] which arrived out of the blue in my mailbox. It was on newsprint, about eight pages, and it was unlike anything I'd seen. It was contractors talking to contractors and revealing, not only what their solutions were, but what their problems were. It was, "Oh, this guy has the same problem that I've got and doesn't know what to do about it." But a lot of what I learned came from a couple of established contractors in my area who were willing to suffer stupid questions for fifteen minutes at a time. I wasn't shy about asking, but I didn't ask enough because I was as reluctant as the next guy to reveal what I didn't know.

What formal carpentry training did you receive?

Mostly on-the-job training from other carpenters. I was fortunate because I learned from those guys I mentioned as my first job—they were key individuals in my career—who were interested in learning, educating, and discussing with others who wanted to know. But that's rare. They taught me the proper sequence and made sure I practiced it. If I asked a question about framing, they didn't just explain how to lay out a stud wall, they explained the load path.[3] It wasn't, "Put the studs on 16-inch centers," it was, "Put the studs on 16-inch centers because we're working in 48-inch modules with 4-foot by 8-foot sheets of plywood." In terms of the procedure and process, it's not just using tools, but knowing the proper sequence and thinking through the project.

They did some clever things to teach me the trade. One day a skid of studs [294 pieces] was dropped by the lumberyard, and the guy who was heading up the job explained how to measure and make a line and how to use the circular saw. He watched me cut a couple of studs and said, "I need this whole stack cut to 92⅝ inches." By the end of that pile I could use a circular saw and a tape measure. It was only later that I learned he could have

2   *New England Builder* later became *The Journal of Light Construction (JLC)*^.
3   Load path is the route along which a building's weight passes from the highest point, downward through its frame, ultimately transferring the entire load to the footings and the surrounding soil.

ordered pre-cuts but had deliberately ordered full-length studs so I could learn to use the saw. When I had employees, I remembered that.

What drew you into the trade and what was most rewarding and most difficult about it?

It wasn't a well-reasoned choice. I needed a job, this was available, I liked the physical activity and working in the open air. I really liked standing back each day and being able to say, "Wow, we got a lot done." A building, even a residential building, is a complex structure, and I was involved in everything from excavation to finish work. That is a huge body of knowledge, and although I didn't master it all, the sheer variety was rewarding. What is most difficult is keeping up with the physical demands of the work as we age. That's obvious now, but when you're in your twenties the physical part is not an obstacle and the work is interesting and it keeps you engaged intellectually.

I was learning carpentry in Vermont in the 1970s, a time when energy efficiency was gaining attention among builders in a state with an extreme climate. The debate over vapor barriers was raging. Old-timers said a house needed to breathe, which kept the structure dry but was not energy-efficient. But concern about condensation from moist indoor air was leading builders to seal the heated side of the walls with a polyethylene vapor barrier. Fortunately, the wall could still dry to the outside, but later, when we started to insulate with rigid foam on the exterior side of the walls, we risked trapping moisture between the foam and the poly. You would never do that today in this climate. We all made decisions back then about things that were buried in the wall, but building science^ has made great progress and we now know that some of what we did is not recommended.

What academic education do you have, and has it helped in your career?

I have an undergraduate degree in the philosophy of religion and a year of graduate coursework. One of the weaknesses of people in the construction business is their impatience with paperwork and detail. Unlike most contractors, I liked the business side and my education helped me pay attention to those details. A broad intellectual base is an asset—there is no doubt about it—and the broader that base, the better off you're going to be and the better able to handle, not just situations you run into, but working with different kinds of people.

Talk about your goals and ambitions when you started out.

When I started it was, "Okay, I'm going to spend the summer doing this, and then I'm going to go back to school." But I liked the work, I wanted to learn; I knew I didn't know what I was doing and that I needed to find out. In 1977 when I came back to Vermont, it was with the intention of getting serious about the business of construction. In my years with Circus Studio I realized that in both the craft and the business there was more than one way that worked. I started thinking, *Why can't I take a job and be in charge of it?* Circus Studio was a well-organized company, but like most carpenters, I had no clue what was going on in the background. I thought, *I can do this, make more money, and do it better than them.* Most guys like the work and get good at it working for friends and family, then suddenly they're in business—about which they know absolutely nothing—and they make it up as they go along. They get into business almost accidentally, which is what I did.

Talk about memorable mistakes.

I had a project that had water problems with the foundation. It's one of the reasons that I left the business. It was a slab on grade with a frost wall—I'm not sure what happened—but I think there were springs in the ground that washed the sand out from under parts of the slab. I think that because the contractor who repaired it dug the sand out from under the entire slab and replaced it with crushed stone, which was wildly expensive. There was a lawsuit, and I could never convince anyone the springs were there, so we settled. Ultimately, it wasn't so much that it cost a lot financially, it was that I realized the risk that the business carries. It made me think, *Maybe twenty years in this business is enough.* That was 1985–86 and it was the beginning of the end. I went on to do a couple more successful projects for that same architect before getting out.

The biggest my business got was in the late '80s and my biggest year was about a million dollars in gross revenue. I had a run from 1985 to 1989, and part of my demise was that I realized it was too big for me to manage—it had been for a couple years—and I went into a partnership that didn't work as well as I had hoped. The recession of 1991 finally did it, but after twenty years I'd had enough.

If you were to start over, what would you do differently?

I knew what I hoped to earn, but I had no idea what my costs were and therefore how much work I needed at what margin, so it was one job to the next, "Do the best we can, get in, get out, get our money, get more work." Most guys start out like I did, playing it by ear and losing money for years because they're not doing the math right. Later I understood how important budgeting was and I started to take the week between Christmas and New Year for planning, to set goals, and to determine my overhead for the next year. Overhead started with what I needed to earn, so I would set that goal, and then figure out how much work we needed to accomplish it. Also, I had no sense of marketing—mostly I had enough work—but marketing is part of the package and I didn't have the whole package. I wanted to run my own business, but I did not have a plan of any kind.

If I were starting now? I would pay more attention to the business side. I would learn how to price work, how to calculate profit, and understand what a budget is. I would hire an office manager to handle incoming calls and cull leads and a part-time bookkeeper so the administrative tasks were handled. I would market—you need to market, whether you think you need to or not—because when you run out of work, it's too late to get more. I would do conscious culture building. I would not assume everybody's motivation is the same as mine. I would talk to employees about why I'm doing what I'm doing, my plan for the future, and I'd talk about what it means to them, to get them more engaged.

Fifteen years after I got into business, I was still intending to put my tool belt on every day. Gradually I realized it wasn't happening because I was putting out fires, doing estimates, and working with clients and subs. The problem had been coming for years and things like marketing, customer relationships, training employees, and looking at the big picture all suffered. I was trying to give everything a little attention and ended up not giving anything what it deserved. It was a Catch-22; the business was too big for me to handle and I didn't have time to make the hires needed to build the business. It also put a strain on my personal life. I remember not joining my family for Thanksgiving one year because I had to complete an estimate. That was crazy, and I did not get the job. When my back injury reoccurred, it brought all of these issues to the forefront. I can remember recuperating while lying flat on my back in my living room, thinking, *I have to reorganize the company.*

Have you ever wished you had done something else?

Not only did I wish I were doing something else, I did something else. But being a contractor for twenty years led to another fulfilling career, and for thirty years I wrote and published for trade magazines. I was fortunate to be able to use what I knew and loved. Also, I know what it is to begin not knowing anything about the business and what a struggle that is, not just personally, but for my family. All of it could have been so much better if I'd had a plan and started out knowing what I was getting into.

What do you love?

Music. There was always music in my family; my father was a musician and always had a side job with a band. I play acoustic and electric guitar, and I'm learning banjo. There is something about picking up a guitar and feeling the strings on my fingers, and the kinetic and tactile pleasure I get from it. I like making sourdough bread and do it almost every week and I love: board games, video games, the Vermont landscape, wine and winemaking, basketball (especially the Celtics), science fiction, my fifteen-month-old grandson, golf, and woodworking.

What advice have you given most to tradesmen?

It is hard to convince somebody who's twenty that he needs to pay attention to hearing protection and general safety. Almost everybody in the trade has a back problem or arthritis or tinnitus. I suffer from all of these things to some degree. All that repetitive motion, all on one side—swinging a hammer, holding a drill or nail gun, or cutting lumber—bent over all day long. When you're twenty, you're a little sore and the next day it's like it never happened, but that stuff catches up with you. Lately my advice to tradesmen is to pay attention to your body because it may not affect you today, but it's going to affect you tomorrow.

What is the best path to learning a trade?

There's an argument to be made for vocational training—I don't see it coming back anytime soon—and unions do a good job training. On-the-job training is mostly what we've got, but the question is, "Who is the trainer?"

If he does it correctly, then you learn correctly; if he's making it up, that is what you learn. The industry needs to pay more attention to how it trains.

In 2007, while building a deck on the back of my house, I needed a special tool to remove vinyl siding, but I couldn't remember what it was called. So I Googled "vinyl siding repair" and immediately found a ninety-second video that showed the whole process, including the "zip" tool. That kind of search experience is old hat now, but back then, before the iPhone, it made quite an impression. It was the seed of an idea that eventually became ProTradeCraft.com, a web-based collection of short videos of best practices from working contractors, optimized for mobile phones. There is no feasible substitute for on-the-job training, but it's a great complement to it.

What is a good and a bad tradesman?

Certainly, they need to have mastery of their trade, but I want somebody who can solve a problem, think on their feet, and wants to say yes. Someone flexible, organized, willing to take some risk, intellectually engaged in what they're doing, conscientious, and able to keep their job site well-organized. I want the sense that he's aware of how his work fits into the broader context and how it affects the work of everybody else. A bad one is the opposite, rigid, a "my way or the highway" kind of person, or the guy who says, "We can't do that."

What's the best investment you've ever made?

Besides real estate, I did a couple of things that were critical to staying competitive. One was converting to pneumatics,[4] the other was using computers. Today it's battery powered tools and, on the business side, your online presence. You have to be willing to take a chance, but most guys in this business are reluctant to try new stuff. When I first started, the older carpenters—guys who were my age now—said, "Plywood will never catch on." (*Laughter.*) The industry is slow to change and early adopters get burned on some stuff, but over the long haul the earlier you adopt the right new technology, the bigger the leg up you get.

What purchase has had the most effect on your life?

Computers. I took out a $5000 loan to buy my first computer in 1986. It was a CPM system, MS-DOS wasn't popular yet, and I said, "The

---

4   Pneumatics are used in the industry as, for example, nail guns powered by compressed air.

government is using CPM, so that's obviously the way to go." [*Chuckles.*] It had an eight-inch disk drive, no hard drive, and I had to learn the software. But it not only helped my business, it has been critical to my entire career since then.

What about your best and worst customers makes them that.
The best customers let me do what I did best without a fuss, and they understood the project required a lot of resources; most had budgets beyond what the contract specified. And they were not as price conscious as some customers. They wanted to know what it was going to cost of course, they haggled a little, and they compromised where they needed to; but they understood the value of the work and they trusted me to execute it well. Another characteristic was someone who had been there before and said, "I know it's going to be a disruption, and I know you will do your best." There were lots of customers from hell. They are the opposite: they meddle and question everything, they're involved in your business and how you are going about the work. They are distrustful of the process—maybe not you personally—but they change their mind so much it makes the job impossible. Then there is the arrogant customer who knows it all and thinks of you as just a mechanic.

How did you shape a new client's expectations?
Not as well in the beginning as toward the end, and there's a lot more I could have done. I told customers I could almost guarantee the job would cost more than the contract stated because of issues we couldn't anticipate or changes they would make. In either case, they would have to sacrifice something or come up with more money. In time, as I came to understand the client's point of view, I tried to give them a feel for what it would be like during construction—dust, noise, the disruption to their lives—but it's hard to convey the experience of living in a house while a remodeling project is going on.

Did you turn down customers and if so, why?
I didn't turn down enough of them. Late in my contracting career, I turned down picky meddlers and tire kickers. But there were too many instances where I volunteered solutions to problems and someone else ended up getting the job. I finally learned to recognize that person.

One of the biggest changes I made was how I worked with architects. Often, I would compete on projects where there were four, five, or six bidders. Crazy, right? At one point, an architect called and I had the sense, finally, to ask who the other bidders were. They listed five contractors, one of whom was always 20 percent below my cost, so I said, "Thanks, but no thanks." I told them why and said if they had clients who wanted to negotiate a contract—so I could get involved early in the process to work on budgeting—I'd be interested. I was never more surprised than to hear them say, "We'll put you on that list." Within thirty days I was sitting across the table with a client, and we eventually signed a contract. It was that simple. I had always assumed competitive bidding was the way of the world.

What did you look for when hiring and what do you expect from employees?

I would evaluate them by looking at their tools, but more importantly I wanted to feel comfortable with them and to hire somebody who was honest and reasonable. I wanted a forthcoming attitude. When things go smoothly it's easy to work with anybody; when there are issues, attitude is what really matters, and I got a feel for that in the interview. I told people that no matter what happened or how bad something was, I wanted to know about it immediately. The more I knew and the sooner I knew it, the easier it was to solve the problem. It wasn't a formal process, but I was good at hiring and I was also lucky. When I had a lot of jobs going and rearranging schedules was a nightmare, reliability was really important. I never expected anybody to stick around forever, but I tried to keep people.

Did you have an educational program at your company?

Not really. If we were using a new material, I would informally explain how to install it. If I were running a company today, I would direct people's attention to *JLC* and ProTradeCraft.com, and I would bring in articles and encourage guys to read them. I would get together weekly and talk about trade issues. I would, in a rudimentary way, tell them how the business runs, because they would be more engaged. I would explain in more detail why change orders^ are important and how to differentiate between an extra and what's in the specifications^. That is always a challenge.

How did you let people go?

I can't remember firing anybody for cause. I was unhappy with some people, but mostly they left of their own accord. The one that stands out was my first employee. At the time he left, the company was growing and the work was less suitable to his skill and temperament. He was easygoing, he was not going to up his game, and people felt he wasn't pulling his weight. So I talked with him and said, "Here is where the company is going, I don't think it's a good fit for you. You've been with me a long time and you'll always have a job here, but you might be happier doing something else." He left and went into a handyman business where he did well.

How would you tell someone to find a contractor?

Look for somebody you feel relaxed with, that you have no doubt has your interest at heart, somebody reliable, who has a track record and a list of past customers to talk to. And spend time with the references, because it is hard to draw this information out in a quick conversation. Most people go to friends and relatives—that's good—but remodeling is happening all over and if you see a project that is going well, note the company. Mainly I want to know, when there was a problem, how did this guy solve it? Regardless of how their client felt about the solution, evaluate for yourself: "Is this the kind of person I want to work with?"

Talk about marketing and sales.

To the extent that contractors succeed when they start, it is because they are natural salesman, comfortable with people, use colorful language and descriptions, and have a flair for design. Like a lot of guys, I naturally listened to what people were telling me, though I wasn't consciously thinking, *They mentioned this, I'll tuck it away and bring it up in my proposal.* I've learned, but back then I did it by accident. Most contractors dislike sales and are offended by the idea of selling and therefore don't get sales training. But everything you do is sales; you're selling yourself to everybody you deal with.

I didn't understand the value of marketing and I didn't feel I needed it, because the work showed up, and when it didn't, it was because the economy was down. Most of us think of branding our company as getting a logo and having people see job signs. That's a start, but marketing is much more complicated and more useful. You cast a net, and from what you catch, you pick the jobs you want. Now I know it is absolutely essential because I have seen how relentless marketing guarantees leads, which allows you to discriminate in the jobs you take. Word of mouth works for a while, but marketing is more sophisticated and more deliberate.

Nobody does marketing when they start out because they think jobs come like manna from heaven. That works, until it doesn't, and it takes a few cycles of feast and famine before it becomes clear that actively marketing will generate enough leads to meet the company's sales goals. Those who are good at marketing learn that not every lead is worth pursuing, not all prospects are a good fit, and not all jobs have the same profit, so they screen for those that are most likely to be successful. Today, because of the internet, marketing is vastly more important than sales because often the customer has vetted your company before contacting you, so you can start talking about the details right away.

When work slowed, or when you had too much work, what did you do?

When worked slowed we would do anything, and I would call customers and architects and let them know we were available. Also, rather than make new hires when we weren't sure we'd have work, we'd partner with other contractors and work together temporarily. If I were doing it today, I'd stick with marketing my sweet spot so work wouldn't dry up. Having too much work is another problem for contractors. They don't like to say no because they are letting people down and, because they are not marketing and don't know why the work is coming, they take what they can get. I would sub extra work out, but mainly I didn't handle it well and it was a strain on everybody, and I disappointed a lot of people. Toward the end I learned to turn down work.

What belief or action has most improved your business life?

Planning for time away from work. Something that new contractors don't think about. I can't remember taking time off until I had a desk job. When I went to work for the magazines, I had vacation time and I could schedule regular time off. It was hard to do when I worked in my business because I always felt that if six laps around the track was good, twelve was better. It might be true of every business, but certainly in contracting, because it is often feast or famine I felt if I were not going after it every day, I would miss something.

Was there a conflict between working in the field and running your business?

That was one of the largest challenges I had. As the business grew, I was doing the books, sales, estimating, and trying to work in the field. I did not have a management structure in place, because I believed the biggest mistakes happened in the field. But that is not the case. They happen in the contract, the estimate, a poor sales process, and a lack of marketing: those are the *really* big mistakes. I ended up putting out fires and sacrificing both sides; not producing much in the field or in the business. My back injury is what woke me up, but it shouldn't take that, it should have been built into my plan from the beginning.

How would you respond to this idea: If your goal is to be a tradesman work for someone else, if your goal is to establish and build a significant company, put your tool belt aside and focus on business as soon as it is practical.

I agree with that idea for most people. If you want to build a company, you need to learn about business, but a lot of guys are not well suited to it. They're good at building and selling, maybe design, but they're not good at building systems, managing employees, relationships with subs, scheduling, and paperwork. It's hard to admit, "I can't do this, I'll let somebody else do the business part." It is admitting failure and who wants to do that? It might work if you stay small, doing one job at a time of a certain size, but there will be a lull between jobs as you do estimating and sales for the next one, so there's overlap—now you're doing two things at once. As a practical matter, it does not work. In my writing, I've tried to convince people of the value of learning about business right away; but it's an uphill struggle.

Why did you open your business and what were the first three things you did?

I was not unhappy with my employer, and I work and play well with others, but it was an urge to do it my way. Also, I thought I was capable of doing it and I could make more money. But I didn't know what I was getting into and I discovered quickly that it was a lot more effort than I realized. The first three things? I had to learn accounting to keep track of expenses, I had to perfect my estimating and come up with systems to know if my estimating was correct, I had to cement my relationships with subs and set up accounts with suppliers.

While opening your business, how did you learn what you needed to know?

Business information for contractors was virtually nonexistent in the early '80s. There was *JLC* and *Fine Homebuilding*^, but they did not have much information about business. Traditionally, the way contractors learned was by dragging information out of other contractors, or they made it up as they went along. Now there are trade shows, magazines, consultants, and books. But a smaller company doesn't need all of the complexity of a big one, so you have to be aware of where the information is coming from and how much of it applies to you.

Talk about memorable mistakes in business.

For me, the biggest one was not understanding the difference between margin and markup and shortchanging myself on every project. It is something I continue to write about because many people still don't get it.[5] My other mistake was not keeping track of job costs^ in real time, so there was never enough information during the job to say, "We're in trouble, we've got to do something to make money on this job." Also, it is hard with small jobs because there is not enough time to adjust, which means your estimate has to be right to begin with.

A lot of companies talk a good game and are successful by some measures, but when it comes down to it, the business is raggedy. There's a small percentage of companies who are tracking what they need to and using that information to succeed. The replacement industry—siding, windows, roofing—does this well. They are great marketers because they need lots of leads and they are good at tracking costs.

---

[5] See these sites for more information: WWW.PROREMODELER.COM/FOOLPROOF-MARKUP-MATH and WWW.REMODELING.HW.NET, search for Margin and Markup for a video representation, and HTTPS://WWW.JLCONLINE.COM/BUSINESS/STRICTLY-BUSINESS-VISUALIZING-GROSS-PROFIT_O

Did you do a business plan or company goals?

When I was in the business it was just a vague idea and I never did one. It wasn't until I took over the editor's job at *Remodeling* magazine that I wrote a mission statement with goals and objectives. Would we have been more successful with a business plan? Probably. But now I think a big audacious goal for the business is not as important as "What's my goal for next year?" Starting out, it makes sense to ask what you want to accomplish, and then to repeat that next year and maybe extend it out a couple years. Still, there are successful companies who don't have a clue where they put their business plan, so I guess I'm still something of a business plan skeptic.

This can be a tough business, talk about being a hard-ass?

I like the cooler, rational approach. I'm not great at confrontation and I want to be liked, but when something has to be the way it has to be, I would get it done without being nasty. You need skill in mediation or negotiation because ranting and raving works only one time, and if you've got a reputation for being that guy, nobody wants to work with you. So it's a balancing act. Sometimes somebody doesn't want to do it the way you want to do it and you have to put your foot down and throw a tantrum or make a threat. It is not the best way to motivate people, I have done extra work to avoid doing it, but sometimes it's a reality in construction.

What did you like and dislike about running a business?

I liked planning, meeting with clients, understanding their problems, and coming up with solutions. I liked setting the project up and getting the job started. That was the fun part. The excruciating part was the punch list^ and wrapping it up while I was trying to start another one. Part of this was because I was doing too much and didn't have people to help me; I was the prototypical remodeler in that respect.

How did you decide what to focus on in business?

Early on, as work came to me, I took it. There were projects I liked better than others and later I worked more with architects and I tried to have a custom home project every year and fill in our schedule with various sized remodeling jobs. The custom stuff was fun, but because I didn't do formal marketing, I wasn't filtering jobs by type.

Talk about learning to estimate.

That was a tricky process. I never trusted the books that had prices, because they were based on national averages, not on my local market conditions, and costs varied every year, so this year's book wouldn't work next year. Then I found a couple of books that gave man-hours for labor. If I knew how long it took on average, I could plug in my own labor or sub costs. That made sense to me. When it came to estimating, I knew how to do it by imagining the building and counting every piece. It was on legal pads until I discovered computers and Excel. What it amounted to is that I made it up as I went along, so I'm self-taught. But I liked estimating so much that I got good at it and by the time I left the business, we had less than a 1 percent error in costs. We would side a building and the scrap would fit on the front seat of the truck.

How would you tell someone to learn to estimate?

Do a bunch of reading. You want a unit cost^ system. To get meaningful numbers, you must carefully track your job costs to know what it costs to produce each unit of work, so you can plug real numbers into the next estimate. And your estimating and job costing^ have to be done in parallel because, after you've built a project, you have to know how close you came to your estimated cost so you can adjust your unit cost prices as needed. Cost books don't help, but there are still systems like Home Tech that you can start with and adjust their numbers to match your actual costs. It is challenging to learn to estimate and, for most remodelers, it's the work they don't like to do.

Talk about bidding.

Bidding is always going to be, because it is the way consumers learn to buy remodeling services. It doesn't hurt to be involved in that process—you will learn a lot—but you're better off learning how to market and sell to maximize your chances of winning jobs. In architectural work people often take the lowest bid because architects claim they've vetted the contractors, worked with them, and therefore each will provide the same product. Architects are claiming there's no difference between the contractors so the lowest price wins. That's not the case of course, but they do it anyway. Getting away from bidding is ideal, but it's not always possible. If you have to bid, there are ways to differentiate yourself in the process, and price transparency becomes important, because you can't simply say, "I'm better than the other guy." All the customer sees is that one price is higher than the other, so you need to show them where the value is in selecting you.

Talk about working with designers and architects.

This is a sore point for a lot of contractors. I've always enjoyed working with architects—not all of them, some are better than others. They look for the latest and greatest material and this can be good and bad because it means you are experimenting and you're the guinea pig. But I liked that. A good architect understands their success depends on the execution of their vision and if something can't be built, they want the contractor to tell them, and to come up with an alternative that is true to their intent. I also liked working with them because they're systems people, logical thinkers, and generally they manage projects well. Also, once we had a relationship, I could rely on them to mediate between me and the owner if my price was unexpectedly high for a change order.

Talk about the biggest failure in your business.

My partnership. I was busy, I had fifteen guys and I was having a good year but figured I needed somebody to help. I should have hired someone to handle the field work, instead I went to a friend and offered him a partnership in the company. We didn't match up and he didn't have the skills I needed. It might have been because I didn't have a business plan, so a lot of it's on me. It didn't cause me to close the business, but it was a factor.

How did you learn to manage money, and what advice would you give about it?

I learned through hard knocks, it was completely trial and error and self-taught. I did the books myself for a long time, but it's not enough to record numbers, you have to have somebody who says, "This is what it means." So my advice would be to find an accountant who understands the industry and to develop a relationship with a bank. I know a lot of remodelers my age [69], who are still working for a paycheck and they won't be able to sell their company—it is rare that a remodeling company sells—and most don't have any money socked away for retirement. I didn't have any put away until I got a job at *JLC* and had a 401(k).

What would you tell a group of skilled tradesmen who were thinking of going into business?

That they don't know what they are getting into and they are in for a surprise. Contracting is a never-ending process of changing employees, conditions, products, and systems that are never over and done. They think they're gonna make a lot of money—all the money they imagine is going to the front office—but in fact, they're going to be working longer hours and making less money, at least for a while, and maybe forever if they don't learn quickly. It seems like magic, like anybody can do it, but there is so much that goes on behind the scenes and there's a huge learning curve. If they're determined, I would tell them to go to every event they can [conventions and seminars], and don't just say, "Wow, that was an interesting talk"; instead pick one or two things that you learned and every three months implement one of them in your company.

What would you tell them to learn first and what to avoid?

They have to understand their costs, because if they don't, they are out of business right away. Even though I think marketing is wildly important, at first they will get jobs without much trouble because they know people and then from referrals, but they need to understand sales because you can't just say, "Here's the cost, sign the contract." If they understand their costs and how to sell, they can earn what they are worth. A mistake new 'owners often make—I certainly did—is to take every job that comes along. At first you will take much of what comes; but find out what's best for you, what is profitable, and do that work. To decide which jobs to take, think about the opportunity costs,[6] the job that might come along tomorrow that's ten times better than this one, and learn to identify and pursue those. And learn to say no by recommending somebody else, so you don't put people off when turning down jobs.

If you had a method of reaching every builder and tradesman, what would you say?

It's not about the stuff—the countertop and fine trim—it's about the emotional experience of the customer and your place in that interaction

---

6 **Opportunity cost,** the loss of potential gain from other alternatives when one alternative is chosen.

and what you are selling is different for every customer. You go to sales training so you can learn to hear the customer tell you what you are selling. They might say, "I think I need a new kitchen," but if you listen carefully you might hear them saying, "This kitchen is depressing." Depressing? What is that? How do you solve that? So you're not selling cabinets and countertops, you're selling lifestyle and mood and you are appealing to the homeowner on a different level. If you listen, you can understand where their pain is and what you need to do to fix it; you are selling a solution to that problem.

What bad business advice have you gotten?

I've heard a lot of crazy stuff, like "They'll never miss it" or "They'll never notice." But you can't bury a problem. I had my house renovated in Washington, D.C., and the kitchen had a porch above it, so the ceiling sloped three inches from end to end. The guys came to install the drywall and I said, "Are you going to flatten the ceiling because of the slope?" They said, "You'll never notice it." [*Laughter.*] I said, "You won't notice the slope when you put crown molding on it? Are you out of your mind?" "You can't see it from a fast horse," they used to say. [*Laughter.*]

What is success in business?

Obviously, financial success, but beyond that you've created a community that's dependent upon your performance, so it's not just about you. If you're not good at all of these things we've been talking about, you are putting at risk dozens of people's livelihood. I like the idea of B Corporations and the triple bottom line: people, profit, planet.[7] There is a local community and people that are dependent on your business, but there's the larger community too. B Corporations measure what you are giving back to the larger community and that you are doing your best to mitigate the problems that are created by building. So it matters how much trash you create and that your heating systems are efficient

What is a successful building career?

Aside from financial success, if I've helped employees master their vocation, that's success. To have a client base over a long period of time is success.

---

7   Visit HTTPS://BCORPORATION.NET/ABOUT-B-CORPS for more information.

Word Association

Integrity: It is critical. Integrity is a key to your character.

Communication: Vital, and a huge shortcoming of the industry and the trades. Weak communication skills are an obstacle in selling.

Job safety: What's that? [*Laughter.*] When I got into the editorial side of things, every year we had a feature story on safety. Nobody cared. The most success we had was when we told horror stories about amputations and falls. But I don't think it changed their behavior. The industry pooh-poohs safety because it's too much trouble and too expensive, and that's unfortunate and I wish we could change it. On the other hand, there are cases where safety standards are complete nonsense. I use the example of adding a couple of fasteners to a gable roof fascia. If you follow safety protocols, you erect staging with guardrails, but that's impractical if you only need to drive a couple of fasteners.

Fear: Failure.

Company image: It is what people hire. They hire the individual and the feeling they have about the company. What wins the work is the force of your personality and the emotional effect your company produces in a potential client.

Gratitude: Most of my employees seemed to be grateful to be working in the environment they were working in.

Overhead: Higher than you think.

Profit: Lower than you think. You deserve it and you deserve more than you think.

Marketing: Essential.

Sale: Harder than it looks.

Estimating: *Waaaay* harder than it looks. [*Laughter.*] A fundamental, a basic, and you've got to be good at it.

Bidding: It should go the way of the dinosaur; it is not the way to run a business.

Community: Invaluable. The larger community in which you find your business, but also building it in relationships.

Quality: Taken for granted.

Cut-Offs

I fell off a ladder, doing something stupid. I was twenty-three—absolutely invulnerable—and here I am, almost fifty years later, and I still have pain in my back from that accident.

I would never have learned anything if I had not said, "I don't know how to do this, can you help me?"

I used to do a keynote seminar in which I juxtaposed task with purpose. I used an example of an HVAC contractor whose slogan was "We're not comfortable till you are." *Task,* hooking up the AC system. *Purpose,* providing a comfortable environment for the homeowner. Whether you are focused on the task or on the purpose makes a big difference in how you approach the work.

Field work is complex, and it is extremely valuable to have somebody who understands the *what* and *why,* to be sure the work is done right. If you're really good in the field, stay there, and find a partner who can handle the business. Partnerships are not easy, but it can be done.

When you understand your product is the service and how you provide it, it will make a difference in how successful you are.

Your best safety gear is between your ears.
Dump truck bumper sticker

Chris Fralick,
Cabinetmaker

Chris was 65 at the time of this interview. He built organs for twenty years; the huge ones heard in cathedrals. The company he worked for made every part, including the pipes and keys. When the owner of the organ company retired, Chris began his woodworking business. He builds cabinets and musical instruments and other wood projects that interest him, and he is also a dedicated rock climber, and has a rock climber's build, tall and thin, with a sinewy frame and powerful hands.

I was a mechanic when I was a kid, until I was in my mid-twenties, an auto mechanic. And I got involved with a start-up business in Eugene that built bicycle trailers. And I got into helping set up production in welding and so on. And then I moved into a string instrument apprenticeship, and then I went into bicycle building, and then I went into production woodwork, doing components for a kaleidoscope company. Then I began building mechanical action pipe organs. I did that for a long time, until they closed. So I took that step and I moved into doing residential work and doing custom design furniture and making my clients happy. And I was drawn to the craft of woodworking. I wanted to be involved with the people and the process and the product that I was discovering, either through myself or through other people that I was getting involved with.

    Working with my hands was kind of a given, but I was trying to bring that beauty to life and have someone experience it—in their house or by playing it— while I was trying to make a living in all of it. I've never had the business development mind, and I still don't. It's not part of my personality.

Making things is my personality. My business has been growing, and I get good referrals and clients. I like the process of working with a client and helping them envision what they want, and then executing it. But you have to think in terms of, "Yes, I want to work with my hands, but it needs to be something that's going to actually pay what I want to make."

I needed a shop. I had equipment that I shared with my brother, and I inherited some equipment from the organ shop. I started with one kitchen and then in a couple of months I had two more orders. I wanted to get a website, I wanted to get a business name and a shop. All of which I did. I started with word of mouth. I had plenty of work lined up until the stock market crashed and people who were going to have stuff done to their homes changed their mind. That made it difficult as far as scrabbling to pay the bills.

For me, I realize even now that I don't have the energy or the focus to be everything in my business. So I have to give up parts of it at different times. But my business is one person with no expectation of it ever being more than that. The difficult question for me is, "How much more work do I have to get to make my wage?" So I accepted the fact that it's going to be a one-man show, which makes the marketing and dealing with clients take kind of a back seat. I work with my clients to understand their needs, but sometimes, if I'm doing a big kitchen, I have to hire help.

Oh yeah, I have made big mistakes in business. I undercharge for fear of not getting the job and then work forty hours for twenty hours' pay. When I think about that, I think how many hours a month do doctors give free consultations? How many hours do dentists work for free? They don't. In the trades industry, it's unheard of to charge for a quick consultation. It's almost a class difference.

Capital-wise, I had nothing to start. I had a small inventory of wood and I had most of the equipment that I have now. The capital for a marketing program or having employees and knowing I can pay their wages six months down the road: those I did not have. When I first started, the business was a blank wall with no windows. Over time, after dealing with clients and taking a business management class, the wall started getting windows and I could actually start seeing something and getting a sense of things.

I would only advise tradesmen to go into business if they can focus on actually doing marketing and drumming up the business and making sure they have the capital before going ahead with projects. Being the person that does it all is hard. If you're working on marketing and working with clients and doing design, and executing and finishing, if you're going to be a sole proprietor, it seems so all-consuming. But if that's what you want? I can't say no to it, because so many people do it and are happy and successful, and they understood the compromises involved. But I can't see working all the time and rejecting the freedom I have. So I take the blow to the business monetarily for my freedom.

I've had good relationships with all my clients. Every client I've had. I only have ten or twelve a year, and these are important relationships to me. We may or may not be friends in the future, but life is happening between us. This is the dance we're doing, and to me that's worth something. And I also know the game's only going to last so long, your life. And we need to get out of it what we can, when we can. I'm not going to wait until I'm seventy to start rock climbing. I'm going to burn the candle at both ends. I'll do my work and hopefully get enough of it.

It is impossible for a man to learn what
he thinks he already knows.

Epictetus

Stephen Uhle,
Automotive Machinist

http://www.restartart.com/

Stephen was 68 at the time of this interview and his path to becoming an automotive machinist mirrors the way many of us get into the residential construction industry, that is, he slid in sideways. Once in, he was glad to be there and grateful that he had found this occupation. Some months after doing this interview, I learned that Stephen also does metal art, what he calls, Car Part Art. To see his work, go to the link above.

> *Yeah, I don't know what I would do differently, getting that job was such a perfect fit, I can't imagine finding something else that would fit as good*
> ■ *If you're borrowing money and juggling, you're in trouble*

Well, I was unemployed, and I was out of money. I was sitting in a bar, I wasn't drinking because I was out of money, and this guy comes up and goes, "Why aren't you drinking?" and I said, "I just spent my last quarter." It was twenty-five cents a beer. And he says, "I'm going to buy you a beer." Then he took me over and introduced me to this guy, and he says, "Bill, this guy doesn't have any money or a job, take him to work." So Bill gave me his address, and the next morning I went to his house and met him, and he was all hung over. I don't think he even knew who I was or why I was there. He said, "Well, come on, let's go to work." And we walked two blocks to work. It was 1972 in North Hollywood, California. I was twenty-two.

I started at the bottom rung. And that machine shop was like, I was home. It was great! All of a sudden, I'm in a structured environment working with these two alcoholic flathead mechanics that were just geniuses.

They were alcoholics and weird, but they had such a work ethic. I liked the work. I was able to do it. I picked it up really quick. I worked Saturdays. I worked six days a week. I might have worked seven. But it was not like the tennis racket factory I worked at, where I can't tell you how many Mondays I missed—enough to get fired three times. This place, I did not miss work, it just called to me.

In the process, I'm developing a skill that's actually becoming more valuable than I had thought. And my name got passed around to somebody that needed a machinist in Beverly Hills. This guy had a one-man shop, and he wanted me to run the whole place, and do it on commission. I still didn't have a lot of confidence. So I spent another five years there honing what I'd learned and getting better and actually making some real money at it. It worked really good.

I actually got up to 65 percent commission. And the funny thing about that was, I told my boss, "You know, it's not enough, 65 percent. If I owned this place, I'd get 100 percent." So we were trying to work out a deal to buy it but it looked like I was going to have to pay him way too much money and too much rent. And that's about the time I moved to Oregon. The first place I went into was an auto parts store, and I asked if they were interested in running a machine shop, and they said, "Sure." And that was $150 a month rent! My brain could handle that. So I set up my business immediately—it was 1982—and I've been in the same place ever since.

My education in business? I did a three-year small business class at the local community college. It was really interesting, a good thing. I would recommend it. But what was really valuable was all the networking. There's all these people and everybody starts talking about what they do, so there's all this brainstorming, about what other people have done. That was a valuable thing for me. So yeah, that was good, and I've done metallurgy classes at another community college to understand metal and learn how to run the machines that test for hardness, and I just learned a lot about metals in general.

Nobody would bring me any work when I started, because they didn't want somebody, they didn't know working on their car parts. I advertised in a local paper. Being hooked up with the auto parts store helped too. Periodically I would go around with their outside salesmen and I'd introduce myself to their customers. Then the walk-in trade started coming through, and it just built on that. And I'm doing a good job and if I made a mistake, I made it right, and word of mouth works, sooner or later. My marketing was minimal. It's was hard to say what ads were effective. They were all equally effective, I guess. Going out and meeting customers always generated more business. Any time we were slow, I just went out and did cold calls.

I had some guys who wanted to work for free, just hanging out and wanted to be doing something. The one guy was an acquaintance of mine; he cut his finger on an oil can and said he was going to sue me. I don't know how serious he was, but it taught me a lesson right off, if you're going to hire somebody you have to have Workers' Compensation. It was fortunate for me to learn that early on.

At one time I had five people, but it wasn't working. It was way too many and I wasn't there enough to organize it. I've had three guys, and that worked good: a solid machinist, a helper, and an in-between guy. I love working with my hands and playing with metal—but I did not want to be just a tradesman—and I liked my customers and that is what got me into the business.

Here's the punch line I never got to. Working for that boss in LA at 65 percent, that wasn't enough because I wanted 100 percent; when I got the 100 percent, I made like 10 percent! I would have killed for 50 percent. [*Laughter.*] And I never made as much as I made working for that man in 1981, but it's okay because working for someone else was not enough.

I turn customers away sometimes. If they are really pushy and they're angry and they're not going to listen, I will turn them away. I make a point of setting expectations for my customers. Well, it's not that I'm setting them up to expect to fail, but a lot of times you're compromised with what you can do, so I try to let them know what they're getting. People are basically good, and they're honest. Most people are in a state, they need their car fixed and they're agitated and need to get back on the road. You've just got to be real kind with them and help them to understand what you're doing and give them the information so they can make a good decision.

Employees! Hiring is a very tough thing, and I'm not very good at it. Sometimes, I lucked out. I learned that you can't make employees do anything they don't want to do. [*Chuckles.*] You've got to accept people like they are. You've got to set your rules and limits, but you're not going to change people. It's something that I just had to work at. My three best machinists, you could not talk to them. They were the biggest hard heads. I also don't want to be around somebody who's just saying yes to please me. I like things to be nice and even and for people to be happy where they are and want to come to work.

I've learned a lot about business. I can only guess at why my competitors and customers go out of business, but I think you have to really watch the money and not go into debt. So many businesses don't make it. You need to have that cash reserve. All the books I read when I was starting out talked about having six months' or a year's' worth of money on hand; I took that seriously. So I had my home expenses covered for six months and my business expenses too. I think it was probably my grandfather, he was not a tightwad, but he managed money. I know what money I have, and I don't spend more than I have. I'm very disciplined in that way.

There's a great advantage to doing a trade instead of just a school education. We don't know what the job market is; it will be one way or the other at different times. But you don't know. There are a bunch of college graduates right now that can't get jobs, and a bunch of tradespeople that can. One of the things that fascinates me in this country is the idea that everybody needs to go to college, that's the thing. And I love education; I love it personally and think it's a wonderful thing for the country and for individuals, but for some strange reason we don't encourage people to do trades, and that's a huge problem. Yeah, we need to do something for trades for the kids that cannot stand school, like me. Tom Sawyer was a genius, but didn't fit in.

You'll have more fun and success when you stop trying to get what you want and start helping other people get what they want.
Dale Carnegie

Morgan Reiter,
Retired Yurt Builder

Morgan is a fifty-six-year-old, semi-retired carpenter and builder, who once owned a yurt-manufacturing business in Eugene Oregon, where he still lives. He's a self-proclaimed onetime hippie, although it is hard to see that now.

If just your labor and material are paid for, you don't have a business ■ I felt I did the best possible work I could for my customers and part of that—some of my employees hated me for this—was that I was more concerned for my client's well-being than my employees. In retrospect I feel badly about that ■ I have never wished I did something else. I feel blessed; I built a lot of incredible structures for people who were appreciative of what I did

Building for me really became the essence or the pure definition of right livelihood; I was so doing the right thing. I felt there was a real need, and a resolution of that need, by what I did. Whereas pushing papers, I just couldn't get. What I loved about building—I would use the word freeform—is that there were so many realms that you could express yourself in as a builder. Do you want to be a remodeler or do a restoration? Do you want to do new homes? Do you want to work for somebody as a finish carpenter or framer? Where I started was a carpenter, where I ended up was a businessman. I still, to this day, love the smell of wood; part of it is smell, part of it is visual, and part of it is practical. Turning a tree into a board and then to see it become something; it is almost a religious experience. There is a physical and emotional satisfaction to create something beautiful. It fills my eyes. I love the touch.

I ended up moving to Eugene, Oregon. It was more economically vibrant and diverse than southern Oregon. There were certainly more opportunities here. I walked in and got a job the first day as carpenter with a large tract builder and I did that for two years, which gets me to about 1976 and then I took off on my own. Not just building yurts, because it still did not feel like I could make a living at it. But whenever an order came in, I would build a yurt because that was a lot of fun and more satisfying than traditional building.

Mostly I was self-taught. Initially it was spontaneous. But I started asking, *How do I do the business part of this?* Then I took some classes. After I was building yurts for six or eight years, I went to a business program at a community college, which was intense. I was with other small business owners. I learned, in so many ways, why a business plan would have been really helpful when I started.

One of the things that become clear as I matured—I wish I had understood this a lot earlier—is that growth is not inevitable, but it is absolutely critical to keep a business functioning and essential if it is to succeed. And I did not get it for a long time. Because I had this ideal: "Okay, if I can make this much money each year, that's great! And then I can take more time off …" Well, nope, the numbers have to increase every year because employees expect increasing benefits and compensation.

I had a lot of pain learning the business. The best example is the night I came home from work, I was building a conventional house, a custom house, and everything that could possibly go wrong, was going wrong. I came home that night and I just broke down in tears and I sobbed on my bed with my wife holding me and it was just this—there were so many things that were going wrong: I was hoping to make money and I wasn't. I was hoping to keep up with the construction schedule, and I wasn't. I was hoping to create a beautiful product, and that particular day some of my subcontractors were making that impossible. So, I was at the bottom of the barrel wondering how I could keep doing this with everything I was trying to achieve and failing at it.

There was no sophistication in my understanding that a business needs more than charging for labor and material. That is, understanding that Time & Material doesn't grow a business; it gives you a job. I would say it took me five years to figure that out. I think that a lot of people who go into the trades don't understand that or they get confused by it.

And the best and most simplistic story I can tell you about that—I was living on Grant Street in Eugene, and I would go to the mailbox and come back and say, "Bummer, there is nothing for Oregon Yurt Works today, no orders." And my wife said, "Think about it." You don't advertise and you don't even have your name in the phone book". It was a simple conversation, but it jelled the concept that to create a successful business you need to have more than just a good product. You need to understand how business works. You need to understand the advertising component of it. You need to understand the image component of it.

I was a hippie. I had long stringy hair and dirty clothes, ripped, and so on. I had earrings. I copped to all of that, kind of in one moment: "Image is important." I took my earrings out and never put them back in. I cut my hair. I started wearing nicer clothes; nice clothes being jeans that weren't ripped. I started advertising in magazines. I started hiring graphic designers to do presentations of my work to go in magazines.

In some ways building awful, ugly tract houses helped me generate a vision of what I really wanted to do. Seeing the stuff that I disliked helped generate the vision of what I really liked. Here I am doing something during the day that I'm not proud of and going home and living in this tiny yurt that I felt comfortable with. People would see it and eventually, finally, someone asked, "Could you build me one?" It was like a bulb went off, "Sure, I can build you one, because that would be fun." And I did. I built a yurt for someone in southern Oregon. But that yurt led to two more, and two more led to four more. And then what also happened, someone said, "Can you build it this bigger?" I had no clue, but my immediate answer was yes, and then I would go home and wonder, *Now how do I do that?* And to be honest, I did not know what was possible and what was not possible. Well, part of my education in being a builder was learning how, and I learned through consistent and regular failure.

There were no books about business.[1] None that really addressed the type of issues we are talking about, in a format that was readable and accessible. I read a series of books on carpentry, plumbing, masonry and so on; I devoured

---

1   There were few if any trade magazines or books in the '70s that addressed the business of residential construction. It is also true that building details and business requirements were not as complex as they are now.

that kind of stuff. I think anybody can do this. I never thought it was rocket science, it just takes desire and the ability to learn. But I still thought in my heart of hearts that I was going to be a custom home builder here in Eugene.

Now we are in the late '70s and early '80s. When 1980 came around, the economy started tanking, and then in '81 it accelerated, and in '82 it really hit bottom. Here in Eugene anyway.[2] Even though I had done some successful things and had name recognition, the market squashed all of that. At the same time, amid the building downturn, I was getting more requests for yurts and demand was increasing. So, in 1982 I decided to hang up the conventional house business because I thought I could make a living building yurts. And yet, I still did not know shit about business.

I think when you are talking about a business that is truly organic—you start by swinging a hammer and it gets bigger and then you are hiring guys and building three houses—you are so close to it that you can't see what is keeping you from going to the next level. I needed somebody who could look at the business from the outside, someone not attached to it. The business classes and a friend allowed me to see the universal business problems that I was having, and how to identify and address them. I had to learn to delegate, and it took me a long time to realize that I needed to hire people. Everything would have been different if I'd had business acumen. I hired an office manager who had a wonderful demeanor and he liked me and loved what I was doing. I knew this guy had my best interest at heart, so I could listen to his criticism. It wasn't an epiphany. It was not book learning. It was actual advice from a trusted source, that made all the difference in the world. He also said "Morgan, you need to choose. There are so many demands in the office that every time you are in the field, we are losing money and going backward." But that is after ten years of doing it all myself.

The end of that story is that I worked too long and too hard and I have a great wife who bore it with me. But my marriage suffered. We would have had kids if I were not working so hard. I worked all the time. I worked sixty hours a week and more, and weekends, and holidays sometimes. And there were stretches where I would work fourteen or seventeen days straight. It was too much.

---

[2] The United States, and to a large extent the entire world was in a recession during the early '80s.

If you want the best the world has to offer, offer the world your best.

N. D. Walsch

Nick Nott,
Fixer-Upper / General Contractor

Nick was sixty-three and lives and works in Eugene, Oregon.³ He has been a preacher for much of his life and general contractor (GC)^ for a time. He is an earnest man of quiet humility and strength and without pretense.

> *I went to community college classes. It was a series with some books walking you through starting a business. I never wrote a formal business plan.* ∎ *I never marketed. It was nice that I didn't have to promote what I was doing.* ∎ *I thought about running a business, but I always thought, I'm glad I'm not the boss, having to hire and fire and oversee.*

I can see pretty quickly what a house needs to resell it. My wife would look at it and say, "Are you sure?" I'd say, "Can't you see it?" So it was part of my artistic bent, wanting to make it nice again. I would inspect a house and sit down and make a list of the work needed and a timeline and ask if the real estate market was good enough to make it worthwhile. It was all handwritten in ledgers, with pen and paper.

A couple of times while I was in college, I worked for a builder for the summer. He was building little utility buildings and we built a restaurant/office building. I was learning, that's for sure. In a way it's nice to just do your job and go home and not have to think about it. But pretty quick I thought, *I don't want to work for people.* So, I was a one-man contractor for

---

3   Nick is retired, but in 2018 he bought and moved into an 1880's log home that he plans to renovate.

seven years, I had my license. Before that, I bought and flipped houses. I had some rentals for a while and decided I did not like the landlord business.

I went to college, Bachelor of Science, and then I went to seminary, got a master's in divinity to be a preacher. I became interested in fixing up houses, right after I was married—I was twenty-four—and I bought my first house. My wife and I would have five kids, and preachers aren't paid a lot, so I was motivated to make extra money. My first project was built in 1860. It should have been torn down, but I thought it had enough character, and it still stands today. I didn't know what I was doing at the time, but my dad had tons of remodeling and fix-up experience, so I asked him to help me. I lived in that house for a year and sold it. I did that six or seven times over the following years.

That first house I did was in 1978, and it did well on the financials. Another one I got for a steal and the market happened to be going up, and I bought it for about $34,000, I put in about $15,000 and my labor and sold it a couple of years later for $135,000. I rented it in the meantime. That was the best one. On some houses I made a killing and on some I did not make a penny. The last one I did was in 2006. I got this house—I thought it was a pretty good deal—but it needed a lot of work and I spent several months on it. I could tell the market was going down and I was talking to a real estate agent, and he said, "You are about ready to sell. Good. Things are looking bad." So I hustled and dropped the price a couple of times until it was bare bones and it finally sold. Whew! I got out of that just in time because the market kept falling. If I could do it over, I would have done the house flipping and fixing earlier or stayed with it more consistently. I know I could have made a better living just doing one after the other, doing ministry on the side, and doing the building full time.

I hired subs for special projects, but I never had an employee. I hired a plumber friend; the agreement was I paid him to show me how to do some stuff. From then on, when I needed to, I hired trades to be my teachers. That was money well spent. And I had a couple of books, so I was kind of self-taught too. I used contracts when I hired subs. The drywall people created their own contract.[4] It was simple, put up so many boards for so

---

4   A general contractor (GC) sometimes provides the contract for the trades and sometimes they add addendum to a contract that the trades provides.

much money. I hired electricians several times, because if I'm working on a place and it has permits, I can't do the electrical.

The only formal education I had for building was a log-building school. I signed up for this school with Allan Mackie.[5] He was kind of a guru of log building in Canada. I went to this school; it was ten days of intense training with chain saws and then question-and-answer. By the time it was done, all the questions were handled, and I was ready to go. At home I started in and built a log house, and it became my home.

And then, quite a few years later, when I was about to get my contractor's license,[6] I thought I'd build log homes. I looked into that, talked to insurance guys, and was told that log houses were a risky business, the insurance and liability runs about $20,000 a year—something like that—for a one-man show. That shied me away from doing it. I've often wished I had stayed with log building after I built my own log home and jumped from there into building log project. I did get hired to work on some log houses, doing repairs and that was satisfying. But I got scared off by the insurance and bonding and all that because I was poor. But I don't have a lot of regrets about it.

The advice to myself is, *Don't be too quick to jump on a deal that looks good.* Just in the last six months I've walked away from half a dozen old houses. I look at them and think, *I could do this*, but I start putting numbers down, realistic details, and add it up—my time is worth something—and they just don't pencil out to making money. Yeah, it's hard to get a steal on a fixer, there's too many people doing it. I don't jump on things now. I do my homework, give it some time, and if it gets snapped up by somebody else, *oh, well.* A couple of houses I bought quickly when I knew there was competition, I didn't do so well.

I take my time on estimates and I write down everything and then add 20 percent for things I might have forgotten. I had a friend who was a contractor, and when I first got my license, I picked his brain, and that was a part of my education, the business side. He talked about estimating, and I learned

---

5   Allan Mackie ran a log-building school in Prince George British Columbia for years. He is no longer offering courses.
6   Nick did not need a contractor's license because he owned the houses he was working on, although he did need construction permits and inspections. When he began working as a general contractor (that is, building for other people), he needed a contractor's license. Licensing rules vary by state and often from town to town within the same state, and many rural areas don't require construction permits or licenses.

to be really careful. Typically I do fixed bids^. And, you know, all of my jobs were small. I might build a deck or an extra room on a house. I learned to estimate from all these houses I fixed up. I had one job, I figured all the roofing time and hiring a couple of guys and had everything written down, but I forgot to include the cost of shingles, so I ate $2,000. I can't go back and say I forgot. Before I submit it, I let it sit a day and give it some time.

I do Time & Material sometimes, if I'm fixing things, maybe a rotten wall or something. I'd tell the customer, "You're probably safer because I won't charge you as much as if I had to bid the work". But on those kinds of deals I would always say, "If I find a problem other than what we talked about, I'll show you and we'll renegotiate." If you tell them right up front, they seem to be fine.

Several times I've worked with people, and they asked, "Can I help you?" This one guy I said, "Every hour that you work for me, if it's really helpful, we'll deduct twenty dollars an hour." And it was good, he was a friend and we worked well together and had a good time. He saved a couple thousand bucks. I enjoyed doing it that way. I've done that several times now, because they want to learn, and I enjoy being the teacher. They're not an employee and it's a different feeling. But it's not a way to get rich.

If I were starting again, I might be more businesslike, make a business plan, think about what I really want to do, not just take what comes. I'm driving an old van. My wife always said, "You ought to get a nice new big pickup; that's what contractors drive." But a van was more practical. I might have been more businesslike with a sharper image.

A good customer listens, they're reasonable. It means when we're talking money, they're not going to think, "How I can chisel this guy?" They're considerate. Also, they leave you alone, they're not coming around all the time and watching everything you're doing. A bad customer is somebody who doesn't pay. I haven't had many bad customers.

There's a certain drywall guy I used over and over. I never got other quotes from anybody else, even if he charged a lot more, because if he said he'd be there Tuesday and have it done, it was. A sub who does what he says is worth a lot. A bad sub is somebody who doesn't come when they say. Everybody's busy, but if they don't show up or call, I pretty much write them off. Also, a bad sub is one that doesn't listen. I want somebody who is humble and can appreciate what I want.

If I were talking with young guys about going into business—I should have taken more of this advice myself—I'd say:

- Work for somebody in the specific thing you want to do as an apprentice for a couple of years. I got into carpentry jobs where I really didn't have enough experience to know what I needed. I should have worked for a log builder for a few years. It's probably why I didn't get a big log job, I didn't have enough experience. So I'd tell them to get experience if you want to have your own license—don't do it too quickly.
- Be nice. Don't burn bridges. Grit your teeth if somebody mistreats you—be done with them—but don't bawl them out. You don't want to get a reputation of shooting your mouth off or being angry.
- Don't underestimate; don't undersell. Be careful and detailed, give it time, and then always add a certain percent because you're going to forget a few things.
- Don't undervalue yourself. When I was first working on log home projects, I'd do it for twenty-five dollars an hour, using my equipment. I wasn't charging enough. I should have figured out equipment, time, and insurance, instead of saying, "Twenty-five dollars sounds like a good number."
- I'd say, "First make sure it's what you want to do. Talk to a contractor in the business you want to work in and ask if you can shadow him for a while, maybe in a different town so you're not a competitor." I spent a couple of days hanging out with a two of log home builders to see what they did. Most of the bosses never touch logs, so I was glad I saw that before I committed to being a big boss. I'd tell them to make sure it's your style to be a boss.
- Don't hire anybody to do something that you can't do yourself. If he suddenly quits there's a problem. If you're going to be a boss of a company, then you'd better have gone through the hoops, so you know a little bit about all of it.
- Having a general education is useful for the kind of customers you have. Sitting down with coffee, talking about a project, I think a customer can tell if you're just a dumb laborer. But if you can talk about subjects they're interested in, it helps. An education will help you relate to people.

Cut Offs

A couple of times I was low on an estimate. I was always trying to make bids that would sound good to the customer—this is what I did early on—and it was a mistake. Instead, I should have said, "I need to make this much," and just lay it on the table.

A few times it occurred to me I should start a business with an office and employees. But I enjoyed working by myself so much, the simplicity of it and the free schedule. My personal life has just as much importance to me as work.

I didn't have any big goals. My goal was to find satisfying work. I think my goals were always kind of immediate: am I going to enjoy this, can I make a little money at it?

A friend of mine loved playing golf so much that he bought a golf course. After that, he said, "I never play anymore because I'm running this goldarn business." He sold the golf course and now he plays golf again. Same with a business. I think there's a certain mentality who enjoy the management part, but to people like me, and most of the common guys out there, it just isn't attractive.

Difference among builders aside, it takes
longer and costs more to do a good job and
the biggest influence on the success
of the client's project is who builds it.

Jim Locke

Matt Risinger,
Home Builder, Blogger

www.youtube.com/user/MattRisinger
Instagram @RisingerBuild
Twitter @MattRisinger
Blog www.MattRisinger.com

Matt is a clean-cut, upbeat business owner who lives and works in Austin, Texas. One of his companies is an upscale residential contractor and another produces videos focusing on material application and use and the business side of building. Matt turned forty-five the day before we did this interview. He is a frequent contributor to *Fine Homebuilding* and *The Journal of Light Construction* and the only interviewee who was not a tradesman before transitioning to business owner. The interview took place at his office in Austin.

> *One of the things I love most about this business is that it's tangible; the houses we're building should be around for at least a couple hundred years* ■ *I always had this desire to be my own boss* ■ *I'm not a great planner or organizer, so starting out working for a company that was fantastic at both, that was good for me*

I was recruited by a national builder out of college and started as an assistant superintendent. I was twenty-two years old and I had worked in construction for many summers, mainly through a church ministry. I didn't realize it was a career. In college, my degree was industrial management and I thought I wanted to build cars. A builder came to recruit on campus. I was like, "Man this sounds incredible." So I started with those guys in 1995. I was with them for seven years and worked my way up the career path. When I quit that company, I went to work for a semi-custom builder in Oregon.

That's when the mold crisis[1] happened, in 2001–02, and I learned a ton about building science^ and had to take apart a bunch of leaky houses and fix problems. The builder I was working for had to buy back a bunch of houses. It was a hard time in the construction world. That is when I really became passionate about building better. I had no kids, so I had plenty of time to devote to long workdays and lots of research.

In 2005, when my wife finished her medical program and our first child was born, we moved to Austin. That's when I started Risinger Homes. I didn't quite know what my niche would be or how to start a building company because I had very little business knowledge. It was a busy market in Austin. I hired an architect who was really smart about climate and building science and did a spec house in a fancy part of town. That was a hard one for me. I was still trying to figure out, how do I make money at this? I didn't know a thing about the office side. I got information about business from as many places as I could. I joined the National Association of Home Builders^. A lot of things about money, lawyers, and how to set up an office just fell into place because I asked the older builders I was networking with, "Who do you recommend for an attorney? What accounting program are you using?"

Would you change anything about your career?

Hmm. That's a hard question. I believe that my long-term experience has helped me. Had I not built some junky new houses for a few years and had a ton of experience with foundations that leak and bad trades, I don't think I'd be where I am today. Also, because we did so much remodeling work during the recession, it helped us understand how houses fail. This really informs how we build now, by seeing the old.

In your experience, can a tradesman do their trade and run a business?

It's doable to work as a craftsman and run a business, but I think you are going to have a hard time doing both. Some guys that are able to do

---

1 The "mold crisis" began in the United States when a family in Texas sued their insurance company for failing to repair water leaks in their new home, which led to the growth of mold and, the family claimed, caused brain damage in the husband and asthma in the son. A jury awarded them $32 million, although it was later reduced to an undisclosed amount. Known as "sick-building litigation", similar lawsuits spread throughout the country, and insurance companies and builders were inundated with claims. The building industry and product manufacturers responded with improved construction methods and products while insurance companies raised rates, tightened policies, and in some cases stopped insuring in areas prone to mold.

it, but they are rare. The guys that succeed are finish or framing carpenters with one crew. But the guys that I see doing that work fifteen-hour days. It's really hard to have a life outside of work if you're doing both the trade and the business. I get that tension too because I love being in the field, but I need to be selling jobs and managing this company well.

How do you transfer knowledge to your men?

Usually we do the training on the job site with a mockup. One of the things that has gotten us into trouble is waterproofing, and it's costing me the most money in warranties. Most of the time doing it right means using the same trades, working with them to make sure that their bid is in line, not simply going to the next guy who's cheaper. He's cheaper because he doesn't know how to do the work. We've used a lot of products over the years; we use the tried and true ones again and again.

Talk about mistakes you've made.

Oh man, I've made a lot of them over the years. I think one of the bigger mistakes that I've made repeatedly—because I reacted so much against production building—is focusing on building such a good house that I forget to make a profit. As I've gotten older I've realized business needs profit; it's the blood of the business. I've got a client now who owes us a large final draw. We have a lien on the house, but now I have money in reserve, so all the subs are paid and everybody gets a paycheck. Had this happened two or three years ago, what would I have done? This helped me to realize that it's not bad to have profit [*chuckles*], to have money in reserve, to charge what it's necessary to charge.

Eric is my lead salesman and he does most of our estimates. But we need a full-time estimator in order to divorce sales from estimating because, a couple of times, we've lowered an estimate to make a sale and either lost money or had to tussle over change orders. Almost all of my customer problems are money-related: we're over budget and we didn't give them a heads-up on what it is really going to cost. I've lost several hundred thousand dollars that way over the years.

What do you look for when hiring?

I have lost project managers over the years who've gone on to start their own companies. But I hire people who are entrepreneurial, the type that take charge, so if they go on to start their own business, I'm okay with it. One of the best things I got from my production building days was a pre-employment test.[2] I use it on everyone who starts here. With the test I can see from an objective point of view what 'their critical and logical thinking skills are and where their work behaviors fit into different categories. Generally, it's helped me hire well.

You have been in business for twelve years; would you consider it successful?

I think our business is an overall success, but I see a lot of issues that we need to keep getting better at. It's really easy for builders to look outside their business, and go, *Oh gosh, that builder must be killing it.* But as I get older, I realize, maybe he is killing it, but he also has huge debt and people suing him and people angry with him. My definition of success has changed; financial freedom is more important to me now.

What makes a good and a bad customer?

I've had some hard clients the last year or two. Two of those I took thinking, *Oh God, what's going to happen with this, but we need the money, we need work, and we need to get this job going.* The one we are having trouble with now, when I did the initial interview, I didn't like them and they didn't like me, and I didn't get the job. They hired another builder but couldn't negotiate a contract with him. So we had a chance to run it up again—one of our guys felt like it was a cool house and it was an architect we should be working for—so he took the lead. We ended up getting the job, but I had this prickly feeling; they don't get us, they wanted an ultra-sleek house and there was a lot of tricky stuff. I think back and wonder, should I have said, "Look, let's not pursue this, this is going to be a problem."?

Another house that we had problems with was a super-go-go-fast job where they wanted to do a two-year remodel in one year. I had a project manager, one of my top guys, he ended up leaving and one of the reasons was this job. He was getting it done super-fast, but the problem with super-fast is keeping the budget under control. He had guys working nights and weekends and we did the drywall phase in twenty-four-hour shifts. It was craziness. The clients were loving it, but we knew at the end we'd be a half

---

2   Matt uses HTTP//WWW.PSPMETRICS.COM to test prospective employees.

million, or more, over budget on a two-million-dollar contract. Some of it we covered with change orders and some of it we didn't. We had a bunch of problems with them at the end, and we did a contract closeout so they wouldn't sue us, and we gave them seventy-five grand back.

That's the other thing I've realized over the last year—I didn't want people to be upset with me or not like me. So I was a yes-man, only to have to clean up the pieces later, and then they really don't like me. I've realized that not everyone has to like me. We've adopted a bad-news-first philosophy: give them the bad news early; give them the change order now; tell them what it's really going to cost; don't sugarcoat anything; and don't take jobs because we need the cash flow or whatever. We've done a much, much better job of that lately.

I've got two clients right now that are probably my two best ever. With really good clients, when you tell them how much it costs, they don't want to beat you up on fees or ask you to do the work cheaper. It's more like, "Okay, well that doesn't work for the budget, how do we make it work within the budget?" And they see us as a partner and help to get us where we want to go, rather than acting as a roadblock. It's not so much that they're superrich, or can afford whatever, it's that they see the value that we bring to the table. And when we do make a mistake, when we own up to it, they're upset, but they say, "Look, I know this was an honest mistake, how do we move forward?" These clients are hard to find. But we're trying, early on, to get a sense of how new clients will work before we sign a contract.

How did you learn to manage money?

I've always been debt averse. I got some of that in college by taking finance classes. I never had credit card debt in college. Also, when I was working for the production builder, I was reading financial books by Dave Ramsey. His idea is the way to true wealth is being debt-averse and not living a high lifestyle as a young person. Lately I've been working to pay off my house mortgage and I don't have any business loans.

If you were speaking to a group of young people interested in a trade or being a builder, what would you tell them?

I would say, get as much hands-on experience as you can. If you see a neighbor building a deck, offer to help. My high school and college experience on construction projects helped me to appreciate the guys on the job, to understand what it's like to work in the sun all day and to get a general love and knowledge of craftsmanship. Those experiences still help me today to be successful. Also, working for someone else for ten years, learning on their dime, seeing what I liked and what I didn't like, really helped me a ton.

How important was a college education to opening your business?

I'd like to say that it's really important, and generally I won't hire someone as a project manager without a degree. College gave me confidence in the world, it gave me a few years on my own where I still had a safety net, and a time I could learn different things. But the builder I worked for in Portland was super successful, he was a high school graduate, he was a go-getter, and he was confident, and no one knew or cared that he did not have a college degree.

How would you define personal success?

If you take pride in what you do. If you go home at the end of the day and feel like you gave your clients good value and, whether they're happy with it or not, or whether we got paid or not, you've delivered a good house. A rising tide floats all boats; I want people that work here, my subcontractor base, all of us to keep doing better work, to be paid better, to have a better reputation. And those things have happened. And that's been really cool. The other thing that defines my success is the people that I surround myself with.

Cut-Offs

My college degree taught me how to work with people, how to write and communicate better, and how to organize my time.

I was good with managing subs. I like to know what the trades are doing and how they do it. I was intent that subs made money on my jobs, so I wasn't taking the lowest bidder and I was getting good subs.

I hired an architect in my business and he said, "We need to focus on architects because they have already done the marketing."

The world values what the builder with faith brings to the table: honesty, integrity, hard work, a desire to do well, and someone who has the client's best interest in mind. The customer values these things, they don't necessarily want to talk about them.

I was being used by the corporate builder I worked for. They wanted to build a cheaper house every year and wring every dollar out of each house to show Wall Street they're making money so their stock price can go up and the head guy can make $30 million a year. It put me off.

A rising tide floats all boats. By having better competition building better homes, I'm not the outlier. We all are telling clients that doing it right requires a certain level of work. That is the community spirit we have fostered in Austin among builders: competition yet community.

Our new Chief Operating Officer (COO) has helped to put processes in place to make sure the client signs off on change orders.

I've got a couple of clients who think I'm the cat's meow and a couple who think I'm the worst guy in the world, and now, that's okay.

My advice for young builders is to be cautious about making yourself look successful from the world's perspective. I had a builder that I admired for years who I always thought was killing it; he dressed well, drove a fancy SUV, had a big house. He went out of business during the recession. He had the look of success, but he didn't actually have success.

It was a big benefit to start the business at a time when I didn't have big financial needs.

I started a company with a partner and we did two spec houses and did well on them. I bought my partner out and started my third spec house, I lost almost three-hundred-thousand dollars on that house. I started at the peak of the market and paid peak land prices. I did it because I just felt like things were going to keep going up.

To work with architects all you have to do is say, "I'll be a good builder. I'll treat you with respect. I'll respect your plans. I'll treat you like the client and not backstab you." And that's what we do. We never throw them under the bus and as a result they send us their best clients.

Many people make the mistake of thinking that all the challenges in their lives would dissipate if they just had enough money. Nothing could be further from the truth.

Tony Robbins

Bernie Calcote,
General Contractor

www.meldeconstruction.com
info@meldeconstruction.com

Bernie lives in Austin, Texas. He is thirty-six years old, married with two children. He is the CEO of Melde Construction and The Good Guys Construction Services. He is young and enthusiastic about life, being a builder, and God.

> *I'm a people person. I love talking with people and hearing their story and learning from them ■ When I talk to clients now, I say, this is how we do it, so I don't feel like I'm selling anything and I can be authentic ■ I love working in the field, I still miss it, but I'm better at business ■ I don't think that confidence and humility are opposites. You can embody both.*

I have no college education. At eighteen I left a suburb of Houston and moved to Nashville, pursuing a music career. I moved back to Texas in 2002 and I did music full time for the next couple of years. In 2005 I got married and we moved to New Braunfels, Texas and I started as a carpenter's apprentice for a one-man remodeling shop. I didn't know anything about construction. The apprenticeship was informal, and I came up through the trades. The guy I worked for, Scott, became a mentor in not just carpentry, but life.

I was young, newly married, and needed money, and I had committed not to travel or pursue music during the first year of our marriage. The job with Scott was a great opportunity. When I started doing carpentry … I am very competitive and not being good at something really frustrates me, so as Scott was teaching me, I would work on my own house or make candleholders or tables. This work melded the creative, musician side and the technical side of my brain together, and I started seeing they could function as one and create really cool things. Scott had me holding the dumb end of the board for like six months—it was an old-school apprenticeship. I was young, but early on something clicked and I thought, *Man, I really like this.*

Scott created a culture surrounded with a joy in what we were doing. Had I gotten with somebody who was money and deadline-driven and not interested in teaching people, my trajectory in building could have been completely different. Scott's method is now the core of the leader I try to be. I worked with him for probably two and a half years, and he was letting me and another guy lead stuff. But I was getting impatient to grow the business and Scott had no desire to grow it. I learned the craft from Scott; I did not learn about business.

In 2007 my wife got a job in Austin and we moved here. I ended up getting a job as a substitute art teacher where my wife worked. So I got out of the construction industry for a year. When the school year wrapped up, I found a carpenter's helper job.

When I met the project manager for Melde Construction—the company I own now—I was still a musician and I had long dreadlocks; the project manager gave me a shot anyway. I started at eleven dollars an hour and was told that if I showed up for a week, he'd give me a raise. The bar was pretty low.

The project I started on was overwhelming. I thought it was an apartment complex at first, but it was a single-family home. I had learned enough with Scott to keep up, but I soon learned there was a whole other world of building I knew nothing about, and I was intrigued. This was about ten years ago.

I started as a helper and a carpenter. I showed up and I was well-spoken, so I slowly got more responsibilities on the job. There were three project managers and fifteen or so carpenters. I fit right in. The whole fake-it-till-you-make-it thing, man, I'm a poster child for that, but I was trying to balance the times when I needed to be confident and when I needed to watch the guys that knew what they were doing and ask questions. It was a great group of guys, that is what kept me around.

Leon Melde was the owner of the company, he had founded Melde Construction in 1980. Leon's son John worked in the company as a partner, and around 2011 he moved overseas and left the business altogether. At that point I was a project manager. Leon was getting older and wasn't as involved in the day-to-day operations, so there was a void. I was still a part-time musician and I got a call from a booking agent who wanted to get me on a TV show. I would have had to commit to going to LA and being away for as long as it took, but I'm in the middle of building this project. Music was a passionate mindset, but building was tangible, and right in front of me, and we had just had a son. So I got it. I told the agent no. I had never really given myself fully to building, but at that moment, I took ownership of the business—not actually, but even if it wasn't going to be mine, I was going to do this fully. I decided I had to know everything about the business.

Leon and I had a conversation in the driveway of the project I was managing, about me taking over the company. He had seen my ability to communicate, to maintain and cultivate relationships, to network, to manage multiple trades, and to manage a job; we made an informal agreement and Leon started peeling back the curtain to show me how it was done. Our agreement was informal because I was not certain I could do it and he did not know what the transition would look like. But he was going to retire in a few years, so he suggested we start working toward this. He gave me all the education and resources that he could. I got to learn on his dime, making tons of mistakes.

One of those mistakes—as I became the face of the company—was the first interview I went to. I made a PowerPoint presentation that I thought was so flashy, I was sure the clients would be impressed. The guy that interviewed after me, and got the job, had a conversation with the people. I did not recognize what I should have been selling, which was a relationship. I needed to make a personal connection, that can't happen with PowerPoint. The architect told me later what happened.

The two things that changed the face of this company—these were my education in business—I got heavily involved with the AIA^ because the work we were doing was architect-driven, so I needed to be around them. I got involved in meetings and committees and with the home tours committee. AIA has been an important educational platform for me.

I joke that I built the current company on lunches and coffees, because the second thing I did was to build relationships with other builders and architects by asking them to help me get better. I was not selling our company but asking questions. These guys were generous with ideas and they taught me all they could.

You're swinging a hammer—you're not the owner yet—how do you transition to owning the business?

The project where Leon and I talked on the driveway was the last job that I managed. As it got toward the end I was talking with the interior designer and architect about other projects. I was a working project manager half the time and, although I didn't have the title of general manager, I was doing that job too. So the change was quick. By 2015–2016 I had three project managers, a chief of operations, and an in-house labor staff. When I transitioned from GM to owner in July of 2016, I was already running the company as owner. Leon and I had played golf together for a long time, we've been through ups and downs, but he is a great friend and I wanted to preserve that, so there was a formal transition that was spelled out, and a formal acquisition.

I could see how much dysfunction there was in our processes and bookkeeping and although I didn't know exactly what was wrong, I knew something was. It was a slow process, over the course of three years. On the outside, I was following leads, getting new jobs, and building the brand. On the inside, I was using what we had and tweaking it to make it better. I wanted to fix it overnight, but I was drinking from a fire hose, so it took time.

The more I got into the backroom stuff the more I enjoyed it, because it was another opportunity to broaden my skill set, and I dove right in. Part of my grit—my desire to do things that are difficult—is that I didn't go to college and a lot of my competitors did, so I'm playing from behind.

My first year as general manager we went from doing under a million to almost three million, with the same people, and we started making money for the first time in a long time. If I can provide a healthy, profitable culture, people can thrive and be better when they leave than when they came. To do that, my job is to run a good company. Had I started my own business this may have been harder to do.

I tell my guys all the time, this company could fold tomorrow or they could have a better opportunity, and if they do, I want them to take it. I was listening to Adam Robinson, and he said—and this is what I communicate to our guys, if they are dealing with a client, a co-worker, or a trade—"enter every interaction with enthusiasm, excitement, and delight for the other person." Our people, especially the ones that are closest to me, have to embody that, because if we do, we are playing a game we can't lose.

We don't bid competitively. We interview for the job—the architects in Austin get builders involved early on—and we're selected based on references and team chemistry, and if we are selected, we submit a preconstruction agreement and get a small retainer. Then we go through the pricing process with the client and architect. We do the job on a Time & Material contract.

My estimating experience comes from doing it. We have developed an estimating matrix on Excel and it is always being refined. It asks me around a hundred questions about the job and links my answers to specifications and a current market price and historical data that we have specified. In an ideal world, the project manager is doing our estimate, but sometimes they don't have the capacity, so our chief of operations and I do it. We are pushing the envelope of how technology can make us more efficient and add value.

I have always been led by the Holy Spirit and it has taken me all over the world. While I'm determined to make this a successful company—the guys and gals working for me have done something special and I've raised my kids with them and we have developed a community that is focused on each other—that is option A, and it's a pretty damn good option. Option B is, I build it up and I sell it to the employees and God takes me on some other crazy adventure with my family.

Cut-Offs

Honesty is telling the truth about what I know.

The reason builders have a bad reputation is because too often we don't do what we say we will.

The guys in town—my competition—took me in. I said to one of those builders, "'Why are you telling me all your secrets?'" He said, "'It's not like that. If each of us embodies a collaborative effort, that is what the community is and continues to be.'"

We don't use AIA contracts and we spent a lot of time and money with our attorney to write our contract.

Builders say they have so many millions in revenue, but they are not making any money, or they're in the red, and I think, *If you're not making money, big revenue doesn't mean anything.*

We're not promised tomorrow, therefore, what matters is how we treat each other right now.

When I started meeting clients with Leon some of them were mad: "You said this, and this is over budget, and we're not paying for this, and this and this." I was thinking, Man, there's gotta be a better way to do this.

Be more concerned with your character than
your reputation because your character
is what you are, while your reputation
is merely what others think you are.

John Wooden

Jarod Teichmer,
Carpenter / General Contractor

www.mysoulspace.com
Jarodteichmer@gmail.com

Jarod is forty-years old. Like most residential carpenters, he does nearly everything required on a home, from pouring footings to building decks to installing cabinets. There is an intense honesty about Jarod that is built into his personality, and his passion for the work he does is infectious.

> *We want to establish a business that is going to take care of us into the future ■ I'm comfortable with what I charge. We put out a good product ■ If a guy shows up on a job in torn clothes, cussing up a storm, that doesn't sit well with me ■ Human beings are ethical creatures, it's easy to get away from that, but it's also easy to nurture it and use it as a moral compass ■ I don't want to be sixty-five and scrambling, trying to figure out how to take care of myself and my wife ■ Money shouldn't be the driving force behind what you're doing; it's got to be about creating a sense of joy and satisfaction*

I started in construction twenty-two or twenty-three years ago. My first job was as a carpet installer. I did that for a while and then I got a job with a general contractor out of Washington state. We did large commercial jobs, mostly schools. I primarily did concrete footings, lots of rebar, and building window bucks^. From there, I got a job with a residential contractor in northern Idaho. We built houses from the ground up and rarely subbed anything out because we had a guy who did electrical and plumbing. My job was everything else, from the foundation to the punch list^. I was not drawn to construction as a young adult, but I found that I was good at it.

Most of my training was on the job but I had some formal carpentry training at one point. There was a program set-up through a job service, I think it was federal. It was called the Workforce Investment Act, and there was some job training with a journeyman carpenter. As part of that program I got a voucher for my first set of tools, to the tune of about four grand. I'll always remember that; it was pretty exciting.

I have a GED, a high school equivalency. I dropped out of school when I was sixteen to work. For me school was a social experiment; that didn't work for grades. My parents' condition for me leaving school was that I'd get my GED. So I did that. I've been working ever since. Formal education doesn't interest me. Especially now, when so many people have degrees and can't find a practical use for them. I did go to college for one semester, thinking maybe I would enjoy it, but it wasn't the direction I wanted. I encourage my kids to try college, to let them know it is a possibility.

How did you move from working for someone to starting your own business?

I worked for the same general contractor for many years, until his company went under. Turns out this guy was sleazy and there was a major problem on a twenty two-house project—to the tune of two hundred thousand dollars—he never recovered from that. He packed up his house and hit the road, owing a lot of guys money. He left unfinished contracts and I took a lot of that work.

How would you respond to this Idea? If your goal is to be a tradesman, work for someone else. If your goal is to establish and build a significant company, put your tool belt aside and focus on business as soon as it is practical.

I agree with that 100 percent. That's where I'm at now, trying to figure out how to do both. I constantly find myself in this situation where I can build whatever they want, but running the business is like reading Chinese. So I'm winging it. Fortunately, I get along well with people, and presenting myself as a good contractor—that comes easy. But navigating the legal aspects of it is really hard for me. I learned about business from watching and mimicking what I saw. René, my wife, has computer skills and I know Microsoft Word, so I can make invoices and estimates look professional. We use Excel to track income and outgoing money and overhead. That's the extent of our business skill. It is all the bureaucratic and legal stuff that is so hard.

I'm looking for a mentor to help with my business skills. I'm asking a lot of questions and navigating the internet, trying to figure out everything from contracts to taxes. But there's so much, I get frustrated and give up and make a commitment to do it at a later time. That's the cycle.

Do you use contracts?

I don't. The extent of my paperwork is writing an estimate and emailing it to the customer. If they're comfortable with it, I'll ask for half down—the cost of materials—and the rest upon completion. My contracts are verbal, there's never any signatures. Fortunately, we haven't had issues. I'm a people pleaser, I go the extra mile to make sure whoever I'm working for is satisfied and I don't collect the final draw until they are.

How did you learn to estimate jobs?

I'm not sure that I have learned how to estimate or bid. I do a thorough material list. For labor I work out how many hours it will take based on past experience. I keep a yearly calendar log tracking how many hours spent doing each job, but I'm not good at keeping the log, so a lot of it comes from memory. I don't charge for overhead or profit, but I'm making travel expenses[1] and a small percentage on materials, though I don't add a specific figure. I don't add anything to my labor rate either. I feel like it gets added, but there's no formula.

I don't charge for planning and design. I spend my evenings and wherever free time I have doing the design. It's a lot of phone calls, research, and tweaking to get the final plans. Sometimes I cut that corner by inflating the estimate so that I cover those charges.

Would you change anything about your career?

I'd be where I am now a lot earlier, bridging that gap between working in the field and running the business. At first, being my own boss, I had a sense of satisfaction and I rested on that for years. I wish I had known that I needed to be educated about business, rather than now—I'm forty years old, halfway through my working career—trying to figure it out. The reason

---

1   In the summer Jarod works in a remote community and makes three-hour-plus round trips to get materials.

I have not slowed down [to learn business] is the fear that one day people won't want what I have. That's been a driving force behind cramming as much work as I can get in. The first few years were hectic; by the end of the working season[2] I was overbooked and committed to so many different places that it was a nightmare to be around me.

What mistakes have you made in your career?

I've made every mistake you can make [*laughs*]. When I first started, I thought there was one way to do everything: one way to set tile, hang drywall, weave a roof valley. I took what was taught to me as fact. Sometimes that worked, sometimes not. The mistake I made was not being open-minded, not searching for new techniques.

What do you like and not like, about running a business?

I like the freedom of being able to come and go as I want and planning my work around life, rather than life around work. I spend more time with my kids, we have the freedom to travel and work here and in Idaho. It's definitely more creative, too. I love being able—from design to finish—to incorporate my own ideas. I enjoy working with and developing relationships with my customers. What I don't like, it's a lot of hours and it's stressful. There are days when I don't want to do the physical labor, and some days I fantasize about working on a job where someone is telling me what to do.

What makes a good and a bad customer?

A good customer is someone I can develop a personal relationship with. It is a customer that understands that I'm passionate about what I do, and of course, people that praise me when I'm done. [*Laughter.*] I get joy out of visualizing something, creating it on paper, figuring out what it's going to take to make it happen, and then building it.

A bad customer? I don't like negative energy, badmouthing someone; or somebody that claims to have all the experience in the world (they should do the work themselves); people who want to be so involved in every aspect of the work, looking over my shoulder the whole time; others, no matter what you do, they find something to complain about; and people who are unappreciative. I've had a couple of people I was unsure of working for, but I've never had anybody that I wouldn't work for. I've worked for people

---

2 Jarod works in the south in the winter and the north in the summer.

that my wife said I shouldn't. I've always powered through until the end. It comes down to the bottom dollar, I'm willing to sacrifice peace of mind to get the job and finish the project.

How do you shape a customer's expectations?

The number one thing is honesty. I'm honest from the get-go, so I develop a sense of trust, and that allows me to lead that person where I want them to go with the design and products we use. I direct a project to get the best overall result.

Where did you learn to manage money?

[*laughs*] Trial and error. Rene has a knack for it. I have a desire to be more responsible about it.

Do you have immutable rules that you follow?

My ethics are based on what I know in my heart—it is the evolution of the human spirit—it's what makes us feel good about ourselves and it allows me to sleep at night. So I'd say, first is honesty, then, I do what I say, and clearly communicate if I can't do something. Overall, being of good character and having integrity.

How did you learn to sell?

I'm not sure. But with experience comes the ability to talk about projects knowledgeably; that sells. A lot of our work comes by word of mouth, people have seen the things we're doing, they seek us out knowing what we provide. There isn't a lot of sales that go into it. We don't advertise. Partly because we don't have to, but also, working down here—because I don't have a contractor's license—I am flying under the radar.

You are pulled toward business—because you know you need to be—but you love being a craftsman. Is there a solution to this dilemma?

I'm one of the guys that think there's a way to bridge that and do both. Maybe it's not having a huge business. My idea of a legitimate business is having a handful of employees, with benefits. Doing what I'm doing now isn't necessarily a business—I mean it is, I log hours and I get paid for what I do, but it won't provide for us when I can't do it anymore. I need my business to be legitimate so that I can legally do what I'm passionate about and get paid for it.

When you hire someone, what do you expect from them?

I expect them to work like I do [*laughs*]. I expect him to free up my time so I can do what I need to do. It hasn't been the case yet. What I would like to do is find somebody green and teach them the way that I want things done.

What makes a bad tradesman?

The quality of their work and whether they have work. In my twenty-five years of working I've come across a lot of people that told me they couldn't find work; to me that's a sign of somebody that doesn't want to work. If you're a tradesman and you don't have work, it's because you're not a good tradesman. I know, it fluctuates with the economy and sometimes things are in demand and sometimes they're not, but I've always been able to find work.

What would you tell tradesman who wanted to go into business for themselves?

I'd tell them how important it is to work with the intention of providing a good product and to have honesty, integrity, and be personable. If you have those things, and are passionate about your work, then the rest of the stuff will take care of itself—until you get to the business. [*Laughter.*]

In business, I would tell them not to do what I did. I'd tell them to do their research on owning a business. I'd tell them to have a business plan, a roadmap of how to get where they want to go. I would tell them to find a knowledgeable mentor they can reach out to with questions. I'd tell them to take charge of their finances. To pay themselves as an employee and to keep personal and business finances separate, rather than saying, "I made three thousand dollars on this job I can spend." Keep the money in the business. I'd tell them to never stop learning.

In my heart, being a successful tradesman is being excited to go to work and loving the work and the enjoyment of doing it, and pleasing people, and seeing them get excited about the project. In my head, it's about providing for my family and having something substantial to lean on and to pass on.

Cut-Offs

I've come a long way compared to where I started, but the business side still seems so far away.

René and I have been together for nine years, she has a wonderful design vision, I can build exactly what you want. We approach it as a team.

My time is spent rounding up materials. Flying solo like I do all my time is spent working and preparing for the next job. My excuse for not spending more time on the business is that I don't have time.

I won't cut corners to build something that just looks nice. We build things that are going to last for a long time.

Putting out a good product is one thing, but being somebody that people can depend on, that is a good selling point.

My driving force is the satisfaction I get creating something from nothing. I am knowledgeable when it comes to creating stuff, I enjoy that.

I get satisfaction from satisfied customers.

I try not to think about getting hurt on the job; I have a family of five that depends on me, so there's a lot of fear about that.

I believe when I'm creative, I'm using the talents that are given to me by the universe, and when the combination is right, the product is divine. That is the difference between working for myself and working for someone else.

Great minds discuss ideas.
Average minds discuss events.
Small minds discuss people.
Elanor Roosevelt

René McIntosh,
Office Work

www.mysoulspace.com

René is married to Jarod (previous interview) and works in their business about ten hours a week. She is thirty-seven and was a real estate agent for seven years in the Seattle area. She is the mother of two small boys.

What do you do in the business?

I help with invoicing, bids, and purchasing materials. What I like most—where the challenges and my talent lie—is design. I like to go into the space with the client and envision what needs to happen. If there are two jobs, I nudge Jarod toward the creative one.

What drew you to working in the business?

I was a real estate agent and served on the Professional Standards Board and the Ethics & Grievance committees and I did the newsletter so I'm good at paperwork and I'm organized and when it came to doing invoicing and things for our business, I jumped on it and started creating what we needed.

What do you like about having your own business?

So many things. I love the physical freedom—we work in the south in the winter and Idaho in the summer—and it gives us the freedom to be creative in our life.

What would you change about the business?

I would bring in someone to put everything in place and tell us what we need. I would like the business to be a well-oiled machine. Right now, it's a Picasso painting, here and there and everywhere. If it was plotted out and organized—if there was a clear vision—I could step right in and do it. The business is its own little person; if I put an age on it, it would be a seven-year-old. [*Laughter.*] But if it is going to survive it needs some mechanisms put into place.

What mistakes have you made in the business?

Not knowing what we're doing. We know creatively and in our relationships with clients, but when it comes to the business—investing or saving or taxes—we're guessing if we are doing it right or not.

Do you help Jarod with estimates, and how did you learn to estimate?

I learned from doing it with Jarod. He takes the reins on the bidding, but we work on it together. I've done every estimate with him and I've watched what he does. Also, I have information in Excel that links to past years and within each job are the costs for materials and labor. Jarod writes them up, I review them and type them up. He reviews them again and changes stuff, and we go back and forth until it is done.

What makes a good and a bad customer?

The good ones are interesting people, the ones who say, "Do what you want to do." Those are my favorites. [*Laughter.*] Also, they have enough of a budget to be flexible, I love that too. Bad customers, hmm, somebody who isn't willing to see things differently. They're not open to new ideas. I know this is woo-woo, but my ultimate goal is to create a sacred space—Joseph Campbell's idea—where we can return to ourselves again and again.

When you meet a new customer, do you try to shape their expectations for the job?

I set an intention; the highest and best good for the customer and me and then I try to see what is unfolding, and if they are stuck, I will offer guidance.

What is a good tradesman?

They have happy clients and a feeling of joy and fulfillment in their work and they are living within their means.

When you feel overwhelmed or unfocused how do you regain balance?

I spend time alone. I revisit my vision and my plan. I open my journal and I read what I've written, to remember what I'm here for and what I want to do.

What would your advice be about money?

Don't take it from me. [*Laughter.*]

Do you have frustrations with the business?

Jarod says yes to everything! That is frustrating. He is really, really nice and he's got like a hundred little old ladies all over the place who just love him and when they call and say their friend needs this or that, he does it. I wouldn't change that—it is one of the things I love about him—but sometimes it frustrates me too.

Never ruin an apology with an excuse.
Benjamin Franklin

Deva Rajan,
Retired General Contractor

deva.rajan@earthlink.net

Deva was eighty-one at the time of this interview. He converted to Hinduism many years ago, hence his Indian name. He is a warm and gracious man, who, it seems to me, has moved beyond the clamor of building. He lives in the hills outside of Oakland, California in an extraordinary home that he began building in the 1960s. The interview was done on a third-floor deck, the outside edge of which is built into a forested hillside.

> *Rarely do partnerships work, because if each one is building from his internal creativity, there's bound to be conflict* ■ *I find a lot of really good sculptors are also good builders, so I hesitate to separate artists and craftsmen as two different fellows* ■ *Profit is your first expense and you should be setting aside that profit to make sure that's protected* ■ *I knew how to fabricate flashing and counter flashing from my eighth-grade metal shop program* ■ *A person can be attracted to the trades and go on to become skillful in them, enough to assure a lifetime of contentment and success* ■ *Learn to sell and protect quality, creativity and durability, not price* ■ *You want good teachers in all of your employees* ■ *Mistakes are important, we learn from them and develop humility because we realize we're not foolproof*

My training was in the arts, sculpture, and art history. I had a master's from UC Berkeley. I later taught sculpture at UC Berkeley, but it was way too slow. During college and graduate years I worked in construction as a laborer and apprentice carpenter through the summers and vacations. But what I didn't realize was, I had fallen in love with it. After teaching and seeing the backside of administrative baloney, I realized, *I'm not gonna throw my whole life into this realm of confusion.* So I got out of teaching and went to work with builders in Berkeley. In a couple years I got licensed and established my own business. Two friends and I did a lot of renovations, decks—all the small stuff—for seven years. Later I began to get more consequential projects. I built my first home in 1964.

What drew you to the trades, what was most rewarding about it?

I'll start with physical things: you get up early, you work hard, you eat well, and you sleep well. Really a great combination. You're in good health because of it. On a mental level, it is satisfying. You start something and, at the end of the day, you look back and say, "Wow, look what we did today." If it's a bathroom or a deck, when it's done you shake the customer's hand and you feel great, because it's finished, and you move onto something new. I liked that about construction. Even if it turns out to be a sour job—a client you misunderstood and should have screened out—it does come to an end.

What do you do if you lose direction in business?

Well, that sounds to me like someone who's not focused on their work. They're trying to do too many things at a time. If you focus on just one thing, even if it just takes an hour, and you complete it, you reach the conclusions that are important to you. That's done and you don't have to put it on the shelf and come back to it.

What's the most difficult part of being in the trades?

I think for a lot of young people it is putting the business together with the trade, because they are a different skill set. Now they have to acquire a basketful of other skills: managing money, employees, clients, architects, engineers, suppliers, subcontractors, bankers, lawyers, insurance agents, payroll, investments in equipment and buildings. These business skills do not come easily and often come with mistakes and lessons learned. You have to love it or you will not get good at it.

Has your academic education helped in your trade/business, and if so how?

That's the beautiful part of it. My education, especially in architecture and art history, included the study of great California builders and architects in the '20s, people like Bernard Maybeck and Greene & Greene, built gorgeous homes. I became aware through the work of these builders and architects what beautiful houses could be built by artists. I love that approach to construction, through the arts, through the craft of building things.

Did you work for someone else, if so, how did it help?

As a laborer I worked for the same general contractor for probably six summers. I kept returning and was a great laborer. They gave me a truck to go to the lumberyard and get this and that and I'd come back and they'd say, "You got the wrong stuff." So right away, that was a great education on how to select straight material, clean material, without knots in the wrong places. The names of moldings, all of that stuff, what a great education. And they were paying me for it too! [*Laughter.*]

When you started did you have long-term goals and ambitions?

I think the goal was to bring back to life, in the '60s and '70s, the spirit of building with artisans, like Maybeck and Greene & Greene. It's incredible the buildings they put together with tile artists making tile, blacksmith artists crafting the hardware and railings, and all the wonderful timber joinery by carpenters.

In my mid-twenties I discovered Fort Ross, north of San Francisco, along the coast. It was a Russian outpost—their most southerly outpost in California—and that inspired me. It was built by shipbuilders, everything was handcrafted. Gorgeous work. I developed a notebook on Fort Ross joinery. I'd sketch how they built doors, with tapered cross bands—fantastic joinery—stop-splayed scarfs with under-squinted square butts and tapered traverse keys.[1] That's one joint. We started to borrow these methods and employ them in our building. It was so much fun.

Do you have memorable mistakes that you made in your trade?

Putting posts right in the ground. We used to build houses with rejected telephone poles we got for free--we used to build with whatever we could find that was free—and we put them right in the ground and the center would rot out in a hurry. Not a good thing. The second mistake was putting rafter and beam tails out in the weather. Looks great, but they're the first thing to rot.

---

1   I searched the internet looking for a schematic, photo, or drawing of one of these joints, as much for me as for you, unfortunately, I found none. Deva no longer has drawings of it either.

Another, an insurance agent, had a bunch of bathrooms that failed in Lafayette and asked if I wanted to bid on them. I bid them and built them, and I lost money on every single one, because the city had to inspect the plumbing, test the shower pan, inspect the lath, and so on. Over and over again, I'd start work for a few hours, and stop for the inspector.

What would you do differently or wish you had done?

I would have gotten a degree or good training in engineering and architecture. All through my career I would intuit the need for structural things in a building, but I didn't have the engineering background. I'd have to hire someone, but I was always fascinated with engineering solutions and respect people who can develop structural calculations for a load, and people who can draw well. What great skills to have! I wish I'd learned more about heavy equipment. One of the guys I trained went into business and bought a high-lift.[2] Man, when I saw what he could do with that, I started renting them from him. I think we would have been smart to get big equipment. We had three Bobcats and trucks of all kinds, but wish I'd gone the next step.

What advice have you given most to builders about business?

Avoid, in every way, the concept of a franchise. You are copying what someone else did and expecting it to work for you. That's not the way to build a business. Construction businesses are different from one another because they emerged from within each person, that's the beauty of it. It's not hard to look within your heart and build it from your internal creativity.

What rules did you follow in business?

Business integrity and honesty among everybody. Transparency, about wages and benefits. I also believe, even more today, that you have to defend the interests of your client. There's an old Indian saying: "Those businesses will prosper who protect the interest of others as their own." When you sign up to build a house for someone, you have to find out what they want—listen carefully—and make sure they get it. If you do that, the money comes, abundance comes.

---

2   A high-lift, also called man-lift or aerial lift, is a hydraulic machine that comes in many shapes and sizes and lifts the tradesmen and materials up to where the work needs to be done, eliminating the need to set up and work off of ladders or scaffolding. These lifts offer more safety and flexibility than ladders and far more flexibility than scaffolding.

How did you learn about business?

I got licensed in early 1966 and created a company called Canyon Construction. I managed it for forty years and sold it. Learning about business was a leap for me. I didn't have that background and nobody in our family was a businessperson, they're all artists and teachers. I had a lot of learning to do. While I was restoring Fort Ross—after a catastrophic fire in the early '70s—I hired Robert Mann, a CPA, and met with him once a week with payroll and business details. After a while I said, "I don't know what a business is, would you teach me about it?" Every time I'd go, he would take me through various steps and explain business.

Robert taught me accounting and it fascinates me, even now, that accounting is really easy to learn. Even though I liked it and became good at it, I realized it was better to turn over the routinized work to a bookkeeper, and to do the things I was good at, which was running a crew and guiding day-to-day decisions on the job. I loved being on the job, ten hours a day.

Do you have memorable business mistakes?

Yes. I didn't realize until we got rolling on this job at Fort Ross—it was a state of California contract with fifteen men on the project—I started with no capital. You can't do that. I ended up having to borrow money from everybody I knew. I even borrowed from one of our construction guys. I wrote notes to everybody and paid it all back, of course, but that was a learning mistake. If you're going to take on a project—particularly one where your payments are 30-60-90 days out—you can't run a business on expected income, you've got to have capital up front.

Were there conflicts working at your trade and running the business?

For me, there was a slow migration from being full time in the field to more time with clients and office work. I didn't see it so much as a conflict, but I know what you mean, you can't do both, particularly with multiple projects. Eventually, our company had sixty employees and many jobs going at the same time. We evolved a mature and competent project management staff. The only way you can leave the field is if you've got competent foreman and carpenters, who can do things just as well as you can. I learned to step back. If you're on site all the time you suppress their maturity; as soon as you get out of the way, man, these guys take off! It's great to see.

How would you respond to this idea? If your goal is to be a tradesman, work for someone else. If your goal is to establish and build a significant company, put your tool belt aside and focus on business as soon as it is practical.

I think there's a natural time for all of us to put our tool belt aside. Maybe age is a factor—young guys are faster and stronger and able to do more in a day than you can—and you ought to get the hell out of the way. [*Laughter.*] Besides, if you spend your time building really good people and fail to let them take charge, you're going to lose them. So, how do you keep really good people? You give them freedom, responsibility, constructive criticism, and lots of support.

How did you learn to manage money?

I learned a lot from Robert, the accountant, about levels of financial management, putting money away consistently, and saving for retirement. Also, encouraging everybody around you to build wealth and to participate in 401(k) plans. It requires discipline, not spending, and always putting at least 10 percent away. In addition, I began to read voraciously and listen to recordings of successful entrepreneurs. I got started building post offices. I still own some. Most people don't know that 90 percent of the post offices in America are privately owned and rented back to the postal service. Once you learn how to work the system and start building, it's amazing. They're great sources of passive income and perfect for builders.

Did you actively mentor people?

Most of our foreman and superintendents eventually wanted to go into business themselves. They'd come to me and say, "Deva, I've got to start my own business, can I use you as a reference?" I'd say, "Of course, let me help you with this." I'd mentor them in all the ways I could, before and after they left. A whole lot of them came back, because they were great at construction, but not at business. It might take them a couple of years for them to find that out though. There have been several exceptions, builders who worked for me who started their own business and were wildly successful.

To be good at business, you have to be interested in clients and consultants and all of that stuff. You have to have a passion for them and then you become really good at it. Over and over I would hear these guys say, "I'm great at building, but I hate the business end of it." If you hate something, you're not going to do it well.

What bad business advice did you get?

Because I lived through the discovery of computers as a business tool, there was a chapter in all of that where we became too dependent on them, we'd buy software that we hardly used and built schedules that nobody looked at. What a waste of time.

What kills creativity?

Two things: budgets and schedules. When clients and architects start looking to reduce costs, they begin by unbundling this creative wholeness, chopping away elements because they cost too much or take too long to build. I know it's a process that everyone does and we have gotten used to it—even aiding by providing line item budgets and schedules that slice and dice the work into almost unrelated elements—but we have to guard against the intellectual and competitive forces that encourage us to abandon our commitment to build projects beautifully. We have to protect the spirit and soul of the work. Wealthy clients rarely have to do that. They want to know all of the ways that you, as the builder, will help preserve and enhance the integrity of the project.

What is great success in a construction business?

There are several parts, I don't know if one is more important than another: assuring the satisfaction of clients so, when the job is finished, they're so happy you built their work they tell everybody about it; bringing on consultants as you grow the business, a good banker, insurance agent, accountant/tax person; and making money, not driving old beat-up trucks and working with old beat-up equipment. You're building the business, constantly improving everything, through making money and building capital.

How did you learn to sell?

Mostly from listening to tapes of real estate salespeople. They're really powerful. This concept of listening to your client and asking questions. Listen, listen, listen. The client will tell you how to sell them. They're gonna give you all the keys.

What is the best investment you ever made?

Midway in our company growth we were renting space in an office building when it came up for sale. I had never thought about it, but the next thing I knew I owned the building and I was leasing office space and moving our company into the available space. It paid for itself. I paid $900,000 for the building, in three years I sold it for $1.7 million. Wow, what a great investment that was.

What makes your best customer?

Well, it's always great when they're wealthy. [*Laughter.*] I had one customer who took his computer business public and walked away with $150 million or so. He asked us to build a house and we set up a joint account and he kept $250,000 in the account at all times. I could draw at will. We moved mountains with that kind of financial power. Nothing like it.

The worst customer?

One who's misrepresented the work and is purposefully setting you up for a fall. It's usually the last payment. That's happened to me twice. The client actually built a scenario where they plotted all along not to pay the last payment, and they didn't. They got me.

Did you shape a new customers' expectations?

I did make some mistakes about that. I was trying to sell bath and kitchen remodels and I would tell the clients that all of our men were artists. They don't want to hear that! They wanted to hear that they're plumbers and bath and kitchen experts, they've done hundreds of them, they're fast, and that they are not going to be creative. [*Laughter.*]

Did you turn down customers and if so, why?

We've turned down several. Some customers are crooked. If you're fortunate—in the process of interviewing them—you can discern who they are at the beginning. One of the mistakes I've made is not discerning that early enough in the process. You're finding out the reason for the project and who in their marriage is responsible for design and who for business decisions. You get them talking about each other and about themselves, they'll reveal a lot. If you find them lying, you stay away from those guys.

How do you respond to this quote: "Clients do not come first. Employees come first. If you take care of your employees, they will take care of the clients."

It's an interesting premise. I suppose that works in some businesses, but construction is more of a direct service industry and I think you have to put your client first, always.

Do you have a favorite failure in your business?

I have a failure that permanently changed how we did things. Most AIA contracts include an arbitration clause requiring one mediator. We signed one of those with an attorney as a client, he was determined not to pay the last 10 percent of our bill. He beat the heck out of us and one of the reasons was that the arbiter was also an attorney and he gave the entire remaining balance to the client. As a result of this, we had an arbitration clause crafted that required a three-person panel: the client chose one, the builder chose one, and those two chose the third. All three of them had to be licensed contractors, engineers, or architects so they knew the industry. That clause worked for us one hundred percent.

What do you look for when you hire?

Of course, you're looking for skill and experience and why they aren't working for their last contractor. Did they leave or were they fired? What's the backstory on this guy? Then you're looking at him personally, using your intuitive eye, asking, *Is he talking straight with me? Is he looking me in the eye? Is he shifty?* I'm looking for honesty. Education is a plus, but not necessarily required.

What do you and don't you expect from your employees?

I expect competence. When they look at a set of drawings, they understand what they are and build it out correctly. It doesn't always happen, but it's great if they turn out to be a good teacher. You hire a lead carpenter; is he barking orders, or is he helping these guys grow? A lot of builders are self-taught, lone wolves who never learned from a good builder. You want to find that out—who have they worked with and how they learned. You want somebody who's positive—first to the job and last to leave—and happy to have the work. That's the thing about Latino workers, they often are singing while they work, wow, what a great thing. I don't expect work they don't get paid for. Some builders want their employees to pay for pickup time. In our company we pay them to wrap up and close up their tools and get off the job. I do expect them to bring their own tools, the company provides table saws and big stuff.

How do you let people go?

There are all kinds of legitimate reasons to let someone go. One dump truck driver couldn't start the day without a joint. We thought we made the message clear, but he left the corporation yard one day with the dump up and ran into something. That was easy. It's harder with a key employee who's been with you a long time. We had one like that—he is still one of my best friends—but there came a point when the way he was as a person became too heavy on the company. It was a friendly fire—if you could ever call it that—and he understood. Somehow his personality and the way he ran work became so strong that it was no longer my company.

I discovered this tremendous relief after he was gone, and the company came back into my hands and I was able to shape it just the way I wanted. A lot of what I wanted was based on what we had promised the client. We told them, "Here's an estimate and a budget, and we're going to track these and make them work." When he spent money that was not part of that picture, that hurt our ability to do what we'd promised and our relationship with the client. Because of my religious beliefs and commitments, I was really, *really* dedicated to bringing that kind of truthfulness into the business world. In the '50s and '60s contractors were known as crooks. In the '60s, '70s, and '80s, there was a group of us in the Bay Area who were dedicated to turning that around and building great companies based on good ethics.

Please talk about the Splinter Group^.

Our regular meetings were fabulous. To share our experiences—mistakes and everything—was incredible. We learned from each other and almost everybody gave away their secrets because there was so much more to gain by giving away all that we knew. What most of us learned early on is, "The more you give away, the more you've got to give." We became each other's teachers. We had wonderful speakers. There'd be smaller meetings, maybe twelve people around a table brainstorming something like, "How do you keep key employees?"

Sometimes a business is based on competition, on who they're up against, and that defines who they're going to be. That's kind of a backward, or uncreative way. A more satisfying way to build a business is from the energy within yourself and the people in your company. If you get a collective agreement from a group of five, ten, or twenty people, it's a powerful thing. For example, if you have one great carpenter, he will stagnate after a while, until he bumps up against someone else just as good. If you get two or three top carpenters, they suddenly make a quantum leap, striking a whole new stride of excellence and creativity. It's incredible to see. My motive was to build a company with great people and allow that natural process to occur.

What's a bad tradesman?

If they're dishonest in some way, or disrespectful of the client, wanting to take all the credit, rather than sharing the achievement with the people they work with.

What do you love?

I love taking used materials and finding a new use for it. If you look at my house, much of it is reused materials. When I built this house, I didn't have any money, it was hard work and finding used materials.

Did you have educational systems in place for employees?

When I was on the job full time, the first half hour of each day the whole crew met. We discussed the work for that day and got a joint vision of what to do. Then we'd have a demonstration, one of the carpenters might say, "Here's how I sharpen my chisels." Did you know there are six ways to sharpen chisels, and they're all right? When we were a larger organization, we'd have weekly meetings with project managers, superintendents, and estimators. So we were always in agreement on what the priorities were for the company.

What books have been most important in your business life?

Brian Tracy's work. He has written a lot about business and sales. I listened to a lot of his recordings.

Have you had a mentor who has influenced your career?

Steve Oliver, ten years my senior, built larger projects. When I had this fourteen-million-dollar project for the state of California I went to Steve and said, "I haven't done a project of this scale, what kind of contract should I use?" He told me, and then he said to subcontract everything. I said, "Why? We've got excellent carpenters, foundation, and finish people. We do everything." He said, "I know you do, but hold your forces in reserve, get them involved in other projects, and sub everything. Make sure all of your insurance umbrellas name you and the client as additionally insured[3] and put an extra five million insurance umbrella over the whole thing." He said sooner or later subs are going to fall down, you rush in, with your people, and take over the work. Another sub will roll up some huge extra work order, and you say, "Thank you very much, we'll do that." So we had this terrific arsenal of builders to throw into the work whenever we needed to. At the same time we took on other work and we had terrific income all the time. He gave me that kind of advice. Wow was he ever right.

What would you tell a new business owner about marketing and sales?

When I was a kid, we had a fire in our home and my mother had it renovated. A month after it was done the contractor called and said, "Your thirty-day warranty is coming up, we're sending over a carpenter, whatever needs to be done we're going to take care of it." In six months they sent another guy and again at one year. All of this was free. My mother was talking to everybody in town, "Guess what happened to me." Now that's great advertising! I learned this from my mother; your best marketing is a satisfied client.

We never put ads in the paper or TV shorts. It's a waste of money. Sales is primarily listening to your client, finding out what's important to them, and prioritizing that. Maybe it's a move-in date or landscaping— "Whatever you do, don't step on the petunias."—so you put fences around them. You include that in your sales presentation. We had a rule that when the job is finished, we would find something that wasn't on the client's punch list and fix it; a gate that's not working or we put a new post on the mailbox. We didn't brag about it, or even show it to them, but when the client discovered it, they were delighted. I saw early on the power of a contractor who made their client really happy.

---

3   An additional insured is a person or organization insured under an insurance policy purchased by someone else.

How do you feel about high-pressure sales?

I've never done that. In fact, I've done the opposite. When they tell me who they are interviewing, I tell the client they can't go wrong with them. "However, if you go with us, this is what we can offer. We've got depth and experience in our field. When we say we're going to start, we're going to be there, because we've got the men to do it". You sell the company based on their strengths. If they pick another contractor, compliment them, tell them they've made a good choice and they're going to get a good project.

In sales, you have to leap over and past the process of choosing and find yourselves already in the future reality, time travel. Like courting and wooing a woman, it's not, "If you marry me this could be great." Rather, "Wow! Look at the dream that we both have for our lives and here are the details and how we can fulfill them." Clients want to sign up with a time traveler who already knows where they are going, how to get there, and loves the journey.

What if the contractor they choose is not a good choice?

Without putting the questionable guy down, you say, "These guys you are looking at are good people, I don't know the other guy."

How did your marketing and sales change as you got bigger?

In the early years of our company people selected us because they'd heard good things, and they were going to go with us. But later, we were bidding multi-million-dollar projects and there was competition. We included in our presentation the idea that, once they got all of their bids, if they were still interested in working with us, they should come back and see what we could do. That's when we fine-tuned our approach. Instead of making our subs shave their bids, maybe the work can be changed. We'd ask the architect if they needed all of that gravel behind the walls, or trimless finish work, which is way more work than conventional trim, maybe we do trimless in these rooms and conventional in the other rooms. We look at whatever is driving the cost up.

Did you get to a point where you stopped bidding competitively?

We got to a point where we recommended a cost-plus-a-fee^ approach. We determined the cost of the work with subcontractor bids, developed an estimate and a budget,[4] and added our fee. This allowed the client to change the scope, which changed the final cost. This is the fairest way for them and us. Our clients liked it because it was full disclosure; we showed quotes and billing from subs and suppliers and provided copies, so they could see what the actual costs were.

Do you have an interesting construction story?

The city of San Francisco wanted two more sinks for a café in the Ferry Building, which is on a pier. In order to put in sinks we had to core drill through a 24-inch-thick concrete slab. How do you get your cast-iron pipe through the slab and hooked up to the sewer below? You send a skiff with two union plumbers, with all their tools, under the pier and two other guys on top who drop a light through the hole so the guys in the skiff know where to go. Then you hand materials through the floor opening, and just then, here comes a ferry and a surge of water goes under the pier, flips the skiff, all the plumbing tools and materials go to the bottom of the bay, and the plumbers are swimming to where they can get out. [*Laughter.*]

When business slowed, what did you do?

Having side businesses was one way to keep busy. In the '80s there were tremendous rains for a couple of seasons in a row and the hills became unglued. If land wasn't coming down on top of your house, it was going out from under it. There was a new business for structural repair of retaining walls, foundations, and earth work. We jumped into it. We got equipment and developed specialized crews. It was a great avenue for work when we didn't have remodeling. For several years it was covered by insurance, but they backed out of earth movement insurance, so it dried up. In 1989 there was a big quake so through the '90s everybody was scrambling to make their buildings safe with seismic retrofits, that was another sideline for work.

---

4   I asked Deva how he differentiated an estimate from a budget, his email response: "An estimate is often a first pass at establishing cost. An estimate—often after several revisions—becomes a budget when it is accepted by the client and the contractor. The budget then becomes a management tool to track costs for time and material and cost-plus-fee contracts."

Word Association

Integrity: Integrity is something that we find within ourselves. Later in life, through trials and errors and mistakes, we learn a lot of basic principles and develop integrity. It doesn't come automatically.

Job safety: Essential. Get really good habits in your crew and establish patterns of safety that are very, very firm.

Fear: In terms of business; not allowed. You have to be really strong and firm and committed to certain standards. You just don't allow fear to be any part of that.

Company image: Critical. It's more than just the name of your company, it is what clients and subcontractors come to associate with that name.

Gratitude: Show gratitude on specific things. It doesn't mean much when you say, "Joe, you're doing a great job." What's that mean? Nothing. When you catch them doing something right, "Man I love the way you hung that door," or "I love the way you built that schedule out, great job!" Find something specific and that is what you compliment and appreciate.

Overhead: You have to understand it thoroughly, from your own numbers, and put a realistic figure on it. And don't give it up.

Profit: That's your first expense. You decide what you need for business expansion—which always comes from profit—and you don't give it up.

Marketing: Your satisfied customers are your best marketer.

Sales: Get people talking, listen carefully, and they'll tell you how to sell them.

Estimating: Critical. It's the hardest job in the world. The estimator has the most difficult job of all; if the estimate is too high, you lose the work, too low you don't make out well.

Employees: Hire the best people you can, protect them, take care of them, get genuinely interested in them; find out the names of their wives and all their kids. Make sure their personal goals are met. I went to a funeral of one our foremen a couple of weeks ago; all of his men, other foreman, and contractors he'd worked with showed up.

Cut-Offs

The conflict in custom timber work is that a lot of the joinery is not in the codes. You're executing a joint that hasn't been engineered and it's not in the books and the inspectors will question it. The solution is to have a structural engineer's signature endorsing the entire project—front and back end—and a letter from them at the end of the job saying everything was built according to plan.

What do you do with payables? You set a schedule that on the first of every month you pay certain bills and on the eighth, the fifteenth and the twenty-second. That's aging payables, so your cash isn't rushing out the door. What a beautiful way to manage cash.

A fellow selected us to build a fourteen-million-dollar estate. I turned this job down at first because it was too big for us. He spoke with other contractors but he didn't trust them—even though they were more experienced and capable than I—but we'd worked for him on a major remodel and built credibility, and more than anything, he wanted somebody he could trust.

I told clients to get the best materials available. Why? Because every day, several times a day, your hands will grasp those drawer and door handles and you want to feel the quality in them and touch again the creative greatness that is your new home.

Latinos are the most loyal of all your racial groups. They want a really good job, and they'll stick with you for decades.

You can't leave subcontractors out of the equation. If they get paid regularly and there is good project management, they're going to want to work for you again. When times get tough and you are sweating to get a really beautiful job, you go to your subs and ask them to shave another 3 percent off the bid, they'll help you out.

We had one project that was fourteen million dollars, imagine, we had ninety subcontractors. Why? Because the owner wanted to finish on a certain date, but he kept changing and adding scope without changing the completion date. We had five tile-setting companies, three cabinet companies, and so on, just to stay ahead of everything, and they were still designing and giving us new drawings.

Once a banker gets to know you, your business and banking history—cash flow and so forth—you begin to build a credit line. You want $100,000; now you want $300,000; now $500,000; and now a million. It's a slow process and bankers are slow to take risk.

…people will forget what you said,
people will forget what you did,
but people will never forget
how you made them feel.

Maya Angelou

Otis Miller,
Home Repairs

Borregoglass@gmail.com

Otis is a thirty-seven-year-old handyman who does glass work (showers, doors, mirrors) and carpentry. At seventeen he began working as a helper in a glass shop in Florida and he worked there for many years. In 2018 he began working for himself in a small town in Southern California. He freely admits that he does not know how to do some of what he is asked to do, but he is upfront with the customers about his abilities and charges accordingly.

> *I learned a long time ago that not all money is good money ■ I turn away people who have a negative attitude ■ I would tell guys who wanted to start a business to get a contractor's license. That should be their first step. Keep everything on the up-and-up and life will be a lot easier*

Talk about actively working in your trade versus running your business.

When you work for someone else, you pretty much know what your day is going to be, lunch is at noon and you are going home at five. Working for myself, I'm working on a job, I get calls, I need to get materials for a job in three days, and somebody needs me to measure for something. It is hectic.

How did you learn to estimate?

Google. [*Laughter.*] As far as percentages and stuff, I don't estimate like a contractor. I probably get a lot of jobs because when the customer sees I'm charging them a decent amount for labor and no overhead, they know they are winning. I don't add profit to my labor or materials. When I put my estimates together, I charge for getting materials and 20 percent on the cost of the materials. My labor rate is between forty to sixty-five an hour—depending on what I'm doing. On some jobs it's by the piece—if I'm changing a light bulb, I charge five dollars. I try to get a forty-dollar minimum for showing up, but some people have a problem with that, so I find a balance. I'm not here to get rich. Making enough to feed my family and be comfortable, that's all. I'm simple and I get joy when a customer knows they are getting a good deal and when I do good work.

Do you market your service?

No, I don't market. It is by word of mouth only.

What makes a good and a bad customer?

Good customers are the ones that say yes, with no questions! [*Laughter.*] My best customers are the ones that have an idea of what they want and what it will cost. I'm already giving the best price; a good customer knows that. The bad customers are the ones that want a lot of work done for nothing. When a customer says, "So-and-so said they would do it for much less than you," I'm like, "So why am I here?" Those are the worst.

On one of the first jobs I did—I should have paid more attention—the women threatened to sue all of the companies that came to her house; the propane company, Lowe's about a refrigerator, and others. I did little stuff for her at first and she seemed okay. Then I fixed her driveway, and while it was still wet, she drove over it. I could see her tire marks in the concrete. I was willing to give her back the money for the concrete work even though she had driven over it, but she wanted all of the money for everything I had done on her house! That was not okay. People like her are the worst thing about owning a business.

Do you shape your customers' expectations?

Yes. I let them know they're going to get what they want and—without getting all technical—I tell them what I'm going to do.

What would you look for in an employee?

Someone young, with a determination and drive to learn and who shows up on time and gives their best.

Describe a successful business.

I used to think, the bigger the truck, the more success someone had. Now—after working in different companies and watching some go under because of the owner's poor attitude—I would say, success is being in business for many years with lots of happy customers.

A business should be friendly to the customer—what we call Southern hospitality in Florida—knowing their name and getting repeat business. There's the initial process of meeting the customer and being professional and troubleshooting problems that might occur, even if it wasn't the company's fault sometimes. I learned a long time ago to leave the job site looking better than when I got there. If you are working in a bathroom and at the end you sweep up, sweep the whole area, not just where you are working. These are the things that make a good, reliable business.

What is the best path to learning a trade?

To learn from somebody and schooling, you can't go wrong with school. If you come out of high school and you know that you want to build, further your education. It's not going to hurt and in our society, it helps you get along.

When you feel personally overwhelmed or unfocused, how do you regain your balance?

I get prayerful. I go outside and walk in the desert. I sit behind a mesquite—to make sure the kids can't find me—and lie down and look at the sky, take a couple of deep breaths and talk with God.

If you were telling a successful tradesman how to open a business, what would you tell them?

Make sure it is something you want to do. Then, get a business name and insurance and a tax ID number. I would tell them to cross their t's and dot their i's, because it will make life easier. I'd tell them, if they worked hard for someone else, expect to work one hundred times harder now. They should avoid customers they get a bad vibe from or who think they know everything about your trade. You're the boss now, you don't need to take bad jobs.

What advice would you give them about money?

Save it. Save money because you don't know what will come up.

What bad recommendations have you had about business?

The worst advice I ever heard was, "Tell the people what they want to hear, get their money and keep it moving. If you mess up, don't call them back." [*Laughter.*] And "Work under the table. Don't do paperwork and don't give receipts."

What books, teachers, and mentors have influenced your life?

Mr. McSheehy, a middle school shop teacher—I was thirteen or fourteen—he took pride in what he did and he taught us well. He was one of my favorite teachers. We worked with wood and it has interested me since then.

I had a mentor, Mr. James Ward, a retired Florida senator who opened a glass shop in our town. In high school I was a football player and a knucklehead and I was getting in trouble. My dad was military, and he said, "You need to buckle down, get a job, and move out." I remember vividly walking down the main road in our town, and I was going to stop by every business to look for a job. Mr. Ward's was the first place I stopped. He remembered seeing me play football—he was a prominent guy and didn't have to take a second look at me—but he called me into his office, sat me down, and said, "If you want something that could impact the rest of your life, I'm willing to teach you, but don't waste my time." Which meant, "Don't quit on me."

He hired me to clean the shop. The Old Man loved to tell stories and when the guys would go into the field he would come back to the shop and talk about being in Washington, DC as a senator. With my background—I lived in a rough neighborhood with drugs, gangs, and prostitution—it opened my eyes, his stories made me be more in tune with, to feel part of, regular society.

When Mr. Ward said he could give me something that could benefit my life, I didn't understand at all. It's like that saying, "You can give a man a fish and he can eat for a day, if you teach a man to fish, he can eat forever." Also, he didn't just make me a laborer. He had me cleaning the shop and cutting metal and glass and going to installs; he was teaching me everything. Now, no matter where I am, I can go into a glass shop and get work. With hindsight, I can see what he did for me.

Now that you are in business for yourself, what are the hardest and the best parts?

The technical parts are hardest, doing the estimates and sending them out in a timely fashion. Also, when I'm are busy, it's giving everybody the same attention to detail and giving everybody my best. The hardest thing for me is the growing pains of running the business. The best parts are being able to do the things I'm comfortable doing and I'm exploring things I have not done. It's the freedom to adventure into things that interest me, that is awesome.

Do you have long-term goals and ambitions for your business?

To take on a couple of employees and grow the business.

If you could, would you change anything about your career?

Right now? No. I'm brand new on the journey and it is interesting and there are good and bad days and times when I've never felt so comfortable. Other times, I'm like, *Where's the money?* Right now, it is enjoyable and exciting and scary.

Have you made a mistake in the trades that you laugh about now?

Yes. It's a common practice when putting up a bathroom mirror, when the owners are not around, to take your shoes off and hop up on the bathroom counter to install a mirror. This one job, we did not know anything about floating counters, so me and another guy are standing on the countertop with this big old mirror and, boom, the counter broke! The owner said, "You cost me twenty grand, but I can't get mad because I would have done it the same way." Another one—if you have not done this, you have not been working in the glass business long—is to drive off without tying the glass down. I did it once. I made it a good eight miles—I must have been making all right-hand turns—but all of a sudden, I looked in the mirror and three units of glass were falling off. My boss said, "How did you make it that far?"

Perfection is not attainable, but if we
chase perfection we can catch excellence.
Vince Lombardi

Desiree Bolman,
Remodeling Contractor

https://aurorasf.com/

Desiree describes herself as an introvert, and seems shy at first, although she is a general contractor and is around people all day. She is sixty-two—intensely loyal to her small crew—and for someone in construction, physically small, although she seems surprised by this observation. She has a thriving business and—like every builder—has mixed feelings about some of her customers.

> *Figure out what you stand for, what your values are, what's important to you* ■ *I get annoyed with clients when they say, "I don't have a check" or "I'll pay you in a couple weeks." It's the only thing the client has to do! I'm like, "No. It doesn't work like that, look at your contract."* ■ *My contract is the scar tissue of my mistakes* ■ *It's important to make notes each time the schedule is derailed because of new decisions, or a lack of them* ■ *I've compensated for my weaknesses with a payroll service, having help estimating, and having a bookkeeper who is smart and makes me stay on the straight and narrow* ■ *I told a sub who was bullshitting me all the time, "Tell me something that I don't want to hear, because that is what I need from you. Tell me the truth"* ■ *My estimator is certain clients show my bids to the other guy to get them to lower their price*

I've been doing this work since I was thirty-two, I'm now sixty-two. I am a remodeling contractor in San Francisco, California. Aurora Builders is the name of my company. We do residential work, no commercial. We do small additions, and there's a lot of them to build in San Francisco. We do foundation to finish, but we don't do a whole lot of foundation work.

I had no formal training in the trades. I was in my early twenties. I wanted to be a carpenter, because I was in conflict with the idea that girls had to be nurturing and I did not want to be pigeonholed or limited by gender expectations. I was creative and wanted to express myself, to make tangible things. You build something and there it is. It lives there. Walk away, and it's still there. Also, it was a self-image that I was aspiring to, of competence, being grounded, working with my hands.

I was raised in Hawaii, and I got a job with a cabinet builder. I was twenty-three when I started working there. He was growing his business and he started hiring guys and he was giving them more opportunities than me. We were sanding, doing bullshit stuff, so it wasn't because they were more skilled. I was too young to be in the boys' club, I was quiet and kept to myself, and I didn't stand my ground. I went back to cooking and I moved to San Francisco when I was twenty-four. Then I was working as a counselor and childcare worker in a group home for emotionally disturbed kids. Because of that, I'm well suited to work with the guys I do, they are not the most mature bunch all the time [*chuckles*].

When I was thirty-two, I met a woman carpenter who needed labor help. I said, "Okay, I'll do it." She was a one-woman show and I worked for her for a little while. There was a huge community of self-sufficient women in SF and there was a book called *Against the Grain*[1] and there were magazines and publications with women doing stuff. This was inspiring. Then I met a woman general contractor with an all-women crew. I thought, *This is going to be good; I won't be discriminated against and I'll get opportunities.* The women carpenters were good, but they were tough on me and very critical. It was their brand of support. They were older than me and had difficulty coming up in the trades, and they were damned if I was going to have an easy time of it. Which is ironic. I lost the key for a job once. I had to go out, with my own money, and buy a new lockset and figure out how to install it, because no one was going to help me. It was difficult, but I learned a lot.

That general contractor took a long vacation and everybody scattered. I got a job with—I forget who the first guy was—but I learned that if the guy at the top is good, everybody else on the crew was decent. It wasn't like you

---

[1] Against the Grain: A Carpentry Manual for Women, Dale McCormick, Iowa City Women's Press, 1977.

had a great guy at the top and assholes working for him. I had no problem getting work, and everyone was supportive and taught me a lot. I worked really hard to be accepted by the guys I worked with. My physicality was never an issue because I was trying hard and I had a lot to prove. I started out digging foundations and doing rebar, I was tough. I was on a job where they were forming foundations and the end blew out.[2] Coming up, I learned a lot from other people's mistakes.

I subscribed to The *Journal of Light Construction* and *Fine Homebuilding* and that's how I figured everything out. There is information out there if you look. I would characterize myself as, not the best carpenter or the most knowledgeable, but resourceful. In a way, that is better than having a wealth of knowledge, because that can make you lazy.

What did you learn by working for other companies?

I didn't like the way my last boss responded to problems. On my first job as a lead carpenter—a long time ago now—there was a problem with a wall. So I think, *I'm the lead guy, I need to take responsibility for it.* I say to my boss, "I'll figure it out." He says, "You come here this weekend and fix it on your own time."[3] I was floored, it was like getting punched in the gut. I thought, *Really, it's me against you, we are not in this together.* It's still painful.

Also, the women contractor I worked for would come on the job and say, "Am I running a fucking daycare center?" She did not handle stress well and she was dollar oriented. She was a good businessperson and charming if you weren't working for her. What I learned from her was, *Don't be like that!* The whole stress thing is so inefficient. I never feel okay if I get mad at somebody, even if I feel righteous about it. And it's never useful to treat people badly.

What's the most difficult part of what you do?

The paperwork and the little bullshit things—running around for all the options—is tedious. Emails and chronicling the information so I have a record of the important stuff. Also managing clients. It depends on the client, of course. Right now I have a young couple who are rich and incred-

---

2   A blow out is when a concrete form bursts from the weight of the newly poured concrete. It happens because the form is not braced adequately and, among many things that can go wrong during a concrete pour, it is likely the worst.

3   It is illegal to require an employee to correct a problem on their own time, without compensation.

ibly entitled. They are designing on the fly, and because of that we have rescheduled the subs so many times they can't keep our schedule. I have good relations with my subs, but now, when I say, "Okay, I'm ready," they don't come running. That frustrates the homeowners and they say, "I'm going to call my lawyer" and "You're the professional, you should have known, that's why we hired you." I have to back up and explain what the limits are and what my job really is. Often clients and contractors don't have a clear idea of where our responsibilities start and end. We provide a host of services and there is a constant push-pull on the perimeter of that effort. Part of my job is educating clients about what each of our responsibilities is.

When clients are frustrated, their memory can be self-serving. The hard part is when I find myself in a defensive position because they are blaming me. It requires extra patience, deliberation, and checking notes. On the other hand, I take responsibility for my team's delays, and it helps to have a plan to make up the time.

What do you like about what you do?

I like the relationships with my subs and everyone involved in the process. I like the problem solving, that is rewarding. Every day is different. I keep to-do lists, but the day is different than that. It's challenging. It's fun. I'm comfortable in my skin now, and although there are certainly difficult situations and people, I don't have a lot of ego about it and I have everyone's best interest in mind.

What do you do if you are overwhelmed or lose direction?

I make time. I sit down and pull out my yellow pads and make lists. I put it back together again. It doesn't happen that often, but if I get overwhelmed, I'm resourceful. Sometimes it means picking up the phone and calling somebody, getting information, or hiring whatever kind of help I need. I make sure it gets done.

Do you still work with your tools on jobs?

I have to sometimes. Punch lists, or if a client needs something and my guys are tied up on another job. I don't have the focus to help on a job. I've tried a few times, but I'm so distracted I'm useless.

What did you like about working for someone else?

I liked being exposed to jobs I wouldn't take on my own and doing work that was challenging. I liked one boss's quality standards. I liked going to work at seven and being off at three.

Did you have long-term goals when you started in business?

I went to a conference about women in construction where I listened to a woman speak who was a commercial contractor. She said to the group, "You need to know; business and the trades are two entirely different things. Don't become a contractor, many more people fail than make it, and it is *really* difficult. If you want to be a contractor, take business classes or go to business school, otherwise it's impossible."[4] I never wanted to have my own business. I absolutely did not have goals. I went into business because of an economic downturn and a guy I knew said, "Go out on your own, you'll do great." I needed to pay my rent, and then, I was just doing it.

Have you had any failures that set you up for later success?

All of them! Now, when I have a bad day or make a mistake, I don't kick myself. It's just, *Okay, so what do I need to do?* And I move on. A lot of it is maturity and some of it is learning. Maybe it's maturity 70, learning 30.

What mistakes have you made in business?

My contract is the scar tissue of my mistakes. In the past, I was often not clear and didn't spell things out in my proposals. That's another thing that is really difficult about this job, you have to back up *absolutely everything*. And for a long time—it was a lack of confidence—the biggest mistake I made was not charging enough.

How do you estimate?

Now, I have an estimator who helps me. I started working with him because I was underestimating my jobs and because I hate estimating. It would take me forever and I was like, *Oh, I can't charge that much.* Also,

---

4   Although I agree with the speakers ideas—contracting is "...really difficult," "...more people fail than make it," and "...business and the trades are two entirely different things"—it is untrue that it's impossible to succeed without a formal business education. Countless contractors have and those that succeed learn—intuitively, piecemeal, through education, or with a mentor—what is required.

now, I don't have the time or the bandwidth to come home after working all day and do an estimate.

For the last five years, since I've been using the estimator, I've been making over a hundred thousand a year. I should have been making that a long time ago, but for years I did not get the concept of charging enough, and I did not understand overhead and profit. Now my estimates are very detailed. If the customer asks, "How come you didn't do this?" I say, "Look at this line item, it's excluded, it's to-be-determined, or there is an allowance."

My estimator tends to be high; he is very much for the contractor. While doing the estimate he does material take-offs. I do my own material take-off for the jobs. He and I do walk-throughs with the subs and the homeowner. I'll collect information, he will build the estimate, I'll get the subs going on bids, and we'll flesh the estimate out together. He is not using a cost book; his prices come from his experience. He charges me seventy-five dollars an hour.

How did you learn about business?

Doing it. Being in it. Making mistakes and talking with people I respect.

Do you charge for estimates?

No, I wrap that cost into my project supervision. If they have chosen me as their contractor, I'll do a detailed preliminary estimate for free. If they want to rework the estimate or do value engineering, I'll give them a preconstruction contact to cover my effort. Also, on large projects with multiple bidders, I do charge for my estimates. What I charge depends on the project.

I'm getting picky about what I estimate. A client called me and went back and forth, finally they picked a guy and he fell out. They called me back and said, "He was looney toons." I'm thinking, *You're the looney toons*. I'm about to say no to them. When people say, "We want you to bid it this way and that way," I'll tell them we are too busy to bid their work.

Looking back over your career, what would you do differently?

There were a couple years when I was working out of my truck and not reporting taxes. I might have gotten my insurance faster. I don't think I could have done anything different because of who I am and my life experience. I didn't go to regular school and I didn't go to business school. I could say I'd do business school, but that's not me. I think being tenacious and resourceful and honest, and challenging myself, always checking and reevaluating: that's been good.

What advice would you give to builders and tradesmen?

Guys ask me about business stuff because they know I do my taxes, and I have workers' comp. I make sure my employees and I are taken care of. That is my advice: build a good team and take care of your employees!

In the past few years, what behavior has improved your business?

An attitude of embracing the day and having no expectations that things have to go well. Not having a definition of what a good day looks like. Being preemptive. That's the way I alleviate my anxiety. I try to be honest and transparent: it's not a rule, it's more of a personality trait.

Is there a conflict with working on the job and running the business?

Yes. Absolutely, at a certain point I got too busy managing the jobs and overseeing the business to do carpentry. When I started, the conflict was that I wasn't busy enough to justify not working on the job, but when I was on the job, my brain wasn't there anyway. That was difficult. Because it is important to me that my guys see me doing physical work, I still do job layout, material pickup, job cleanup, and small dump runs.

What would you tell a group of skilled tradesmen about going into business and what would you tell them to avoid?

It's *really* important to be a legitimate business. Guys used to say that to me and I'd say, "Yeah, whatever." But they were right. People respect you more, you'll respect yourself more, you can charge more, and you'll have insurance to back you up. You want clients to respect you, so produce a good estimate because you have to put something out there that people can say, "Yeah, okay, I trust this." You have to have a contract, even if it's small when you start. My contract is eight or ten pages. I got it from a lawyer because there are so many laws in California. The contract cost me around three thousand dollars. Avoid being sneaky. I've worked with guys who were always taking shortcuts, it's a personality type, either you do that or you don't.

There are specific values in what we do—it's a class thing—about loyalty and honor. It's old-fashioned. *It's a lot of work.* You better really want it. Nobody understands this fully and so they walk into it with their arms open and get blindsided. [*Laughter.*] It's nuts. Especially in the beginning, the learning curve is so steep. I'm a workaholic, so I'm well suited to this, but it's a weird way to live, working that much.

How did you learn to manage money?

You are born with it. I've always paid my bills on time. In a pinch, everyone gets paid before me. If the client doesn't pay us, they screw us over, everyone will still get paid for their work. I don't have patience for guys who say, "I got hung out to dry, I can't pay you." That's not how it works. It's just wrong.

Do you actively mentor people and if so, what does that look like?

If somebody wants to know and they come to me, that's fun, then I'm engaged. But anything else is work. My guys are picking stuff up, they know what our standards are, and they are proud of their work. That always makes me feel good.

If you had a method of reaching every builder and tradesmen in the U.S., what would you say?

It's all about community and relationships, it's people first, everything else follows. It's not me who's doing this, it's us, as a team. It's super fun! You can't announce it though, 'cause it's a secret. It's why I do this. It's not to give you that fancy bathroom, it's 'cause we're having a good time.

What bad business recommendations have you gotten?

A guy got hurt on my job and got workers' comp. One contactor told me to get rid of the guy because he is going to get hurt again and it will be a problem. But I stuck it out with him and I'm glad I did. I've been told twice to cycle through my subcontractors, because if I use the same ones all the time, they will get comfortable and take advantage of me. I reject that idea completely.

What is a great success in a contracting business?

It's when you know what needs to be done and you capture the homeowner's vision and deliver it in a reasonable time and make a profit.

What would you tell new business owners about money?

Have a business account and keep personal and business money separate. I must have had tremendous stamina, because I didn't make money for a long time, but I am good at managing it. When you asked me about rules, it's an absolute rule: *Pay everybody on time.* Your business is a machine, that's how you oil the machine. Because I'm making money now, I am always shoving money into my business savings, for whatever comes up that I forgot, and the 401(k) at the end of the year. I'm not living high off the hog.

What's the difference between marketing and selling and how did you learn to sell?

Marketing is promoting and I want you to notice me. If I'm selling, then I'm right there with you and I want to convince you. I learned how to sell by losing out to my competitors. Now if I want a job, I get it, although I have lost a few I wanted. It's a momentum I can feel physically. It's about being transparent, explaining and educating about costs. It's the way I do my presentation. It's my ability to communicate and my confidence level.

What's the best investment you ever made?

The first investment that comes to mind is everything that's spiritual and emotional. The first half of my life was extremely difficult, full of struggle. The second half, *Oh, I get it, I figured it out. It's fun. It's great.* The thing that made me happy about starting my business was naming it after my dog; it was me, my dog, and a pickup truck. And buying a house. And I've got some tools that I'm pretty fond of.

What about your best and worst customers makes them so?

They do their homework and they listen. They understand this is a complicated and technical undertaking and they are realistic in their expectations. I have favorite customers. Wonderful clients. They are people who understand concepts. A smart client, that's really good, because they participate in making sure I give them what they want. I find the whole thing of having a client difficult though. I just want to do the work, I don't like handholding, I'm good at it, but I don't like it.

The worst is passivity. People who can't make decisions and don't understand the impact it has on the schedule. People that don't trust me. It's not usually about me, it's their own stuff. They have unrealistic expectations that come from their emotions and they trust their emotions more than they trust me.

Do you shape a new customer's expectation, and if so, how?

Yes. With the budget and schedule, then with the contract. I don't go over the contract with them—the bigger guys go over everything—but I feel so stretched a lot of the time and also because I'm an introvert. I don't like those extra meetings. They'll email me questions about the contract. I need to do a better job of explaining change orders and explaining that there are change orders on *every* job.

Do you turn down customers, and if so why?

Yes. If they are difficult to work with or if they have boundary issues. But sometimes you don't know going in. And it's not always the client, it can be our chemistry. I don't take jobs just because there's a lot of money in it. I asked one guy as I was walking out the door, "How many bids are you getting?" "Ten," he said. That was the end of that one. Another guy said, "Look, this is the only way this will go down." I did not pursue that one either.

How would you respond to this quote by Richard Branson: "Clients do not come first. Employees come first. If you take care of your employees, they will take care of the clients."

No, we're all there to take care of the client. We take care of the client, the client takes care of us, I take care of the employees. Definitely, the client comes first.

What do you look for when you hire?

Somebody who has a certain level of maturity, a nice personality, and who will look after clients. Somebody with good social skills who can talk with clients and represent us well, that's really important to me. Also, organizational skills and job cleanliness are a bonus.

What do you expect from employees?

I expect them to be on time, to be honest, and to care about their work, the client, and the subcontractors. The fundamental things I'd expect of anybody I'd have in my life. I'd like them to be my eyes and ears on the job. To notice if something is untoward and needs to be dealt with.

What's a bad tradesman?

Somebody who takes shortcuts, who doesn't think about their work or take pride in it, and who does not value their commitment to the client.

How do you feel about competitive bidding?

I don't like it, although I take it for granted that I have to do it. I used to only bid if there were three of us. Now I'm more comfortable with two or just me and we negotiate the contract. I don't like that bidding is apples to grapefruit; you don't know the other bidders, the clients are not sophisticated, everybody's bidding and estimating style is different, as is what they include and how they communicate it. It's not fair to the client. Also, unless they have a really good set of plans, there's always room for interpretation. When there's a gray area, I put a big red circle around it and say, "This is our assumption and this is what we're including." Sometimes, if the client is interested in me, we show them the full estimate to wow them. It almost always works.

When you have too much work, how do you respond?

Buckle down. It's one of my assets. Take deep breaths and focus and organize. When it gets too busy, mostly it is when one job is delayed and I can't put another job off for two months. I don't try to have too much work. I turn down jobs too.

You said you communicate well. What does that look like?

Part of it is being articulate and emotionally comfortable. I am intuitive about my client's strengths and weaknesses, that helps my communication. Asking questions, anticipating what they need, and what their areas of concern are, and addressing them.

If work slows, what do you do?

Take time off and feel bad about my employees. It is the thing that I hate most about having employees; it's a big responsibility and tiring. I have enough friends who are contractors that I can get them work, but they don't like it, they want to work on our jobs. So if we take time off, I'll worry a little, but I'll be happy.

Word Association

Integrity: Truth.

Communication: If you're comfortable with me, the communication will be good, because I'm a good communicator.

Job safety: Caring.

Company image: Clean, organized, honest.

Gratitude: I have so much gratitude for my life and my experience and my level of engagement.

Marketing: My personality, who I am. I have a lot of repeat customers.

Sales: I hate sales. Maybe I take it too personally. I don't like the idea of talking someone into working with me. I basically say, "This is what I offer, this is who I am, take me or leave me." When I sell, it is about honesty and transparency and my personality.

Cut-Offs

Building on the fly is the most difficult thing, it is exhausting, and the paperwork is tedious. Just give me a set of plans, we'll hang out for a while, I'll get your vision. Then don't talk to me; in three or six months, I'll give it back to you.

I'm not a religious person but it is good to have a philosophy or religion to navigate life. Recently I've realized I'm in sync with Stoicism; it's about integrity, honesty, and taking responsibility.

I like my work and I'm going do it as long as people will hire me, or till I drop. I'm going to do a big remodel on my house and friends say, "You're 62, why do it, why spend the money?" But I'm a remodeler, that's what I do.

I'm always saying to my guys, "We need to be ready for the subs. We want to take care of them, so they take care of us. We are a team, and that is how teams' function well." For me it's always about community, camaraderie, and mutual support.

We got written up on Angie's list, but we got a lot of tire kickers. I like repeat customers or their friends, those are the best clients.

My employees have ideas about what they deserve and want. One guy I wanted to be a lead carpenter, a manager, but that is not him. It is difficult when you want somebody to be something they're not. But that is life, right?

Guys I know did big jobs. They'd ask, "Why don't you do that?" But I needed to go slower and I'm glad I did. I never made catastrophic mistakes like some of them.

Leaders who don't listen will eventually be surrounded by people who have nothing to say.
Andy Stanley

Stephen (Steve) Nicholls,
Remodeler, Cabinet Maker, GC

https://www.mnbuild.com/
info@mnbuild.com

Steve is British, although I did not know it until he told me. When asked why I could not detect an accent, he said, "Because I learned to speak American." With hindsight, there is a properness about him that might have given it away. He is a principle in MN Builders based in Oakland, California.

> We started in 1982, so we've been in business for forty-plus years ▪ This last recession was horrible. It cut our volume and staff in half. We have been through a couple of other really hard times ▪ We do a lot of community work, we're involved with kids' education ▪ You can get better at managing money, you can learn it ▪ In our world, we do the pricing backwards; we talk about money early, rather than the beautiful project stuff

Our company is about eighty people now. We're called MN Builders and we are primarily a residential building company. We have a large cabinet facility. That used to be our primary business. Over the last twenty-five years it's morphed into more remodeling and some new homes, mainly high-end—Bay Area high-end—where an average construction job for us is north of a million and a lot of them are two, three, or four million. We take a job from the person coming in the door, all the way through to the punch list^. Design/build^ is only for residential work. We do some commercial work, more in the shop than in the field. Casework [cabinets] is done for other general contractors [GC]^ , too.

Did you have a trade when you started?

Yes, I started in finish carpentry, putting trim up, installing cabinets, and paneling. I didn't get much woodwork training, and what I got was on the job. I was learning as I went. I worked for a local contractor in the Bay Area. I liked doing woodwork, which is why I ended up in a partnership with a cabinetmaking friend.

What drew you to a trade?

Because modern society puts so much value on none-built-things and the value of craft is demeaned in many ways. I am intrigued with stuff that's made by hand—built to last—instead of work that isn't describable. The most rewarding part now is seeing excellent work in place. There is nothing like a well-made job, whether it's a cabinet, a building, or a sculpture.

What was your education and how was it useful in your current business?

I trained academically in the U.K. as a teacher. Going to school in the U.K. is, depending on where you go, a privileged route. That was the case for me. Education focused on esoterica and academic things. In my case, it was language and humanities. The process taught me how to question, analyze, and correlate ideas and come out with a thesis. It's not that different from building, where you look around the landscape and figure out what to concentrate on to make a building work. One of the things that education can teach you is that life's complicated and you better have your eyes open. That's certainly happening in the building world; when we started, it was much simpler than it is now. The building industry needs very, very smart people to deal with that complexity.

Did you work for somebody when you began, and if so, what did you learn from them?

When I was in college in England, I called a company called Encounter Overland that was based in London and ran expeditions around the world. I spoke with the owner and said, "Your organization is intriguing. If you will pay my train ticket to London, I'll come to work for you." The owner said, "We don't do that." Two years later, after college, at 22, I got a train ticket to London and I worked for them for two years leading expeditions across Africa. I was responsible for forty people and I liked that leadership role.[1]

In the U.S., I subcontracted for a general contractor when I started out. I was watching this guy run the whole job and I thought, *Man, this guy has a lot on his plate.* I didn't think much about it at the time, but the idea of being in charge was intriguing. I did a couple jobs with a guy, on an hourly basis, paneling a library. I didn't know what I was doing, just watching these guys, trying to keep up. I didn't understand the terminology or the trade language. I caught on pretty quick, part of that is loving what you do; if you do, you'll learn fast.

What is difficult about trade work?

It's tiring, emotionally and physically. There is a lot of skill involved and you have to be in good physical shape to last eight hours rolling joists or working in a cabinet shop. With clients, it is emotionally draining when they don't appreciate things. Also, some design professionals don't understand how things are built, and they want the nigh-impossible. But in general, it's a great business, and our trade is never going away.

What do you do when you become overwhelmed or lose direction?

I usually find somebody to talk to. I like the outdoors a lot, so I go for a walk or a bike ride. That helps. It doesn't happen much because this business is full of lose-direction options all day long, so you just accept it. They are around you all the time, whether you're a one-, a ten-, or a hundred-person company. The bigger you get, the less those challenges go away.

What did you like or dislike about taking direction from a boss?

I accepted the fact that somebody had to be in charge, so it was fine. He was a typical GC; he knew a lot about not much and had an opinion about pretty much everything. He was paying me to do something I loved so it was like the Africa experience: *They are paying me to do this?* I still feel that way in the building business sometimes.

---

1   Author note, I did not know Steve before doing this interview. The expedition company he mentions was owned and run by a Brit named Tony Jones and I met the same, now nearly eighty-year old Tony at his small hotel at the end of 2018 in the city of Pokhara, Nepal—nine months before being introduced to Steve. Tony and I spent time together, often with me listening to stories of his adventures starting and running Encounter Overland.

What did it look like as you transitioned to running a company and did you have long term goals?

We were a subcontractor to the GC, so even then, we had our own business. Starting off, some of what we did was legal, some was not. The more we did, the more we realized we needed to be compliant: taxes, bookkeeper, accountant, all that stuff. But it was gradual. We did not have goals. It was more like, "Let's get this project done." To some degree that's still happening, "Let's get this thing built." We didn't have any long-term goals, except to build good stuff and to be involved in beautiful projects. That was definitely something that we loved to do, and we still do. We are not a commodity builder. Our ambition was always to be known as one of the best in the business, to be on the top of the heap.

What are the issues that you are having now, with eighty people, that you did not have when you were ten people?

Personally, letting go of things, and what to do on a daily basis that helps the company. We recently became employee-owned, not a hundred percent, but on that path. Now my focus is primarily on making sure that we have a sustainable business. For me and everybody else, the long-term strategy is for the business to thrive and continue without me.

What mistakes did you make in business, any whoppers, and looking back, what would you do differently?

Oh yeah. There were plenty of whoppers. We purchased another cabinet shop about twenty years ago. We didn't analyze what it was or where we were going to take it or how we would get there. We closed it after two years. It was a million-dollar mistake. Our mistake was not realizing it was somebody else's business and not knowing what that business was. It was partially bad timing and possibly bad management on our end. That is a mistake that sits with me still. Then lots of others, not big physical mistakes, more like strategic missteps: hiring the wrong people or not getting rid of people when they are overdue to leave. Also, taking the wrong jobs, at the wrong price, at the wrong time.

I would have got into remodeling earlier—there is more liability than shop work, but it is more profitable. I would have tried to work less; but I don't like to sit around, so I probably would not have got too far.

What business advice have you given most to builders and tradesmen?

A group of us started a builders' support group in the Bay Area years ago. It was called the Splinter Group^. The idea was not to pay for the advice that we needed and to get this information into our daily, weekly, monthly consciousness. We started having dinners together every couple of months and talk about what we were paying for workers compensation, how we were dealing with flaky subs and clients, lien releases, insurance, all that stuff. At the time there was no training, no books, or resources about the business.

What habit has most improved your business?

All the way through it's been outdoor life, exercise, and sport. Family has been my biggest grounding in life. When you have kids, things get real, fast; it is no longer the framing and plumbing that is most important.

Do you have principles that you follow in business, and if so, what are they?

Our general manager has a Spike Lee street sign in his office that says, "Do the right thing." That is certainly what I try to push. You don't always know what that is, but usually, when you do the right thing, you'll be okay.

In your career, have you invested money outside of your business?

Yes. Absolutely. In fact, we say to everybody, "You'll earn a decent wage doing this, but you'll earn a lot more from real estate and other investments, beyond your salary and wage." That has been huge. We encourage people to buy a house, and some—including my wife and I—have kept the first one and bought others as rentals.

What do you like and dislike about being in business?

I don't like it when people are not appreciative. Either clients or employees or design professionals. We work hard to build nice stuff. Badly executed work, I don't like that, and people getting away with shoddy work, that bugs me.

We have an amazing team, the people that work here, they are what keeps me here. We want people to tear our work apart in a hundred years and go, "Wow, these guys knew how to build." Some of the most interesting people we know are clients, and some of the most amazing human beings are designers and architects. Youngsters are a big deal for us. We want the kids who are twenty-five now to have a career. Old-school: you find a good company, they take good care of you, they pay healthcare, they take care of your family, they give you a retirement. We've got a company where people are retiring with money, that is cool! You asked what we like about business, that's one of the things we love.

We're a company, a team. There are three partners and there is an executive team that's running the place too. The way it runs now is, we talk about an issue and try to come to a consensus, but if someone needs to cast a deciding vote, I do that.

How has the partnership worked out?

Partnership is never a smooth road. The company originally was called Mueller/Nicholls [it still is], it was Mike Mueller and I in a 50/50 partnership. The arrangement of the names came from a coin flip. I bought Mike out twenty-five years ago and was too cheap to change the logo. [*Laughter.*] I got a good piece of advice in the split, which was, "Be generous." At the time it was a big settlement. We're still good friends, but the 50/50 partnership thing was a lesson for me: *Don't do that.* I became 100 percent owner and brought in two more partners, who had been long-term employees, with an ownership percentage. Even that morphed around a bit.

Was there a conflict between moving from tradesman to business?

No. I was intrigued by how to run a business, challenged by what I could do. There are several kinds of businesspeople. The kind who wants to have his own business, gets it set up, tends the garden, and makes sure there's a fence around it. There are other people who are like, "Okay, where can we take this?" That camp falls into two groups. One wants to set up a business and retire as soon as they can. The other says, "Let's create something which is going to last, that looks good, and feels good when you're in it." That's what we do. That's what I spent the last twenty years doing: creating a business that is as good as the buildings we put up.

Where did that idea come from, to create something that lasts, gives the twenty-five-year-old a career, and helps the community?

Deva[2] was one of my early mentors and his way of doing business was intriguing. His thing was, "If you do it right you will be rewarded, but you

---

2   Deva Rajan was a founding member of the Sprinter Group and is also interviewed in this book.

won't always be able to measure the reward." We live in a society where you're measured in odd terms: your car, your house. But that's not what's real. Your definition of reward changes as you get older.

How would you respond to this idea? If your goal is to be a tradesman, work for someone else. If your goal is to establish and build a significant company, put your tool belt aside and focus on business as soon as it is practical.

There is a lot of merit in it. When a business grows to ten or fifteen people, you don't have much choice about putting your tool belt aside. But you can never lose respect for the trades. I'm not talking about fine gold-leaf work, but all trade work. If you lose respect for the craft of building, you might as well not be in business.

How did you learn to manage money?

People fall into two categories: people who are naturally good at managing it and people who aren't. It is an innate thing. We have two daughters, one is really great at it, the other is not. The money part of it has always mattered to me. I've been a good manager of money, and I don't spend a lot of money and we invest heavily in the business.

How do you decide how much to charge for a job?

It is based, in part, on the competition. You can always find out what the competition is charging. Also, we have trained in the sales process; we figure out what the client wants to spend and make the project work around that. Someone told me way back, "Cost is fact, price is policy." What you get for the work is separate from what it costs you to do it. If a client comes to me for a kitchen, my role is to find out where they are comfortable with pricing. What you can charge is more client-dependent than job-dependent.

We want to make 5 to 10 percent profit over a hundred years. But I'm not interested in making 100 percent on one job and losing money on the next one. I want to be steady, all the way through, steady, steady. No matter how much the client spends, there's a consistent profit margin. Sometimes we can't get it, we take on work because we need it—like every builder—but it does start with the client's comfort level.

Do you actively mentor and what does that look like?

Yes. I check in with them a lot. Part of mentoring to is showing human interest in who they are, what they are doing, and how they are doing it. We do a lot of safety meetings on technical stuff.

What would you tell a skilled tradesman about going into business? What should they learn first and what to avoid?

I would say they should surround themselves with people who are better than they are at doing something: sales, administration, human resources, building. Most people that work here are better at their job than I am. I'd tell them to take a sales training class. I learned to sell in two ways. I was born being able to connect with people and I took classes and courses on how sales work. Again, it's like money, some people are good at it, some people are not. A lot of people in construction are not good salespeople. Also, avoid clients you've got a bad feeling about.

If you had a method of reaching every builder and tradesmen in the U.S., what would you say?

Build to last!

What is a great success in business?

Watching people grow into a career. Good people. Integrity.

What's the best investment you've ever made?

Two things. We bought this building when we first started, way back, and had the business pay it off over thirty years. That's been a good financial investment. It was a real struggle in the beginning. And the emotional investment we have made in our people. Watching people stick around for thirty-plus years. That's been amazing. I think a third of our staff is ten years or more.

What makes your best and worst customers?

In our world, the ideal client can afford to do it. It's very expensive to build these days and the San Francisco Bay Area is one of the most expensive places in the world to build.[3] You need wealth depth and an appreciation for nice stuff, because that's what we do. The best customers appreciate craft.

---

3 According to International Construction's website May 2019, the three most expensive cities in the world to build in are New York, San Francisco, and Hong Kong, in that order.

The worst don't care about us as people. We've had customers watch people get injured and go, "Where's the next guy?" They are the very worst.

Do you shape your customers' expectations and if so, how?

Yes. We talk about schedule, a lot. We talk about things that will go wrong. We sometimes show customers a happiness graph. The day-by-day schedule is a big deal. So those two things, time, and money. And the fact that things go wrong.

Do you turn down customers and if so why?

Lots. There is a woman in the office next to mine, and one day she said to me, "I watched you, all you seem to do is turn work down." We do turn down a lot of small stuff: weird stuff, weird people, weird projects, the shoppers, and the tire kickers. We have a list of questions that we ask: Have you remodeled before? What was the experience with the previous builder? We try to figure out if they get along with their significant other, whether they've been planning this for a long time, whether the money is going to work, if they have a weird relationship with money, the cars they drive, their living condition, if they live in chaos or are they living an orderly life. We interview over the phone, we go to their home, we meet with them in the office. There's usually two or three pairs of ears and eyes on every decent-sized client. If anybody goes, *this one looks weird*, we will not work for them. It is a gut feeling, not an intellectual response.

How deeply do you get into a client's financials?

We don't ask, "Can you afford this and where's the money and show it to us." Although sometimes we feel like we should. If there's a question about it we'll ask, "Are you financing this personally or is it a construction loan?" Because once the thing starts, we are going to want to be paid, a lot of money, quick. We don't get into financial statements, although, if people ask me for our financial statement, I ask them for theirs. That usually stops that conversation. Most people, if they're doing a two-million-dollar remodel, are smart enough not to embark on it if they don't have the money. Some people do, although you can usually suss those out in the beginning.

How do you respond to this quote from Richard Branson; "Clients do not come first. Employees come first. If you take care of your employees, they will take care of the clients."

That is a Steve Nicholls quote! [*Laughter.*] I feel the same way. Take a look at what we do for our people. They get full healthcare coverage and we pay for their families too. They pay a portion of the premium; we pay everything else. And we have an employee stock option plan. Someone left the other day—he was here for eight years—he will get at least forty-five-thousand dollars. The quote is correct. If you look after your employees, they will love where they work and they'll take care of the customer. The ones that don't, won't last long because their colleagues will ask, "What are you doing?"

Has an apparent failure set you up for later success?

Yes. We often learn from failures and missteps. We analyze our failures to learn what we can. We do what we call "job autopsies" in the construction end of the business. We take a look at what goes right and wrong and what we could have done better. It's a group discussion with all of the job financials on the screen—gross profit, net profit, and anomalies between them. We also share general overhead figures and overall volume numbers, but not specifics. We don't show anybody's salary, for example, except the salary range when we advertise for a position. As we go forward with employee ownership, other financial information is becoming available. There are still some limits to what we show though.

What's a bad tradesman?

Somebody who doesn't care about the work or the process, their coworkers, or clients. We have a great Latino guy who runs our shop. He said to us one time, in his thick accent, "It's very simply, all you gotta do is care." And in the context of cleaning up a table saw after you have worked with it, he said, "What about the next guy?" It is simple and perfectly obvious.

When do you let people go and how do you do that?

When they reach retirement age, even though we don't have that in the manual. If you are getting toward the end of your career, we encourage you to retire. In the construction world, if we have a crewmember another crewmember doesn't want on their job, that's an indication. We'll let them go. Gotta be careful how you do it though. You don't do it through seniority, but merit, although the seniority thing plays into it inevitably. If you have been here for twenty years, everybody thinks you shouldn't be laid off.

What do you look for when you hire?

Motivation, honesty, and last, skill and experience. We'll teach them the skills. They have to be able to connect with people and to work with others. We let a young guy go last week, he never showed the motivation that we thought he should. We let people go by peer review.

What do you expect from employees? I recently asked this question of two people, and they said, roughly, "My people worked as hard as I do, and they cared as much as I do."

Bullshit! [*Laughter.*] This is an employee-owned company and we struggle with people not working or caring as much as they should; no one works as hard as the founder, the owner, the main partner. It is changing in our company; we've got people who work as hard, as committedly, as I do. The difference is, they are part-owners now. Ownership changes the dynamics. I believe that if more companies were prepared to do what we do, the United States would be a much better place.

What don't you expect from employees?

I don't expect them to dedicate their whole lives to this endeavor. They've got to have something else going on: a hobby, a sport, family. I don't expect them to be fully committed all the time. That's what's happening in the high-tech world. Those companies have all these benefits and perks—eat at work, day care, medical—and the expectation that comes along with that is that you work eighteen hours a day.

Do you have an exit strategy for the owner(s)?

The ESOP [Employee Stock Ownership Plan^] that is what we're been working on. It's not just an exit strategy for the owner, it's an exit strategy for everybody. This is the sixth or seventh year we have been working on it. So my exit is taking place as we speak. I'm pulling away from a lot of construction stuff, so the ESOP is an exit strategy that will get me and others out of the business gracefully. I don't know how long I will stay; I still like what I do and I have been doing it for a long time and I have a lot of friends in this business.

Word Association

Integrity: Basic to everything we do. Doing the right thing.

Job safety: Number one. Daily, constant, everybody. It's getting more important as we get bigger.

Fear: Early mornings, sometimes. My Africa experience taught me that fears are just in your head. We were dealing with situations, all the time, when you are taking forty people across the continent, where if you allow it, you can get stuck in fear. You have to control that. You just keep rolling, keep rolling. That was my attitude when we were dealing with crazy border police and out-of-control customs people, and crazy clients. That is building too, just keep rolling, you just keep rolling the joists out.

Company image: Crisp. Crisp website. Crisp job sites. Crisp building details. Crisp appearance.

Gratitude: Employees aren't grateful for what they've got. A lot of people who work here haven't worked for other firms, so they don't know what it can be like.

Overhead: Minimize it.

Profit: Maximize it.

Marketing: Do it all the time.

Sales: Everyone is in sales.

Estimating: The last thing you do in the sales process.

Employees: They are your capital.

Cut-Offs

We had to not be afraid to be expensive. When people say, "You're too expensive," my thought is, *What's your point?* It is part of our business model; charge a lot and do excellent work. The cheapest go out of business.

You may take your tool bags off and put them in your office, but you have to remember, that is what it's all about.

You've got to know how much it is costing you to build something, including overhead.

You have to make the budget work for the client, while making money.

I never thought to myself, *I'm going to be in business.* I just did it

We hired a bookkeeper early on—Lisa, she is still with us, thirty-two years later; she was among our first three or four employees. Everyone needs a Lisa. [*Laughter.*] We had someone to keep us in check.

If you have the right equipment, you can make more money.

I was doing something I loved, but I injured my back carrying a big cabinet up a steep stairway, and I thought, I can't do this forever, I better figure out who we can hire to help.

Define your business goals clearly so
that others can see them as you do.

George F. Burns

Paul Eldrenkamp,
General Contractor

https://www.byggmeister.com/

Paul does not look like a builder. Instead, he would fit in a university setting as an emeritus professor. But a builder he is and has been for his entire career, and he speaks and writes about the remodeling business with an uncommon intelligence and clarity, born of many hard lessons. In 1981, just out of college, he worked for a small-scale developer, and in '83, along with two partners—although it was not long before he was the sole owner—he founded Byggmeister Design/build,[1] a residential remodeling business based in Newton, Massachusetts, which he still owns and operates.

> *Remodeling contractors should recognize that many nightmare clients are of their own making* ■ *The seeds of humility can be sewn during a liberal arts education* ■ *It's by learning what you are shitty at that you understand better what you're good at* ■ *What you say about your work may be understated or self-deprecating, that only enhances your credibility* ■ *You must have a clear understanding of what's not acceptable on a job site* ■ *In the heat of battle there can be a tendency to accept and assume that things are the way they are and they're not going to change* ■ *I learned that sales is fundamentally a service process* ■ *We not only respect the trade's wisdom and experience, we rely on it* ■ *You're not known for what you say, but for*

---

1 Paul: "Byggmeister is a simplified Swedish word for 'master builder.' I founded the company the same day my Swedish-born wife and I were engaged, so romance played a bigger role than marketing. I'm still in business, and I'm still married, so the odd name seems not to have hurt."

> *what you do* ■ *Our rules deter problem clients from hiring us, and they restrain us from bad habits that can turn a good client into a monster*

During high school and summers in college, I was a job site laborer—a carpenter "wannabe"—and I developed some familiarity with the building process. College wasn't a great fit for me—it took me seven years to get a bachelor's degree—and I knew I didn't want anything more to do with higher education. I enjoyed construction work, and just out of college, I responded to an ad for a light carpentry job and was hired by a developer. He paid me four dollars an hour, off the books. He asked if I had a circular saw and if I knew how to hang doors. I said, "Of course." I bought a Craftsman saw and a book on hanging doors that afternoon and showed up the next morning. He knew quickly I was an utter fraud, and I don't know if he was desperate or he admired my chutzpah, but I didn't get fired. For jobs requiring real skill, he would occasionally bring in an actual carpenter. I worked for him for two years and he was not a great mentor, but I learned a lot about remodeling and how not to run a business. I learned the value of hiring good people and giving them room. I improved my carpentry skills and I read books and magazines. It was in the early '80s when *Fine Homebuilding* and *New England Builder* [now JLC^] started publishing, I got subscriptions to both and ate them up. I was never going to be a great carpenter, but I learned the order of construction, the planning, and the thinking required to build.

What academic education do you have, and did it help in your career?

I have a bachelor's degree in history. I believe a liberal arts education is a great preparation for a career as a remodeling contractor. You learn to write, to communicate, to evaluate a range of sources in order to make thoughtful, intelligent choices. You're able to apply lessons learned in one domain to other domains, you're able to close feedback loops[2] by learning to compare actual results with anticipated results and to think about what the root cause of that gap might be.

---

2   Paul's definition of "closing a feedback loop" (edited for brevity): "Verifying what we think is true, is in fact, true. Examples: Job cost accounting—are our estimates as accurate as we think they are?
    Client satisfaction surveys—are our clients as happy with our services as we think they are?
    Annual profit and loss statement—are we charging enough and running the business and projects efficiently enough to stay in business?"

What was most rewarding and most difficult about your trade?

The most rewarding—it's a cliché, but it's true—is the tangible result. The immediate feedback and the ability to quantify a good job versus a shoddy job. To see the progress over the course of the day and to see the change over the course of a project. The smells and sounds—and yes, I should have worn hearing and respiratory protection [*laughter*]—the integration of muscle skills, muscle memory, and thinking things through, it takes the whole person. Also, the endless variety of a day.

The most challenging is falling short of what you hoped to produce, and the frequency with which that happens. Also the periodic realization that what you have been doing for many, many years is not best practice and you didn't know it. And that frustration and embarrassment that frequently becomes defensiveness when you find out, because "What do you mean, I've been cheating my customers all along by doing it this way?"

What mistakes did you make while learning your trade?

I remember custom building a fixed roof skylight. I set a nail in the wrong place and watched the tempered glass crackle in slow motion as it started in one corner and made its way down to the far corner. And I remember a plumber coming down from an attic once, scratching his head, looking at me and saying, "You know, it's not code to nail framing right to a chimney."[3] [*Laughter.*]

As you started your business, did you have clear goals and ambitions?

I don't remember any goals or ambitions. We fell into it and that's how we started. One of the great things about residential remodeling is the barriers to entry are almost nonexistent. My ambition was to do something modestly quirky with my career, a born-slightly-too-late hippie, a shy small-town Iowa form of rebellion. I was doing this work and a couple people found out and they asked me to look at their job. I put together a budget and they hired me. I needed help so I talked to two buddies and the three of us started doing jobs and doing less and less work for the developer. It became clear that we had enough work, so I asked them if they wanted to be partners. We did everything. It was nuts. We built an addition and I put a slate roof on it. I got a slate

---

3   Nailing framing to a chimney is a good way to start a fire because as the flue and block heat up and cool down and heat up again the wood may dry out and burst into flame.

hammer and I read about installing slate. I'm sure I did it wrong. In the early years I joked that our business cards should say "Unlicensed and uninsured."

It was not much of a business in the early years, there was never enough money to argue about, and it was a constant struggle to pay the bills. We had absolutely no idea what to charge—our estimates were guesses—and we did not charge nearly enough. One of the partners left to go back to college after six months, the other moved to Seattle with his girlfriend. I was one of the more ill-suited entrepreneurs on the on the face of the planet. My father is a Methodist minister, my mother a special needs teacher and they instilled in me a strong service ethic and a social justice mandate, and not an iota of business acumen. A strong service ethic, untethered to budget reality, might be noble, but it is a doomed combination.

If you were able to go back, what would you do differently?

That is a tough one. At one level, I would do everything different, but you learn stuff when you're ready to learn that stuff. The main thing, I would charge more. It is what pays for doing everything better and for ongoing education. I would have done a lot of things differently, but hopefully I would still have had the rich career that I have now.

My career has had low moments. There were times when I sat in the car on the side of the road sobbing. Those moments of, *What have I gotten myself into? What have I said yes to that I have no idea how to get out of, or how to get a client—who is sucking the lifeblood out of me—out of my life?* But in these moments, when you have bottomed out, you really learn what you need to learn. When you think, *Okay I really, really have to change something.* You put ground rules in place and enforce them with a passion and a conviction that you never would have had otherwise.

How do you respond to this idea: If your goal is to be a tradesman, work for someone else. If your goal is to establish and build a significant company, put your tool belt aside and focus on business as soon as it is practical.

It's right. Trade skills and business skills are two completely different sets of priorities, although there's overlap. Unless your company is very small, you do not have enough hours in the week to do both construction and management. But it also assumes that someone knows what they want when they start out. With my intimate knowledge of many remodeling contractors through various networks,[4] I know that people go into this business because of the low barrier to entry and because it is fun, exciting, and cool. Then they have to figure out what their trajectory is, and that is the point at which this quote comes into play.

I don't remember being conflicted about putting down my tool belt, but there was about a twelve-month period of disengagement. In '88 we had our first daughter. In '89 I joined Business Networks. In between those two, I bought my first computer. I continued to do carpentry but the computer pulled me into the office; my daughter made it clear that I needed to allocate my time more carefully; and Business Networks made it clear how to get the time and resources I needed. These tectonic forces moved me out of the field. 1991–92 was probably the last year that I put a tool belt on, although in the early 2000s I was still heavily involved in production.

Talk about your career.

In the last thirty-six years of owning the business, I have never had a boring day of work. It's given me a bully pulpit to present information to the industry and the marketplace, backed up by real-world experience. It's given me a lot of freedom and it's been exciting, engaging, and the days, weeks, and years flew by.

My resume is one line—it would fit on a fortune cookie—I've been at the same company my entire career, with four different vocations, each of which built on the other: *Okay, I've got carpentry and production down—been there, done that—that lets me move on to business management. Right, managing and delegating, I've more or less got it figured out—that lets me move onto building science. Okay, I've deployed enough data loggers—that lets me move on to the next thing.*

My third career combined the first two—trade and business—to become more scientific and rigorous, to explore the various ways our projects failed and why. Jobs failed as a service—they took too long, were too messy, communication was poor, or something else caused client dissatisfaction—or they

---

4   The organizations Paul is involved with: Business Networks; Remodelers Advantage; Northeast Sustainable Energy Association's (NESEA), Bottom Lines Network (BLN); Eastern Massachusetts chapter of the National Association of the Remodeling Industry (NARI); HELM Construction Solutions' network of clients.

failed as a product over time. This was a process of introspection, scientific method, psychology, communication, and a large dose of humility.

The next thing—my fourth career—is passing on the business. I'm selling it to the employees, and everybody is keenly interested in making sure they can run the business without me. My formal retirement date is May 31, 2024, so it's a gradual disengagement. Now I'm handing off what I learned in those first three careers to develop an organization and a team that collectively has the skills required to flourish in a way that I was never quite capable of as an individual. It is refining systems, quantifying, and instilling habits and standards, cultivating networks[5] and doing outreach to trade programs and high schools to connect students to good businesses. A friend of mine said, "Your remaining years in the industry will be used to set an abundant table."

Talk about hiring and working with good subs, and what is a bad sub?

What makes a good sub is common knowledge; show up when we need you and on time, work with us to get a full scope-of-work, be certain your pricing reflects the full scope-of-work and help us avoid change orders. There's also a strong reciprocal responsibility to let them know when we need them and to have the job ready, so they can be productive when they arrive.

Inertia can develop in subcontractor relationships. It's easy to accept mediocrity, because the pain of changing is greater than the pain of mediocrity, which is risky, because you're cheating your client and sending the wrong message to your organization. But there is risk in having only one sub in a trade too, and also, establishing a relationship with a new sub is risky and time consuming. We tend to be loyal to certain people—we've been amply rewarded—but if the wrong person got hit by a truck, there would be major scrambling.

What interesting habit do you have?

My email inbox is my to-do list. At the beginning of the day I go to the oldest email and think about why it's the oldest; have I not acted on

---

5   Paul's explanation: "Cultivating networks" is participating in a range of community activities such as environmental and professional organizations, advisory committees, and preparing the way for someone else from Byggmeister to take my seat in these organizations. It's also starting activities and events, such as a monthly "building science for carpenters" meet-up group and making sure a Byggmeister representative is at the planning table.

this because I shouldn't have said yes, or because there's a hurdle I have to get over, or is it causing me discomfort? Sometimes I'll move on to the next oldest one, but sometimes I'll actually change my habits. The oldest email in your inbox tells you a lot about yourself. That's certainly true in my case.

What do you do when you lose direction or are confused?

Break the issue into bite size chunks and start from there. Sometimes it's articulating the issue on paper and acting on the first bite sized chunk. I'm typically able to gain traction and get over the hurdles this way.

What advice have you given most to tradesman and what is the best path to learning a trade today?

It's been a while since I had the audacity to give advice to a tradesperson, but any advice I give is implicit; not beating them up about a mistake they made—trusting they learned from it—and encouraging them to think about what the work will look like in ten or twenty years.

My world is residential remodeling, and in that world the best path to learning a trade is to get hired by a company that respects and encourages learning. There will be some trial and error to find such a company and you are looking for a place where the crew is not constantly under the gun because of lousy estimates, a place with a stable crew who know they've got time to do things right.

If you were to lecture to a class of aspiring tradesmen, what would you tell them to learn first and what to avoid?

On a job site, figure out who has the best trade skills and watch them and copy what they do. The goal is to become confident in your trade, but it is easy to confuse confidence with arrogance. Arrogance comes from thinking you know, confidence comes from humility and knowing that often, you don't know. Confidence is being prepared to take risks, while applying past lessons to what you're doing. Also, realize that you can learn from everyone on a job; you might learn what to do, or what not to do.

What would you tell them about getting an education apart from the trade?

It's *really* important to be well informed about a broad range of topics. So much of remodeling involves human interactions and being a valued member of society requires having conversations that are informed and humble. It is easier to have those conversations if you're exposed to a range of topics. Also, understand that your education comes from everywhere and that it is ongoing.

How would you describe a successful tradesman?

Someone who is aware of best practice, while being skeptical of it. Someone who can work as part of a team, with people who have a broad range of experiences. Someone with a line in the sand for behaviors and products they will not tolerate and who knows how to gently move others in the right direction and later, if need be, to move them with more force. Someone who works in a way that doesn't beat up their body over the years.

I don't want to put an undue burden on the trades—we ask a lot of them—but they can add tremendous benefit to an organization if they communicate their ideas about how to improve the company. Plus, they'll have job security and help to create an environment where they're happy to show up every morning. Some bosses are unteachable, of course, and the sooner you recognize that the happier you'll be.

What is the best investment you made in your business?

Responding to a postcard from Les Cunningham's Business Networks [6] in the late '80s—saved my ass. And going to Joe Lstiburek [7] seminar—he is the preeminent building scientist on the continent. Les and Joe made me look at business and building in profoundly different ways.

What about your best customer makes them that?

An exercise I went through after one of my low moments many decades ago—in a fit of total frustration—was to list the last fifty people we had worked for. I crossed off all the jobs we lost money on and those people whom, if spotted at the supermarket, I would run and hide from. [*Laughter.*] That left, let's say, thirty people. I went through those and figured out the common characteristics: two-career couples, working for a living and not superrich; their jobs were typically intellectual, professors, lawyers, doctors; they were early in the process of thinking about their project; they had a long-term commitment to their house; they had environmental priorities; and

---

6   Les's website: HTTPS://WWW.BUSINESSNETWORKS.COM/
7   Joe's website: HTTPS://WWW.BUILDINGSCIENCE.COM/USERS/JOSEPH-LSTIBUREK

they were open to the design/build process. It turned out to be surprisingly easy to put together a list of clients who were good for us and for whom we were a good contractor. Also, I realized our best jobs are 25 percent carpentry, 25 percent material, and 50 percent subcontractors, and it helped us focus. These were useful exercises because it focused our marketing and helped us not work for people who brought out the worst in us.

When a job gets into trouble, it generally is because somehow the client is in charge—the least qualified person—and I have to think about what I said or did that put them in charge so that I can avoid it in the future. I learned to quantify and articulate what I said yes to, so I knew when to say no. Often when I emphasize how important it is that I stay in control of a project it raises hackles. But it isn't about arbitrary power—it's about providing ground rules and holding to them, because we provide our best service when we do that.

A client who is easy to work with has a clear budget and is willing to communicate it to us—which is surprisingly empowering in the design/build process—and to communicate when things are getting a little annoying, rather than waiting until they are way annoying. We like people who are engaged in the process and ask questions and push a little, who are interested in the choices that need to be made and why we're giving them those choices. Not people who are passively letting us do everything.

What about your worst customer makes them that?

They are indecisive or unable to work within our framework: We won't do anything illegal, we're getting a permit, and we use contracts. We bring our team to the table; they may want to bring in some substitutes, but that will affect the team. We're prepared to have the conversation—we've found good subs by being flexible—but in general, we're going with our strength. If you want us break our rules, we're going to charge more and take longer and the people who keep trying to break those rules are difficult to work with.

Sometimes we create monsters out of perfectly reasonable people because we incentivize them to lose perspective—to care about tiny details—and it can backfire. People getting pissed off and being ungrateful wears me down: "Come on folks, step back, how lucky are you to be able to do this project, on this house, in this neighborhood?" But my service ethic is what created that problem to begin with, so it's also motivating and has required me to come up with systems and crews who can deliver that service.

When do you turn away customers?

We're able to exert tremendous influence over who gets in touch with us, in part, by whom and what we say yes and no to. A lot of the calls we don't get are because we understand our geographic area, our schedule, and we are a design/build firm that does not bid. Therefore, most of our calls are quality leads. This is the result of having done the exercise that identified our successful clients.

How would you advise someone to find a good contractor?

Ask for references going back five or ten years. Ask the references how the project held up? Ask at what point in the process they knew what the project was going to cost? Ask at what point they knew how long it was going to take? Ask what the warranty process was like?

You have referred to low times in your career. Would you talk about those?

Here are three examples of when I got in over my head. We have clients in Boston who wanted to build a log cabin in Western Massachusetts. I said, "What's the big deal, it'll be fun. The crew will enjoy it. We'll send them out for a week at a time and in a couple months, we'll build this cabin." Nothing went right and it was a money and time sink. The crew resented going out there; it was not the adventure I imagined. In the meantime, our real projects, back here, were understaffed and underwater. I had no idea how to get through it. I kept beating myself up and just had to plow through. If I had said no, I would have saved myself tens of thousands of dollars and years' worth of business development. That was a very low time.

In the '90s—later in my career than it should have been—a high school buddy, for whom we were developing a $400,000 project, said he couldn't go ahead with the job, two weeks before it was to have started. The friendship survived, but it was at a time when I had a bit of a Ponzi scheme going on with finances and I was in the middle of the renovation on my own house. I didn't know if I was going to get through the summer financially.

Then, there was a lawyer and his wife who were manipulating me left, right, and center. It was emotional torture; I could not end it or take charge of the job. She was indecisive and her husband was refusing to sign the contract and change orders. This was 2003–4, a couple decades into my career, and I knew better, but I was letting it happen. I consider that to be a form of incompetence. Finally, we met and I said, "I don't know how to do this job with you, I've never felt more incompetent and I can't pretend anymore that I know what I'm doing on this job. We have to figure out a way to wrap this up." That honesty had resonance for them, and we put together a list of things I would be responsible for, and they hired someone else to finish.

What do you look for when you hire?

When evaluating someone, I frame it as three criteria: attitude, aptitude, and experience. Experience is the least important—and sometimes it's a liability—usually you can figure that out from the resume and referrals. Attitude has to do with engagement and enthusiasm; it comes across reliably in the interviews. Aptitude is how quickly they get up to speed and how detailed the instructions have to be. Discerning this is more about intuition, and sometimes the only way to know is to hire them. After we hire, we have a framework for frequent evaluation.

For the last three hires, I haven't been involved. But their first meeting is with the management team—business, general, and production managers, and estimator—depending on what position it is. If it's a field position, the candidate also goes to a variety of job sites and meets the crews; if it's an office position, there is one meeting with the management team.

What is a good and a bad employee and what don't you expect from employees?

I have been known to say, "When you hire, make it a spectacularly good one or a spectacularly bad one, because both are easy to know how to handle." The worst employee is mediocre and intuits the minimum requirement not to get fired. A good employee has good attitude and aptitude, they appreciate the experience we offer, they buy into the mission that we are providing a high level of customer service, and they are eager to provide that service and willing to break new ground to do so. I don't expect blind obeisance, for them to take calls or answer emails after hours, or to derive their life's meaning from employment at Byggmeister.

What would you tell a new business owner about hiring?

Hire people that excite you and avoid mediocre hires. Understand that a good hire today may not fit the job as the business changes, and you may need to fire a long-term, loyal employee. That can be wrenching. And be careful about automatic raises; if someone's wages get too far ahead of what they can get anywhere else, laying them off can be devastating. Also, learn how to fire quickly and compassionately and understand that there is a correlation between the two things, and know that your worst employee is sending a message about what minimally acceptable behavior is.

How do you let people go?

Only after we've tried everything we can possibly do to make it work. We have five lead positions in our production team and if someone can't function in the first slot, we try them in the next slot down, trying to match responsibilities to performance. And then if it does not work, we say, "We've run out of ideas." We've learned the importance of having a job description and fitting the person to that. For a long time I customized the job to the person. It was ripe for abuse, and it prevented us from having shared enforceable standards of behavior and performance. Now we have the same expectations from all of our leads.

It is satisfying when you fit an employee to a set of responsibilities that allows them to flourish: to see their competence become expertise; to see their pride and eagerness to come to work; to see them become a valued member of the community and to grow with and push the company. That's what we all strive for, right, helping to create a job that really means something to someone. It's one of the most satisfying things in the world.

Do you have a mission statement?

The short answer is no. I'm skeptical of mission statements. The guiding, organizing, and focusing philosophy that I've had for decades is "We do work we can stand behind forever and we do it within 2 percent of the estimated costs." And yes, that is realistic.

What educational programs and benefits does your company offer?

We do company meetings four times a year with a variety of educational topics: a warranty talk and slideshow by our warranty people, a safety talk, a discussion about what has worked and what hasn't. And periodically we'll bring in a speaker for an in-house seminar. We have a budget for conferences and subscriptions to online resources and print periodicals. We give paid time off—flex time—the first year there are twenty paid days off, including holidays, sick day, and vacation time. After ten years, it maxes out at thirty-five paid days. There's a 401(k) with an employee match: 50 percent up to 6 percent of your wages. We contribute about $6000 a year toward health and dental insurance plans. Conferences, cell phones, a $1500 per year tool allowance, and T-shirts and hoodies for the winter.

Talk about the idea that perfection is a moving target, and that no one gets everything right.

You have to make mistakes. That is part of the dynamism of the world we live in. The right person is never going to be satisfied, their ambition always exceeds their grasp. I mean, it better. An organization has to be prepared to stretch, make mistakes, and to try new things—in the product, the service, and the people they hire. Making a brand-new mistake is exciting—it's repeating mistakes that is discouraging—and it's important to have an organization resilient enough, with resources and time enough, to fix them.

The better you get at estimating—the better handle you have on your costs—the higher the costs go, so you must get better at sales. You're selling higher prices so you have to deliver a better service. You think, *This lead carpenter is not delivering a premium a job, I've got to replace them.* You replace them with someone who is better in all regards, and the wage scale changes as a result, and you've got to keep that scale fair across the board. So you're raising your prices again, which changes the estimate and the sales price, again, which means your marketing has to get more creative to communicate the additional value clients get in return for paying more.

How did you learn to estimate?

I didn't really. I did not turn things around in my business until I stopped doing my own estimates. My longing for approval affected the accuracy of the estimate because I told the customer what I thought they wanted to hear and it made me deflate my estimates. Eventually, I got so tired of not making money that the pain of doing job cost accounting was less than the pain of my poor level of compensation. It was a paradigm shift. If you can hire somebody who really likes to do it, then it gets done right. It took four tries, but when we finally had a good estimator, it not only improved our profitability, it improved the sales process because I knew the numbers were right.

The mechanics of estimating are pretty basic, so it has to do with the discipline you bring to it. But you learn to estimate by doing job cost accounting, that is, comparing the estimated cost with actual cost. It's a process and a slog. First, you have to document your estimate well enough to compare it with the actual cost of doing the work. To do that, you need to track your job costs, rigorously, so that you have something to compare. You have to do it even when it's apparent that you screwed up the estimate. You have to continue doing it, forever, even when every job cost accounting report is making you look like an idiot.

Do you use cost estimating books or do you have another method for developing the numbers you use to estimate?

We do fixed price contracts and we need really good estimates. Our goal is plus or minus 2 percent accuracy in the estimate, but it's a bell curve, and we hit that goal on 40 to 50 percent of our projects. Plus or minus 5 percent covers 80 percent, 10 percent covers 99 percent, and there are some outliers.

Because we're design/build, an awful lot of our estimating is done in the specification writing, and the estimate is in response to those specs^. If you've got loose specs, you've got a bad estimate. With our ratio of 25 percent each, labor and material, and 50 percent subs, 75 percent of our job cost is easy to pin down. The sub costs—there might be a smidgen of a change order—are a guaranteed 50 percent. Materials can be slippery, but it's not hard to get them right. Labor is the error zone. The big variables are—guess what—framing and finish carpentry and client management. You will get a better number on labor if you think of the project in terms of how long it will take and how many people it will need, rather than breaking it into minute components. That's been our experience anyway.

Where does someone starting out get the numbers to estimate with?

They can manage the risk by locking in as much of the cost as possible for subs and material. Then do the component parts, and the guesses, and step back. If you're realistic about how long the job will take, and the labor hours are showing the renovation will take eight weeks with two people, and you know that's not enough, adjust the hours. On the first one you lose some money—hopefully you can afford to—or you make less than you need to, but you learn for the next time.

If you expect to collect your last payment, you better be able to predict, with a reasonable level of accuracy, the cost of the job. The client's biggest fears are budget, the job is never going to end, or poor quality; but the greatest of those is budget. It is one of the biggest investments a client will make—and they've heard stories about out-of-control budgets—and they want to know what they're getting into.

What books have been most important in your life?

The Old Man and the Sea is one of the most powerful metaphors of the remodeling industry that exists. I've dreamt of writing about the how *The Old Man and the Sea*, *A River Runs Through It*, and *Moby-Dick*[8] describe the three primary types of Remodeling Contractors.

In *The Old Man and the Sea*, the old man goes fishing alone because he can't find good help. He's struggling to catch anything and, all of a sudden, boom, he's got this incredible fish on the line. He fights, his hands are bloody, he can't sleep because he fights it into the night, and finally he brings it alongside his boat and he's counting all the money in his head, and he thinks, *This is going to change my life*. On his way to shore with this magnificent fish, the sharks come, and by the time he gets back, there is almost nothing left of the fish. That's the legion of one-man shops, they love the excitement, but they're never able to get ahead in their business.

A River Runs Through It is cerebral—I'm in that category—they have a respectable practice, but they're not really entrepreneurs, they're in it for the intellectual engagement. And *Moby-Dick*, the real entrepreneurs with big dreams and visions of growth. "We're riding the wave; we went from three million volume to fifteen million, in two years. We're geniuses!"

Have you had a mentor that influenced your career?

I've had a range of influences. Two I've mentioned: Les Cunningham's model is powerful and it brought me many mentors and peers. Joe Lstiburek changed the way I think about buildings. Marc Rosenbaum,[9] an engineer, has been referred to as "the most annoyingly curious person you will ever meet." He's a skeptic in the classic sense, taking little at face value, digging deeper, and he is quick to admit when he doesn't know an answer. I learned a lot from him.

8   The Old Man and the Sea, Ernest Hemingway, Scribner, 1952; A River Runs Through It, Norman Maclean, University of Chicago Press, 1989; Moby-Dick, Herman Melville, Harper, 1851.

9   Marc's website: HTTP://WWW.ENERGYSMITHS.COM/INDEX.PHP

What behavior has improved your business?

Learning to let critical responsibilities go to people who can handle them better than I.

Please talk about marketing.

I would say a new business owner needs to figure out who they are, who they want to be, and a way to communicate that. And that trying to be all things to all people—not being discerning about the jobs taken on—might satisfy short-term revenue needs, but it will work against long-term success.

In the early years it was all word of mouth and 90 percent repeat clients. Then the web was invented! Our primary connection now is our website—it is the nexus of our activity—and it is fun watching where the leads come from. Otherwise, we're doing the same things that worked when I started because they still work. Marketing is communicating who you are through a range of networks. It is a conscious cultivation of those networks that enhance what you want your business to be. You are not necessarily getting new jobs and employees from your closest networks, but you're getting them from the people they know. It is what Mark Granovetter, a sociology professor at Stanford University, calls "the strength of weak ties."

Do you like marketing and if so, why?

I adapted our marketing strategy to what I like, so yes, I like marketing. I like communicating who we are. I like doing a good job for people—that is *the fundamental* marketing strategy for any service business. And I like joining organizations and getting on their boards—that's fun for me. And speaking to a range of organizations—that is a great marketing strategy. And I like writing, which is a great way to reach people. Developing a reputation for credibility, I mean, who wouldn't be rewarded by that?

How did you learn to sell and what does it look like now?

When I wasn't charging enough, sales were easy. [*Laughter.*] Joining the peer review group made me understand that I needed to raise my prices, and through them, I was introduced to Sandler Sales Training.[10] I don't think Sandler intended to teach me this, but I learned that being a good salesman was taking my parents' service ethic and applying it to the act of fixing people's homes. It became a ministry. It was understanding that "if

10 HTTPS://WWW.SANDLER.COM/

I'm going to be of service to these people, I need to learn why they want to do what is one of the most expensive, intrusive, pain-in-the-ass endeavors a homeowner can undertake, and to respond to that on a personal level." That is what my sales process became. If I couldn't make that connection, then I couldn't, and shouldn't, take the job.

The majority of people who contact us now say, "I've got a project I want you to do." Now our sales process is evaluating whether we're the best fit, communicating when we think we are and why, and building their confidence sufficiently so they're prepared to sign a design agreement. Then we continue selling by reinforcing the notion that they made a good choice by selecting us.

When work slows, what do you do?

Using our revenue projections, we've been able to anticipate slowdowns. Our production schedule is laid out and when someone signs a design contract, we know, roughly, what the budget is and when we're going to do it. It's not guaranteed, but 95 percent of the time it becomes a job, so we know a year in advance if things are going to slow down. Usually. A while ago, a $1.2 million job went away, eight weeks before it was supposed to start. That hurt. In that case, we went through our past client list, picked fifty, and sent them letters saying, "We've got an unexpected gap in our work schedule." We were able to fill in 50 percent of the hours we lost.

When you have too much work, how do you respond?

We scramble, but we try to avoid it by being realistic about our capacity. We have two things we look at: projected dollar volume and production hours per month. Both are based on the anticipated projects and if they get outside of a certain range, we are aware of it. Being over budget revenue is not always a red flag, it depends on why. If revenue is high because the ratio of materials or subs to labor is high on one job, it's not a huge problem, but it's also not without risk. We solve it by being vigilant about material ordering and handling and subcontractor management. The production hours is a deal breaker; we reorganize and spread projects out over a longer timeframe to deal with that.

How did you learn about business and what mistakes did you make?

Joining Business Networks is when I first started thinking about business at any level of sophistication. I barely calculated what I was earning in a year or how many hours I was putting in. I didn't think about job descriptions, operating budgets, profit and loss statements, job cost accounting, or marketing, and I had no idea what was possible financially.

In the peer review group, companies prepped for each meeting by filling out financial forms and bringing marketing data and business documents. As the facilitator, Les told us what forms to fill out and what documents to bring. The host company rotated, and when you were the host, there was even more preparation. In the beginning I was thinking, *I have so much to learn*, and *This is going to be hard*, and *I can't tell my clients how much more I need to charge*. But I did it. Walt Stoeppelwerth said, "In the remodeling industry, you will either learn to mark up by 1.5 to 1.67 percent, or you will be working for someone who has."

My business mistakes are easier to speak of in categories. One is not doing job cost accounting. Two is not firing in time, because I was trying to be accommodating. Three is not developing a business plan and a budget by asking, what do I need from the business. If I were to do it again, I would start with what I wanted to do: Here's the skills I bring and the things I like doing and the amount of time I'm prepared to spend doing them. Here's the money I need to make. What structure do I need to build to make that possible? What's the cost of that structure and how does that translate to sales price? That's the core of it.

This can be a tough business, talk about those times when you have to be a hard-ass.

You've gotta have a line in the sand. There are some things that are acceptable and some that are unacceptable, and I had a hard time learning the importance of enforcing that line. But as I got better at it, I needed to do it less often. The rules you enforce most effectively and consistently are the rules you learned from the most painful and expensive lessons.

Talk about contracts.

One of our first clients—he was a lawyer, now a judge—gave me the best legal advice I've ever gotten: "Do fair contracts, that meet the letter of the law, and run the project in such a way that nobody ever looks at the contract." That's what we aim for. We had an organic contract for a while, something I pulled out of a book or a legal seminar. Over the years we've worked for many lawyers, and they would frequently hand me a signed contract with one hand and a page of notes with the other, detailing things that we might want to include in future contracts.

Talk about your company's specifications.
We call them scope notes. There are three documents that we develop to describe the project: the drawing, a comprehensive product/finish list, and the scope notes, which cover everything the drawings and product/finish list does not.

Talk about the company's method of developing a job.
There are three budget milestones in our process. The first is the "ballpark budget"—we've always put dollars on the table in the first meeting. It's a broad range: $3–400,000. This is based on our database of past project costs. Those come from our bookkeeper. We tell the client this figure includes design, which is likely 6 to 12 percent of the construction budget. On the basis of that conversation, they either sign or don't sign a design agreement. If they sign, our next meeting and budget milestone—we call it a "feasibility budget"—there's a flurry of schematic design where we agree on the job. With that information, our estimator prices the job out to plus or minus 10 percent. They say, "Do it all," or "Do these six things," or they fire us. If they fire us, they've spent some money, but they've been given useful information. It's never a happy meeting to get fired, but better then, than later. If they hire us, there's an extended period of design development and filling in details. The third major budget is the "fixed price contract." We work hard to make sure there's continuity between those three budget numbers. There will be updates between the feasibility budget and the contract, but they just are tweaks. Sometimes a bit of work gets added after the feasibility budget and we'll drop that down to a separate line to show, "Yes, that aggregate number is off, but it's because this scope was added."

Talk about change orders.
A lot of change orders is a problem. We manage it through planning up front and not starting the job until we're ready to finish. That is our goal

and often our reality. This year we're budgeting $3.6 million in revenue and our budget for change orders is about $75,000, that is a tiny percentage of volume [0.02 percent]. But that is not zero—and some years are more than that—and years with lots of change orders have typically been years of lower profitability.

It's the lead carpenter's responsibility to get all the information for a change order to the salesperson, and they turn it into a form that the homeowner signs. Sometimes we get the signature after we've done the work, but there is always an email trail communicating that it is a change order. Payment is due with the next milestone payment and because they are small, they're easy to collect.

Do you ever fire a client during a job?
Usually we do the firing before any paperwork has been signed, but yes, we get into jobs where we cannot make them happy and we agree to part ways and give them a list of contractors who might be a better fit. It's usually a consensus in the company. Regardless of when I have to say no to a client, early or late in the process, the conversation is the same: "I'm sorry, we're not the right company for this job."

In the past fifteen years, we've not fired a client after having signed a contract. I'm not saying it's going to be all sweetness and light, but we're going to finish the project and we're going to get paid in full. There have been times when I should have fired some clients.

Talk about bidding jobs.
It's been more than twenty years since we bid work. Bidding incentivizes knowingly leaving things out that have to be done and it puts all the focus on price. It makes it impossible to schedule—I shouldn't say that, people do it all the time—but if I'm looking at four projects and I don't know which I'll get until a couple of weeks before they are ready to start, how can I possibly put together a team to do it? If you get all four jobs, you're in way over your head. Bidding is unpaid consulting and ultimately it's a service to nobody. Maybe the architect and client get useful information out of my bid—it's hard to say—but is that commensurate with the amount of time I put into it? *Absolutely not.* I would rather invest my team's hours in people and projects who have made a commitment to me.

Talk about Time & Material (T&M) versus a fixed price contract.

There are people who do T&M profitably, but I could not make it work. What I can make work is fixed price contracts, where the project is defined up front, and I communicate useful pricing information without getting into the details of my operating budget. It is hard to get the markup required to survive as a remodeling contractor doing T&M jobs. I tried, but frequently there were bills I chose not to submit because they revealed how faulty my initial estimate was. You still have to do a damn good estimate up front with T&M—so why not do a fixed price contract?—and it encourages starting too soon because you have a pathway to make critical decisions down the road.

Talk about working with designers or architects.

We almost always work with an architect that we hire and rarely work with an architect who is working for the client, but if we do, it has to be someone we have shared values with. We have a detailed process map—it's about twelve pages of major and minor milestones—with what the deliverables are for each of those milestones and the desired outcome. This is what we use to work with architects. Rachel and I are the project managers—salesperson, project developer, whatever we call it—our primary responsibility is checking off the boxes from the process map.

If we're not in charge, we don't do the job. That was a hard-learned lesson. Basically, it distills to "Do we have a shared vision of what a completed job will look like?" Years ago, had I understood enough to ask that question, the answer would invariably have been "No, because the architect is continuing to design the project through trial and error, as it is being built, when we would rather be working out critical details before construction starts so that we have control over quality, cost, and schedule."

How do you suggest builders learn to manage money and to develop a budget?

I had no idea how to manage money and managing for me was paying just enough to the loudest people to make them a little quieter. Managing money starts with developing a budget and holding to it. Some, through sheer instinct, are able to do it, but they're the exception. Most people without an operating budget are not running a profitable business. Until you have a budget—and hold to it—it will be hard to have disposable income to save. To learn how, work with an accountant and a consultant, go online to Taunton Press and *JLC* and see what budgets people have. Start with that. If you've been in business for a while you can look back on past expenses, evaluate those and develop a budget from them. Everything is in your budget: revenue, cost of goods sold, overhead, and hopefully, gross and net profit. Once you know the cost to produce a job, you know what the sales price needs to be. Just know that if you mess with the sales price to appease the client, it is coming right out of the bottom line.

How do you mentor?

Now when our general manager wants some help, she will invite me for coffee. In the fulfillment of my project management duties, while developing a project, I have opportunities to set a tone and a standard without being intrusive. When we go to construction, I'm on the job site as issues come up and I mentor as we figure out how to fix the problem.

If you could reach every builder and tradesmen in the United States, what would you say?

Do work that you can stand behind forever and do it for within 2 percent of the estimated cost. Which means you've got service, quality, and business management down.

Word Association

Integrity: That is the single highest accolade I can offer to anyone; it is the most important attribute anyone can bring to their life.

Communication: The best communication is proactive rather than reactive; it is initiating communication and using it as a tool to head off problems, rather than responding to problems.

Job safety: It's obviously critical and it's quantifiable by incidence reports and it's hard for a crew to police themselves. So it's critical for the owner to set the standard and not be afraid to show up at a job and call people out on safety; it is not the time to be pals with the crew.

Fear: Diminishes with confidence.

Company image: The image can be communicated in a number of ways, one via website and another on the job site, and if there is a disconnect it can really hurt you. Consistency of image is very important.

Gratitude: Gratitude runs a close second to integrity in those characteristics that you need to get you through life.

Immutable business principle: Kindness.

Overhead: Think of it as money you invest in your business, not as a burden that needs to be covered.

Profit: Profit is what gives you a better business every year.

Estimating: An attempt to predict the future based on past performance and past experience. Therefore, to make a good prediction of the future, you need to have a good handle—and be honest with yourself—about what's happened in the past.

Community: That is the fertile field on which you are growing your and your employees' career, it is where all the value of the company comes from.

Successful business: Having enough financial resources to be accountable for your mistakes and to invest in the future of the business and to be able to treat people with kindness and integrity. A business that is hemorrhaging money is going to have a hard time acting with integrity or kindness.

Successful career: Success is being a valued member of the community; it is being respected by your peers and being able, at the end of your career, not to be worried about money.

Cut-Offs

There is a lot of "ready, fire, aim" in this business, both at the micro and macro levels. It may be true in all industries, but it is certainly true in ours.

I would tell a new business owner to sit down, alone or with key stakeholders, and think about how much money they want to make and how many hours they are prepared to spend to make it.

In the world of residential remodeling, to have a self-deprecating sense of humor is one of the most powerful tools to defuse tension and bring conversations back around to a civil tone. It's an important skill set.

In theory you can have a safety officer on each crew, in practice it is difficult to make it effective.

I had a Protestant version of chutzpah. [*Laughter.*] I could do whatever I wanted.

Many clients ask when we can start; they should ask when we can finish. We do everything we can to hold off starting a project until all of the decisions are made, and all of the products are picked out.

Quality is measured in four dimensions—not just level, plumb, and square, but level, plumb, square, and dry over time.

I took a furniture building course at the Museum of Fine Arts in Boston. One of the best things I learned in that class was how to sharpen chisels. I built a bird's-eye maple block plane that I had for years; it was a fantastic little plane.

I started off learning about and becoming a carpenter. That was the first decade. The second was learning about business ownership and management, learning to apply the craft of construction to the craft of creating a business.

I was disinvited from the management team. Well, actually, I said, "I don't think I should be going to the business manager meetings." The business manager said, "Good." [*Laughter.*]

The owner and the estimator need to avoid the temptation to blame production for cost overruns. If that's their go-to-guilty party, they're gonna be spinning their wheels for a very long time.

Companies evolve over time. There are many people we worked for quite happily, who are not a good fit for us any longer.

I've got a financial responsibility to clients, the crew, subs, and suppliers. The infinite responsibility weighs: sometimes I can feel that weight more than at other times.

I am not a product of my circumstances.
I am a product of my decisions.
Stephen Covey

Iris Harrell,
Retired General Contractor

Iris lives in a spacious, ultramodern home north of San Francisco, which she and her partner remodeled recently. She has a warm, open face, a spiritual leaning, and she answers my questions thoughtfully.

> *Happy employees make happy clients* ▪ *I paired up with a family friend, he was seventy, a retired brick salesman who had lots of tools* ▪ *Killer clients, they are out there* ▪ *Billing quickly is the only viable way to stay in business and not get behind* ▪ *We taught the staff—the carpenters especially—that if you don't plan three days ahead for whatever you need, you're going to fail* ▪ *Cost accounting[1] is difficult and complex in construction* ▪ *If you've got turmoil at home, you're going to have turmoil in the business*

I was a carpenter and a painter, in my own company. I'm experienced in framing, finish, outside fence and gate work, hanging doors, building cabinets, painting, and sheetrock. That's my hands-on experience. I did not have any formal training. I read a lot. I hired people who were experienced. We were a small company, so I worked beside them. That's how I learned.

What drew you into the trades?

When I first met my partner, she had just bought a 1920s duplex in Dallas, Texas. It needed a lot of work. We had day jobs, and I would come home—she had a *Reader's Digest* fix-it book—and we would decide what

---

1   Cost accounting is the process of tracking all business costs in such a way that the information can be used to manage the business, produce estimates, and to save and invest money.

our next project was and we would start doing it. I started working on our house, that was exciting. I was thirty-two before ever touching a hammer. My father had an eighth-grade education—he changed jobs a lot—but he could build, he was a farmer and utilitarian. Coming from a rural background, I knew it wasn't magic.

Being an intelligent, educated woman, teaching was the highest anybody in my family had gotten. When I joined a band on the road, they thought I'd lost my mind. When I became a contractor—and put a tool belt on—they really thought I lost my mind. Once I became CEO and had a successful company, my mother said she had taught me everything I knew [*chuckles*].

What was difficult about working in a trade?

Working with difficult clients. It's not the trade that's hard, it's laying out the scope-of-work and managing the client's emotions and expectations. I wish I'd had a psychology degree. To me, that's almost more important than anything else. I used to say I did marriage counseling.

What academic education do you have and how did it help you in your career?

For my undergraduate degree, I majored in American Studies and studied American art, architecture, literature, and history. That is also when I got interested in music. I also have a master's degree in education administration. College taught me to be well-spoken, to be a good listener, to repeat back what the client wanted, and to translate that into something that was executable. When I moved to Silicon Valley from Texas I was dealing with CEOs of high-tech companies. It was a wealthier crowd. My education—I wasn't a blue-collar Joe—helped me to be treated as an equal by the client.

Did you work for someone else and if so, how did it help?

I couldn't even get an interview in Dallas, so I started my own remodeling company. When I came to California, with nearly four years of experience, I still could not get a job, so I started my own company again. In California—even with all these lawyers around—the construction companies said, "Because you're female, we don't think the subcontractors will listen to you."

When you started your company, did you have long-term goals?

After taking a workshop about long-term goals and five-year plans, my partner came home and said, "You need this for your company." We spent a whole Saturday working out our mission, which was to be the best residential contractor in the area and to be the client's contractor for life. People are like that about hairdressers and dentists, and they should be that way about their contractor. So that was our goal.

I was a legal contractor in Dallas. In California, I started again, out of my house. I hired the first employee; the second year, on my birthday, I hired another employee; I was paying Social Security, holidays, vacations, all that stuff. I figured, I wanted it, they should have it too. Because I had been a teacher and treated as a professional, I felt like that is what everyone wanted.

What mistakes did you make?

I made every mistake in the world. A big one was signing a contract with the wrong client. A killer client can take you down. A lot of people think that they can please anybody if they roll over enough, but some people like to bring people down, that is their *raison d'etre*[2]. In Stephen Covey's book, *The Seven Habits of Highly Effective People,*[3] one of the personality types he describes is a person who does not feel alive unless they have an enemy, and whoever happens to come into their life becomes that enemy. When one enemy goes away, they find another one.

If you're the salesperson bringing in the client, you've got to vet for that. When interviewing them, notice how they treat the gardener, how a couple talks to each other, and how they treat their children. Notice if their attitude—which comes through in every conversation—is filled with distrust: Are they going to be satisfiable?

What do you do if you lose direction in business?

I breathe deeply and look for spiritual guidelines. I have a Christian Science practitioner that I send out an SOS to. What works is pausing, prioritizing, and remembering who you are. Even meditating for sixty seconds really helps. Everyone feels overwhelmed and lost during many periods of life, for a single day or for a week.

2   French: The reason for one's existence.
3   The Seven Habits of Highly Effective People: Powerful Lessons in Personal Change, Stephen R. Covey, Free Press, 1989 (first edition).

If you were to do it over, what would you do differently?

I'd take a psychology degree. Seriously. I think that's what every business owner needs. I had a thirty-year run and was successful because of all the difficult stuff that happened to me before then. If I had started carpentry at eighteen or twenty, I'd have been out by the time I was fifty. It was perfect the way it happened.

What advice have you given most to builders and tradesmen?

Return phone calls—basic things—show up on time. Also, no smoking, no drinking, no cursing, and don't bring your dog to work. Things that seem so simple, that so many contractors have a terrible time with. Listening to people, repeating back what they say so they feel heard; that's vital to success in anything. We did a branding session of interviewing clients and employees, and our tagline became "We never forget it's your home." We taught our people that it was not a job site, but a home.

We had a full-day orientation for new employees. We'd have each department cover different parts of our handbook. The first part was about culture and how we wanted that to be upheld. We included the meaning of integrity and ethics, proper communication, and what to do to maintain high client satisfaction. We discussed what a killer client was and explained that we had their back if they got into a difficult relationship with a client.

What belief or habit has most improved your business or your life?

Listening more, talking less. Listening better.

Did you have rules that you followed in business and if so, what were they?

Absolutely! No smoking, drinking, or cursing; show up on time; return phone calls; show up clean, with a uniformed logo shirt; no hats that say whatever. These are all so basic.

How did you restart when you moved to California?

I was working on getting my contractor's license. You had to show four years' experience, I had three and a half, so I took a home-study class. I was looking for jobs and interviewing, but they did not think a woman could control the job site. A woman painter's team was running into dry rot repair on some of her jobs. She would call me and I would do hourly repair work.

I started getting more and more contacts like that. After a year I hired a woman who was building dollhouses; she had all the tools and knew how to use them.

For two or three years it was just me and Beth. We would remodel bathrooms and kitchens. We had door hangers for marketing. With two people, you only need a few jobs. As I got more repeat jobs and clients and referrals, I hired more people so we could do more work. Eventually, after seven years, I took my tool belt off, we had eight people. As the company got big enough, I needed to do the things only I could do as president.

How do you respond to this idea? If your goal is to be a tradesman, work for someone else. If your goal is to establish and build a significant company, put your tool belt aside and focus on business as soon as it is practical.

It's harder for people in the trades to become businesspeople because they have no training. Because I wasn't a tradesman from the start, I knew all that, and I collected money before the paint was dry. The strength of the working class is that they can work "till the cows come home" and do a good job, and they're proud of it. But work is all the mental stuff too, and if you don't want to do that, it's best if you don't have your own business.

How did you learn to run the business?

I did a lot of home-study courses and workshops. I went to National Kitchen & Bath Association [NKBA][4] three-day workshops. I learned how to draw through NKBA. I joined National Association of the Remodeling Industry [NAIR]^.[5] I joined Business Networks^ and I went to Remodeling Round Tables.[6] Those peer advisory groups were fantastic! When I joined them, we were maybe a $300,000-a-year company, when I left, we were $8 to $10 million, in maybe thirteen years.

Have you had failures that set you up for later success?

Every failure sets you up for later success. We had weekly staff meetings. This question was always on the agenda: "What have you learned that you want others to know?" Say it in a positive way: not placing blame but sharing

---

4   HTTPS://NKBA.ORG
5   HTTPS://WWW.NARI.ORG/
6   HTTPS://WWW.QUALIFIEDREMODELER.COM/EVENTS/

what you would have done differently. People didn't feel they were going to be crucified and this kept them from hiding their mistakes. This really helped.

What was your biggest failure in business?

I was trying to build the company so that I could come out of it over time. I hired and groomed somebody to be president. Within six weeks of promoting her, it was a disaster. We had fights at the managers' meetings—which we'd never had before. I wasn't listened to or invited to meetings. *It was like a seventeen-year-old had taken the keys to my Ferrari and gone away!* I went with her to a counselor. When I said, "If I want to stay in the company till I'm eighty, that's my privilege," she said, "I'm out of here." The founder of a large commercial construction company described it best: "Once it is known you are leaving at some time in the future, the door cannot hit you in the butt fast enough." After all the bad hires I did over the years, I thought I was better at sensing people out.

I had to retake the company. It took me another five years to put the ESOP^ in place. Instead of calling the next person president, he became the general manager. When he did well, he became president; when he became CEO, I was out, but I was on the board of directors. I think an entrepreneur, in general, is unemployable. We don't like having bosses. Even if a construction company had hired me, I'd have been well-behaved, but I would have gone off on my own at some point. I like having control.

How did you decide what to focus on in business?

When the federal government had the rule about companies with female owners getting certain commercial jobs, I got calls that would have taken my focus off residential work. I never let that happen. I became a general contractor because of my personality and my degrees. I'm a generalist, like an orchestra director, I like to put things together so that the team works toward an amazing outcome. I enjoyed painting and carpentry, but being a generalist, making a project happen, to me, is art. It's exciting.

You are in the field, you have seven or eight people working, but you need to pull away to run the business. What does that look like?

I had a carpenter apprentice and one day she took the broom out of my hand and said, "You know, we really need you to go back to the office and sell jobs because I can't do that." It was so visual. I thought, *Ok, I really enjoy being here, but yeah, I've got to go.* I would work in the office in the morning for a couple of hours and then I would go to the job and check on things, I'd do what needed to be done there, and then go back to the office and close whatever I needed to do administratively. As the company grew, I could not keep going to the field. Either I had to be a practice and contain the size so that I could still wear a tool belt or decide to take the next step and build a business. It had to happen because I wanted bigger jobs, I thought they were exciting.

What would you tell a tradesman who wanted to go into business?

Set up systems,[7] learn to do sales, learn how to hire and manage personnel, learn about design and how to work with outside tradespeople. What you must learn seems infinite.

How did you learn to manage money?

I operated kind of as a nonprofit to begin with. I would go out and buy a truck for cash because I thought I shouldn't have any profit at the end of the year, because if I did, I would have to pay taxes on it. It was simplistic thinking. Being in the Business Networks and the Remodelers Roundtable, that was when I learned I needed retained earnings and to invest that in the company. I learned financial management from my partner, she learned it from her mother. She taught me about deferred gratification and 401(k)s.

If you had a method of reaching every builder and tradesmen in the U.S., what would you say?

"The worker is worthy of his hire." It is from the Bible. To me it means you should value your work and not undercharge. Most trades don't charge enough; it is why so many companies go out of business.

What advice would you give people about money?

Some people think that money is evil; it's not. And it doesn't make a person better or not to have it. Money is barter. Resources are bigger than money: water, housing, fresh air. People know they need fresh air and water, and you need money to be able to live. Learning to manage money is the wisdom of using your resources well.

---

7   See the Appendix for Iris's partial list of the systems required to run a construction company.

How did you learn to sell?

I am my mother's daughter. She was a hairdresser and she had her own business. She was brilliant at getting clients, and I watched her do it. We'd be eating out and she would meet somebody at the next table and say, "Oh, my beauty shop is right down the way, let me give you my card for a 10 percent discount, I'd love to see you." So it is natural for me.

I also learned through Sandler Sales.[8] It's considered a soft way of selling in the sense that you go to places to meet people who might need what you have, and you listen to them, and introduce your business without them feeling you are trying to sell something. You start asking questions. I don't think of sales as talking people into something, it's actually filling a need that they may not recognize. That's a real different attitude. I love selling, it's part of my psyche. We have a band and we sell tickets to our concerts. It's creating an event. It's exciting. It's fun.

What single purchase has most positively impacted your life?

Buying the building the company was housed in, as opposed to continuing to rent. It was a retirement investment. It was in Silicon Valley, about a mile and a half from Google, and it was the best single investment we've made.

What about your best and worst customers makes them that?

I like clients who are collaborative and who can articulate what their needs are as opposed to what the answers are. They don't tell you what to do. They say, "Here's what we are trying to resolve, can you help us work on that?" At the same time, they are vigilant about the things that matter to them, and otherwise they just want you to take care of it. I like people who want to move in a straight line, as opposed to having this wobbly thing going on where they get to change their mind every other day. The thrill is getting it completed and changing a person's life by doing that. The worst is the killer client who is never, ever, going to be satisfied with what you or anybody else does. And they are going to take you down if you let them.

How do you shape a new client's expectations?

You do that as part of the sales process: "Here's what we're going to do today, at this meeting. At the end of this meeting, I'm going to ask if you'd

---

[8] HTTPS://WWW.SANDLER.COM/

like to go forward. If you do, we will put together a design contract based on what you've said. Then we will start doing a preliminary design and budget." I'm setting expectations along the way.

Did you bid competitively?

No! It's such a waste of time! There will always be somebody who's willing to do it lower than you and they're never doing the same thing as you.

Did you turn down customers and if so why?

Yes, one killer client, I could smell out right away. He offered me the moon to do the work, but I could tell he was going to be outrageously difficult. He was arrogant and not respectful to his wife. You can't tell them *really* why, because they will become angry and you don't need to do that to yourself. It's not about lying; it's about saving the person's dignity and not getting entangled.

I had a couple of clients that we fired in the middle of the project. That's hard to do in California. We negotiated that we would go to a certain point and they would hire someone else to finish the work. Killer clients will beg you to work for them—they'll try to be on their best behavior—and then they will abuse every employee you have; it's cancerous. At one point, I brought in one of these clients and one of my senior designers brought in another one. We thought, *We can handle them*. But, as I said before, there is nothing you can do to satisfy some people. When I had other salespeople, we tried to teach them to vet for this—but not being the one vetting, I couldn't protect for that.

How would you respond to this Richard Branson quote "Clients do not come first, employees come first. If you take care of your employees, they will take care of the clients."

I don't think those two are mutually exclusive. A happy employee will make the customer happy if they know that's your highest value. It's our job as owners to make sure employees feel valued, and those valued employees must treat the client as if they are our reason for existence.

What did you look for when you hire?

I look for a light in their eyes. It shows they are happy to be alive. I look at how they respond to questions. Are they personable and at the same time professional? We screened for homophobia and sexism. You could see it in their face, no matter what they said. Appearance is important—not a shirt and tie, but looking clean, orderly, cared-for. Also, hiring the right people with the right skills was hard. Women tended to understate their abilities; men tended to overstate theirs. It was hard to figure out who could do what. We set up a day of work to see what they could do. We started having round-robin interviews, with me, the department head, and maybe a peer. Their skills we could find out in a week, but a bad attitude is what really bites you.

What do and don't you expect from employees?

I expect them to produce good work, to be collaborative and hard-working. I respect people who can really work, whether it's at a desk or in the field. There are professional lines that you have to draw, even when you become friends. We did wonderful things like picnics and all kinds of fun things, but my personal life was mine and theirs was theirs.

When did you let people go?

If they were not hard workers. If they didn't have boundaries, like asking inappropriate questions of clients. If they lied or weren't reliable. When we became an employee-owned company, somebody that might have slid by until their performance evaluation, we would get a call and one of the employee-owners would say, "This guy's not working out." They had skin in the game and didn't want that person to get stock in the company!

What books have been important in your life?

The Seven Habits of Highly Effective People, that was important. It taught me how to be a better partner, co-worker, and boss. Also Linda Case's book[9] was important and all of the manuals put out by the National Kitchen & Bath Association. Those were my bibles.

What would you tell a new business owner about marketing and sales?

I kind of see them all together, but marketing is anything that can be tied to you. Everything that you put in writing is part of your marketing plan, and it has to be consistent and represent who you are. Sales, hmmm,

---

9 Mastering the Business of Remodeling; An Action Plan for Profit, Progress, and Peace of Mind, Linda Case and Victoria Downing, 2008, Remodelers Advantage.

you have to make people comfortable and heard and feel that they are talking to a peer, not a slave. Which is a different vantage point.

How did your marketing change over the years?

We learned in the peer groups how important marketing is and ours became very sophisticated. We hired a marketing specialist. He helped us with branding and to understand who we were and how we stood out in the market. He helped us figure out where to do our philanthropy and what kinds of nonprofit boards managers could join to find new clients.

We did community service projects once a year when we had Christmas in April, helping people of low income get their houses fixed. We did Habitat for Humanity. We also had Girl Scout workshops, we called it "Miss Fix-It," for girls, because I wanted to get more girls involved in construction. We were given guidelines from Remodeling Roundtable about how much to spend on marketing; I think it was 1 to 2 percent of gross volume. We did workshops for kitchen and bath remodels. We had annual parties and open houses and invited past clients. We did everything we could think of to bring in new clients and retain past clients.

When work slowed or when you had to much work, what did you do?

That was a fearful time: How are we going to keep the people we've groomed? I did a lot of praying. Trying not to get discouraged. Making more calls to past clients. I had people—during one of the three recessions—say, "I just assumed you were too busy." Never, *ever*, say you're too busy, because it reverberates, right when you need the work. When we had to much work we would hire more help and bring in more subcontractors. We learned to do that better over time, so we didn't hire and then have to let somebody go.

What do you love?

I love pickleball. I love singing and playing music with my band. I love that I feel alive when I'm active. I love getting stuff done!

If you were to lecture to a class of aspiring tradesmen, what would you tell them?

If they don't communicate well, no matter how good they are at the trade, they won't be able to keep a job. Learn how to write well enough to explain a situation or a problem. Learn how to sketch. It's critical that they become well-rounded to support the trade they want to be in.

What would you say about the importance of a general education?

Education is good, it always helps. If you want to be doing complicated jobs, you're going to be around sophisticated people, and you will not feel overshadowed if you have an education, whether it's formal or not. Some people read voraciously. But I think there is something to be said for a formal education. It was helpful to me, even though it wasn't about construction. And people are more interested in connecting with a well-rounded person.

What would you tell these aspiring trades to avoid?

Learn to not work around the clock. Find a hobby. Avoid drugs, smoking, and drinking. Learn to have a good time sober. Look for a good relationship where your partner and you treat each other with respect. A long-term relationship is one of the best teachers about how to live a good life, and it opens doors for professional opportunities because you are satisfied at home.

Describe a successful tradesman.

Someone who does quality work, someone that everybody wants to work with, whether they work beside them or under them, someone who has progressed to the point where they can teach others their trade.

What is the best path to learning a trade and what would you tell an aspiring tradesman to learn first?

Get somebody to hire you. Do something that uses tools. Take workshops on different types of trades. It's a wonderful career. It's a great business. Construction has such a bad reputation that, even if you are middle-of-the-road good, you're gonna be better than most of them. There's a lot of room at the top. I would tell them to learn how to read and write, *really well*, and sketching is important—in a trade you're doing a lot of three-dimensional stuff—learn to sketch in two dimensions. Take a drawing class.

Word Association

Integrity: Personal integrity is about honesty, saying things that you're going to do and then doing them. You're setting expectations. To me it's one of the most important things that any human being can have.

Communication: Do it! Communication lowers anxiety for the boss and the client. People don't do it enough. I have only known one or two people who over-communicate. The thing about bosses is that they are busy; an employee should say, "This is the problem, this is what I think we should do to fix it, are you okay with that?" In essence: *Be bright, be brief, be gone, I have things to do.*

Job safety: A lot of people think of OSHA. I think having a culture that is attractive for people to stay at, where they feel welcomed, appreciated, and their skills are fully utilized, they're listened to, and they don't have to worry about their emotional or physical safety.

Fear: Panic, that's what I think of. Not being paid and not being treated respectfully. My biggest fear is disappointing people. I'm a person pleaser. But I wouldn't be a nurse, I'm fearful of blood.

Company image: It has to be positive, friendly, welcoming. It has to be purposeful and you've got to convey that in a thirty second elevator speech and in your physical image. It's critical.

Gratitude: A *very important* requirement. Daily. Hourly. About everything: breathing, sunlight, that you can walk, that you could see, that you have the opportunity to serve someone. Gratitude is such an important part of being able to experience joy in life.

Cut-Offs

I took advantage of the fact that I was different. For instance, in Dallas, our marketing was specifically targeted to lesbian couples and Republican widows who do not want strange men in their house. [*Laughter.*] I'm not talking about reality, it's perception, it's about taking advantage of people's preconceptions.

When I advise a potential client, I tell them that they want a company with a deep bench; if the first quarterback is injured, enter quarterback number two. And that the contractor has a good credit rating and that they are comfortable doing the kind of work their being asked to do.

There were earlier women in the trades with a chip on their shoulder. That doesn't win you anything; you don't get clients, you don't get employees, you don't get along with people.

I took Walt Stoeppelwerth's[10] workshop and he taught that it is critical to turn down a job that you are going to lose money on, because, once you get sucked into a job that's taking money from you, you're not free to take a job that will make money.

A lot of tradespeople think you're not working if you're not making noise and sawdust. Just because you're not hammering, doesn't mean it's not work.

Sometimes people get so caught up in community service projects that they get distracted from their business.

I chose residential work because I had more chance of closing jobs if a woman was involved as a decision maker. That's what's so wonderful about being an entrepreneur; you are creating your own world and learning to collaborate with others.

---

10 Walt died in 2013. He was the founder of Home Tech estimating software and an early spokesman for professionalism in the residential construction industry. He spoke adamantly about the need for residential contactors to use a 50 percent markup. My favorite line of his: "Only 5 percent of remodelers run their business; the other 95 percent let their business run them."

The only person you are destined to become
is the person you decide to be.

Ralph Waldo Emerson

David Gerstel,
Retired General Contractor

https://davidgerstel.com/

At the time of this interview David was turning seventy-four. He is a builder and author of construction books. His most recent book, Nail Your Numbers,[1] was published in 2019. We became friends at the time EOB was published and have since spent many hours in phone and face-to-face conversations and countless emails discussing the issues builders must address to succeed in business. David let me into his home—he had an email to finish—and while I waited, I looked around his office. It reminded me of an Amishman's office: matter-of-fact, with everything well used and kept, I imagined, only if it served a purpose. The contents of the bookshelf were dogeared and bags of tools sat ready by the door.

> *If there's any idea I embrace, it's the paradoxical one that being right is just about impossible* ∎ *My dad would say, "The only use of an answer, David, is it gives you a couple more interesting questions to address"* ∎ *Acquisition is not freedom* ∎ *An awful lot of the marketing I see strikes me as not producing a return equal to its cost* ∎ *I mentored my crew when learning opportunities arose* ∎ *They must have a class in architecture school called Arrogance 101*

In college I was being propelled by family tradition and my professors toward academics or the law. I wanted to work with my hands—and I told them so—which was puzzling to the professors, though my parents understood.

---

1 Nail Your Numbers: A Path to Skilled Construction Estimating & Bidding, David Gerstel, Latitude 67, 2019.

I was an athlete and I had a notion that I wanted a more physical life. I conceived, somehow, that I'd find that through learning to work with my hands. When I was a kid, I was naturally attracted to making things. I loved being in the basement shop of a neighbor, who made cedar boxes, smelling that delicious odor, and seeing these beautiful things come together. Another neighbor built hot rods. I loved hanging out in his garage, being around the tools and his competence. That was laid aside as I got into my teens and I was absorbed by sports, which satisfied that physical urge.

When I finished college, I wanted to learn to work with my hands. I had no idea what that entailed or what trade I might take up. I got lucky, I had a roommate who was an architect and a good amateur carpenter, and we worked at a school for kids and we built things. Then I got really lucky. I was living in a large collective that had a strong construction division where all kinds of trades were practiced. I did a bit of sheet metal and electrical work. I met our two top carpenters, Chris and Ted, brilliant carpenters. One of them became a friend; he said, "Dave, if you are going to do this, become a carpenter, because a carpenter runs the job, and you're not gonna be happy not running the job."

I was bewitched by what these guys did. I was taken with it as an athletic endeavor. Chris, my primary mentor, was a high-level athlete, he loved baseball and carpentry. I loved the way he moved and handled his tools and materials—like a point guard in basketball—and how the materials flowed together guided by the tools. It was mystifying and quite beautiful. I was intrigued by the sequencing of tasks in construction, and totally befuddled by it. It was a struggle to figure out how people knew when to bring in materials and move the next trade in and send another one on their way. Now it's so clear, you know, but then, I loved trying to solve that puzzle.

As I moved on from working with Chris and Ted, I got into house building in the Bay Area in the early '70s. I started looking for a job, but I did not realize we were in the midst of one of the worst recessions to grip this country. I'd get on a bus and take it for miles, writing down the address of every construction job, and then I'd walk from one to the other asking for work. I developed a quick three-line pitch, 'cause I knew foremen were busy. And I'd get a job; it'd last three days, three weeks, or three months and it was over. I went through something like three dozen different jobs on my way to becoming a journeyman^. Until finally I got a job on a union project, a big apartment building.

In all of these jobs I'm learning how to install foundations of many different kinds. I learned how to frame and these guys were real production framers. I ran joists and laid subfloor and stood up a lot of walls. My mentor, who was the best carpenter there, did all the exterior trim—it was good training—and that lasted a year. I got introduced to union culture which I found sad; there was no pride in the work and all day long these guys were saying things like, "Nail her, it's good enough for the girls we know."

The next union job I got was working with a trim carpenter, an old-timer, and after a week he said, "David, get out of the union. All they care about now is money and you're not gonna be happy with that. There are guys around who are doing really good work, find them." I had my journeyman's card, I knew how to put in a foundation, frame, and trim. I quit. I was in my late twenties.

A friend bought a $10,000 shack in Berkeley. He asked me to renovate it with him. When that was done, I went off looking for a job as a carpenter. I could not get one. I went back to riding the bus and knocking door to door. That didn't work at all. My friend needed a couple of garages built. So I built them. I realized, *This is nice, I'm my own boss*. I got other projects and was making what I thought was great money—less than in the union if you figured in the benefits—but I wasn't smart enough about money yet to figure that out.

My wife said, "Why don't you go into business and get your general contractors license." But I had never considered going into business. It was an alien world to me. I told Sandra, "That's impossible, I could never pull that off." But she gave me a push and I took it seriously. I studied the manuals, the California state ones about how to become a GC, which were total garbage. I headed out with my license. Early on I was doing time and material (T&M)^, and I doubt if I had contracts.

I can tell you about the next big moment. I was hiring people and beginning to understand the need for markup; there were costs to having employees. I was moseying along in that fashion and I met a guy who had a solid, sixty-five-year-old at the time, remodeling company. He wanted me to become a subcontractor for him and he recognized that I needed to understand business. He invited me into a group called the Building Industry Association Remodelers Council [BIA]^. I started going to their meetings and I heard talks on overhead, markup, and contracts, and I began to realize there were components that needed to be in place to have a business and that I better do that.

You are working in the field and beginning to do office work. How are you feeling about that transition?

I jumped in *hard*. I liked the work, I was engaged by it, and I realized I could make a lot more money than I could working for wages. I liked figuring out what needed to be in a contract. So I wrote one. I built bidding and estimating systems. I set up accounting. I enjoyed that stuff. I liked the guys that I met at the BIA meetings, especially the guys who broke off and formed the Splinter Group^. These guys were very, very smart and they were grappling with the same business issues that I was. We met regularly. We shared ideas. We taught one another how to run a construction company.

When you began in the industry, did you have long-term goals?

Not exactly goals but, sort of a dream. I wanted to create an institution and write a book about it that would be a candle to help other people find their way. The idea came, first of all, from reading a book called *Summerhill*.² It's about a radical English free school. I read books which inspired the social side of my ambitions, but I was more utopian by nature, not political. I couldn't have said it in so many words when I was young, but I can see there were three things I wanted from a work life: maximum personal freedom and intense physical and mental engagement. Then there was this dream of creating an institution and writing a book about it, but all I knew were schools—all my people were professors—so I always imagined the enterprise would be a school, not realizing I didn't actually like school. [*Laughter.*]

There's a great irony here. I've written a book called *Running A Successful Construction Company*³, but the guy who wrote that book didn't know, early on, what the words "overhead" or "spreadsheet" meant. I knew nothing about business. My book came about through happenstance. I chanced to

---

2   Summerhill: A Radical Approach to Child Rearing, Alexander Sutherland Neill, Hart Publishing Company, 1960.

3   Running a Successful Construction Company (revised), David Gerstel, The Taunton Press, 2002. The first edition was published in 1992, when David was thirty-seven.

meet the West Coast editor for *Fine Homebuilding [FHB]*^ magazine in a coffee shop and he was looking for builders to write for them. I told him I was a builder and that I had done a lot of writing. He recruited me. I wrote two articles about organizing job sites, which they liked and were going to publish. I thought, *Oh, God, this will be so embarrassing because this is such obvious stuff, everybody knows this.* I did not understand what a challenge organization is for a lot of people. *FHB* published the articles and got a lot of enthusiastic letters. Deva Rajan,[4] one of my heroes, gave a copy of the article to everyone in his company.

I decided I should write a book about how to run a construction company, only to discover that I didn't know much yet and had little to say on the subject! [*Laughter.*] Fortunately, by that time, I was in the Splinter Group and I was learning along with the other guys. The way I see my book is, I learned ideas from the group and I put them into my company to try them out and sorted and refined them, then put them into my book. It took me about six years to write it.

What advice have you given most to builders and tradesmen?

That the construction industry as a whole is a not-for-profit business. I can't prove it, but I suspect it operates at a net loss over the long term. Second, understand, that to avoid being one of the losers, you must learn how to minimize overhead and not to confuse the so-called cultivation of a "professional image" with astutely investing your capital. And third, along with creating a highly efficient, low overhead operation, you must learn to estimate accurately and bid appropriately. It is hard, hard work. Developing good procedures takes a lot of self-training.

Did you have absolute rules in your company?

We didn't have rules so much as ethics and principles that we tried to adhere to. We were an employee-centered company with generous profit sharing—the most generous among construction firms in our area, according to one survey. We treated employees with respect, giving them as much autonomy as they could handle without compromising quality. The guys worked four days, thirty-eight hours a week, instead of five days and forty hours. They loved it.

4   Deva is interviewed in *BUILDER*.

And candor with clients. We told them when we hit a problem and how we planned to solve it. We completely disclosed our numbers in our estimates. We did not hide profit in direct production costs. Our clients paid us for creating estimates, and they deserved to get every bit of the work product. We owed it to them to make our numbers transparent. Those are some of the principles that really mattered to me.

Did you do marketing?

No, we didn't do the stuff that people are referring to when they talk about marketing. We didn't even have job site signs. My idea of marketing was dead simple: hire serious people—carpenters and trades—with a passion for producing good work and support them in every way. Do that, and they will take care of the projects and clients, and the clients will be your sales force.

A marketing program should be low-cost and simple and do one thing: amplify the good feelings that satisfied clients have about you and enable the people they tell, to locate you via an attractive, good-humored, low-cost website. Sending out a thank-you letter to every client on Thanksgiving—that might be good marketing. And stay in touch with your clients or they might forget you.

Did you have long-term goals for your company?

No. Because I think it's silly. Warren Buffet said that business plans are silly, and at the time I read that, I had not done any, so I decided that I was really smart not doing them. Create a company that can turn on a dime, adapt, and hunker down to ride out recessions. Set goals, write out your plans, and the market will make confetti of them the next day.

How long were you in business—lets define it as when you had employees—and when and why did you close it?

I rolled the company up when I was about fifty. So about two decades. It was a conscious decision, but it started at an unconscious level, I was bored. We were doing sixteen-month-long projects, including complex reconstructions of dilapidated large homes. Even so, it was not challenging anymore. The learning curve had flattened. I had created a portfolio of investments that generated income several times my family's living cost, because we live simply. And my employees were starting to bang their heads against the ceiling, they really needed to form their own companies.

I didn't want to sell the company. If the company were operating as David Gerstel Builder and I wasn't there, that would have been a fraud. Also, I wanted to do projects here and there and I wanted to do them under my own name. Plus, I think, if somebody buys somebody else's construction company, they have made a bad financial decision. If you have what it takes to run a construction company, you have what it takes to build one, and if you build your own, you won't be working with the burden of debt that comes from purchasing someone else's company.

Do you have any memorable mistakes?

We got a job putting a new foundation under a wonderful Victorian home. I looked at the job and thought, *I know what this is going to cost*. I blew out an estimate, more or less on the back of an envelope. We probably covered our out-of-pocket overhead—only because our overhead was so low—but we did not make a dime to pay me and we certainly didn't make a profit. But we loved the clients and their kids loved the carpenters. They named their stuffed pets after them; that was the profit.

What do you do if you lose direction in your business?

I don't, at least not about work, because I am constantly proactive; and because I'm a compulsive organizer and planner and anticipator, I don't get to the point where I get lost.

Did formal education help in your career?

Sometimes I think that the essential education that I make use of, I had by the time I finished sixth grade. Thank you, Mrs. Cross! Beyond that, I'm not sure much of the formal education was valuable. Although high school geometry and algebra were helpful, and I value my study of history in college. We're all whipsawed by history, and particularly in construction. If the country has a recession, construction has a depression. If the country has a prosperous period, construction has a boom. Studying history helps you understand how fast things can go from good to bad and that you better be ready for both.

Was there a decision to stay in residential work?

No. When somebody called about a job, I didn't care what the job was or what size it was. I would talk to them on the phone for a bit. If they seemed candid, I'd say, "Let me come over and we will talk." I'd tell them we don't do free bids and if they were going for free bids, I'd tell them how to do it so they didn't get wrecked by the process. If they were interested, I'd tell them about our approach. If I thought the customer and I wouldn't mind having each other in our lives for whatever period of time, I would take on the project.

You are working with your tools, you begin to work in the business, was there a conflict between the field and the office?

My learning curve in carpentry had flattened. I was good at the basic stuff and felt I could figure out how to build just about anything. But the learning curve for business was steep and therefore exciting. So I took to it. For a while I did both. I was working on the job all day and talking to prospective clients and building my business systems at night. During that period, I worked long hours, but that didn't last long. A guy wandered onto my job, I hired him, and he grew to be an incredible lead carpenter, that happened a couple more times. At some point, I said, "You guys take over the jobs," and I stepped away.

How do you respond to this idea? If your goal is to be a tradesman, work for someone else. If your goal is to build a significant company, put your tool belt aside and focus on business as soon as it is practical.

I don't agree with that. I think it's too absolutist and I know of too many exceptions.

Talk about managing money and how you learned to do that.

There was a foundation from early childhood. My parents were frugal. Probably with their encouragement, I was saving money at an early age. I figured out ways to make money and I saved it up for things I wanted. Then I got together with Sandra, my wife, who is also careful with money. We bought our house when mortgage rates were approaching 14 percent. We didn't know that was high, we didn't understand that mortgage payments were part principal and part interest. That's how much we knew about money. When I realized we had to pay interest every month, that was intolerable to me! [*Laughter.*] Sandra had a good job and I was working hard and eleven months later we had paid off the mortgage. As a result we had low personal overhead.

I learned, over a few years, to charge market rates and markup for my wages as job leader and salary as company manager. Because we spent so little on personal stuff, money piled up quickly, and I began wondering what to do with it. I stumbled into a real estate agent, he said I should invest in property. So I started buying real estate. Cash kept piling up. I thought, *I gotta learn what to do with all this money.* I started prowling around for books and stumbled across *The Wealthy Barber*, which laid out the possibilities that arise from investing in stocks and bonds. The book was a little too cheery, too cute, but the author mentioned two financial sages, Warren Buffett, and John Bogle. I studied their writings. I learned about Ben Graham—Warren Buffett's mentor—and got his book, *Intelligent Investor*[5], and read it four times. That gave me my investment strategy. I had a brief fling at investing in individual stocks but realized that was a full-time profession, and not the one I wanted to be in, so I started investing in index funds, buying during down markets, holding for the long term, and enjoying the miracle of compounding.

Did you actively mentor employees?

I did, constantly. I'm compulsive about mentoring. It was informal, but we did have a weekly safety meeting. When it came to the trades, I'd pull somebody aside and show them a trade trick. I bought guys subscriptions to *JLC*^ and *FHB* and said, "Read them cover to cover every month, it will really accelerate your learning." We had a profit-sharing program and I tried to steer them toward investing their share. Some did, others spent the money as soon as they got it.

If you were in front of a group of tradesmen planning to go into business, what would you tell them to do first? What to avoid?

Do not start on your own until you have a plan for all of the fundamental systems that you need and have them in place. You need a simple marketing plan and estimating/bidding procedures and systems. You need accounting software and you've gotta learn how to operate it. You need

5   The Intelligent Investor, Benjamin Graham, Harper, 2005.

to understand what a capital reserve account is and build one. Don't start on your own until all of that's in place. Avoid trying to shortcut on any of these steps.

If you had a method of reaching every builder and tradesmen in the U.S., what would you say?

Learn to make money by making buildings kinder to the environment so that we don't destroy the world.

What is great success in business?

When I look around and see construction companies that I admire, they're doing work that makes the builder, the crew, and the subs proud, the client happy, and the job sites are clean and safe—I call that success. If I get a chance to look under the hood and I see that the company is being run in a financially sustainable manner, that it is built to weather recessions and thrive during good times, that's even better.

Where did you learn to sell?

I was a tennis coach from the time I was sixteen and I taught in Upward Bound[6] in college. I love teaching. As I established my construction company, I had friends who were taking some of those slick sales programs. I did not like what I heard. I thought they were learning to manipulate people. But they also said things that rang true, like, "When you go in to meet a client for the first time, it's not about you, it's about them and their project. You listen, that's your first job."

I did not sell, I listened and then I educated. I loved talking to people about their project and about how the building business and buildings work. Sometimes I'd talk to people for hours and it would result in a job and sometimes they would realize, *We better not do this*.

On one hand you are listening, on the other you are teaching?

I'm listening carefully, to get a sense of their hopes and knowledge and the realities around budget. The teaching is about helping them understand what lies between them and realizing their vision. I'm talking, and I'm continuing asking questions. I'm explaining how competitive bidding works

---

6   Upward Bound is a federally funded educational program. It is one of a cluster of programs now referred to as TRiO, which owe their existence to the federal Economic Opportunity Act of 1964 (War on Poverty Program) and the Higher Education Act of 1965. Wikipedia

and what the reality of that is, and, if they want to go that route, how to do it most effectively to have some hope of success. I also explain that I don't bid competitively.

What is your alternative to competitive bidding?

I call it cost planning. The owner hires a capable builder, with strong estimating skills, to join the project at the very beginning. The builder and the owner find an architect, or maybe the designer comes first. AIA^ calls what I do IPD [Integrated Project Development]. With IPD the designer brings in a builder immediately, not when the plans are complete, and particularly for value engineering^. The cost figures the builder provides are important, they help the designer get the desired result in the most cost-effective manner. It is so obvious that you need a good builder teamed up with the owner and designer from the outset if you want to avoid a change order battlefield and adversarial relationships.

What's the best investment you've ever made?

My marriage. Sandra is an extraordinary person and a wonderful partner.

What makes your best and worst customer?

The customer who accepts cost planning—who, when they hear that nailing down the cost of construction is going to take a lot of work, that it will benefit them, and that we need to charge for that work. They are not trying to get the service for free and they say, "We want to work with you and this is part of what you're gonna do for us, of course we are going to pay for that."

I love the really bad customers! I've had so much fun with them. I got a kick out of making them behave themselves. I had a cluster of customers who were real difficult, but I never had a bad customer. What makes for the worst customer is a cowardly contractor who wants everybody to like him, who's afraid to stand up for himself at the risk of upsetting the client. There are real sociopaths out there, but even those guys can't severely damage you if you've properly built your bidding, estimating, and contracting systems and are running your jobs and company properly.

Did you ever turn down a potential customer?

There's one guy I would have turned down, but I don't think they actually asked me to do the job. He was the chief counsel for the AFL-CIO. I had a sense about this guy, I didn't want him in my life. There was a ruthlessness about him. I had a couple of other clients who were bullies and I enjoyed handling them, but I just did not want to do it again.

Has an apparent failure set you up for later success?

Lesson learned: don't shortcut estimating, even for small jobs.

What do you expect from employees and how did you let people go?

Steady effort. Passion for the work, want it to be strong and durable and good looking. Integrity: Don't cover up defects. Don't hide mistakes—fix them. Ask questions. It's an axiom: hire people who are better at what they do than you are, because you'll learn from them.

I let people go, twice that I can recall, because of bad behavior. Maybe half a dozen times it was because we didn't need them any longer, but typically those guys were hired knowing it was for a specific job. The way I fired the couple of bad guys was, "Calvin, you got to straighten this out and be quick about it and here's the exact changes you've got to make. I told you once; I'm telling you again, this time it's in writing; the third time, you're done."

What's a bad tradesman?

Doesn't care about the work, makes mistakes and covers them up. Tries to hide whenever he has a chance to goof off, carries a smartphone around with him and is on social media or texting every chance he gets. Is rude to the people on the crew. Is a know-it-all.

Looking back on your career, is there anything that you would do differently?

No. I've lived my dream. I became a carpenter. I've written five books. I loved writing them and hearing from readers that the books are helping them. I got to have a wonderful, compact construction company with great human beings with integrity, passion, concern for others, and a real commitment to the quality of work. Many of them are friends to this day. I achieved, at an early age, financial independence—that's important because that is freedom. I didn't know that when I was younger.

Word Association

Integrity: A nail set properly in shear panel. [*Laughter.*] Not overdriven, not underdriven, set properly, and if it's not, you fix it.

Company image: If you've got a problem on the job you let the owner know. You tell them, "We can approach this in several ways, what would you like?" You keep people informed. You give the best, clearest answer you can. Also, if people try to bully you and take advantage of you, you don't allow it. You have a right to dignity and respect, just as they do.

Job safety: Safety goggles.

Fear: Climate turbulence. What is it going to do to these beautiful, organic things that now exist on our planet?

Gratitude: Appreciated, by them and by me.

Overhead: Burden and opportunity.

Profit: Protection.

Marketing: Sieve.

Sales: Slick.

Estimating: Craft.

Employees: Colleagues.

Cut-Offs

As a young carpenter, every day, after work, I'd stand and stare at the building and try to figure out what had happened that day and why. After a while I got it, and I could see a building as a three-dimensional diagram and see all the parts coming together. Of course that took years.

By pure chance, I was nudged into a world that perfectly fit my aptitudes. The result was that none of it was ever hard in the sense of being a miserable grind. It was challenging because I'm relentless and thorough and there was an awful lot to absorb, but it wasn't hard in the sense of creating frustration, disappointment, or failure. It just somehow came to me and was always satisfying. It still is.

When people were considering us for their project, it felt like a warm gesture to me and I felt appreciated.

I have come around to thinking that, maybe, more marketing would have been smart, it might have given us even better leads to choose from.

In fact, I would sometimes do a job even if I thought the client would be difficult, because these were the people who taught me the most about how to be both patient and firm.

Four common construction delusions:
My labor is covered
At least I broke even
One big job will fix everything
I'll make up for it on the next job
Melanie Hodgdon

Bill M. Fink,
Retired General Contractor

wmfink91@gmail.com
finkaboutit.net

Bill is now retired, although he does woodworking and writes for the local newspaper. He grew up in the business and when working as a general contractor he did many types of construction, from steel and drywall, to building restaurant chains, to fine carpentry, to various types of residential projects.

> *I always made sure my financing was in place ■ I went to court many times, but never lost, because I had a good attorney ■ There are two right answers, yes or no, there is no I'll try ■ I spent a long time learning what's a good job and what's a bad job ■ With all the moving parts, it is no wonder so few succeed in construction ■ A good job runs on good paperwork ■ The ability to deal with people is innate ■ Learn your trade well, then learn all the trades that come before and after you ■ A customer who beats me down for every nickel, I'm going to find a cheaper way to do their job ■ The building business is a hard business and I sacrificed family a lot. I'm sorry I did. It is one of my regrets*

I was always in the construction business, at times in residential, then corporate, then as a subcontractor, then a general contractor. Mostly I did commercial work, primarily restaurants, bars, and food facilities. It was a nice niche. A dinner house contract in the '80s was 7,500 square feet, a million or a million-two. My company did about five million a year as a sole proprietorship.

My dad was a builder. He was single when I was young, and there was no daycare, so I went to construction jobs as a youngster. My first job was collecting bottles on site. As I got older, I was sweeping the sites. Then I was sanding walls for painters, carrying brick and hod[1] for masons, and working on carpentry crews. He moved me around so I got lots of experience. There was no formal training beyond this. When I started there were no schools, and construction degrees were in their infancy. I came from an era when you started off in a trade, moved to supervision—generally as a foreman in your trade—and if you were sharp, you became an assistant superintendent and then a superintendent.

What's the most rewarding and the most difficult thing about running a construction company?

The most rewarding is when you are paid a fair price for the product and are able to deliver the job, on time, on budget, with good quality. The most difficult, hmmm, being short on money. Being pressed so hard you negotiate a poor payment schedule, where your payment gets back-ended and you're strung out.[2]

You have to learn to be hard in this business. The construction industry is different from many other businesses because of the numbers of people involved—it takes fifty to a hundred subs and supplies to complete a project—and those people run the gamut from the highly educated and extremely knowledgeable to the lowly laborer. Any one of them can damage the flow and consequently the profitability of a job. As a company runs multiple projects, that difficulty increases. Most people want to be liked and don't want to be the bearer of bad news, but you often have to do just that as a construction manager. It was the hardest facet of the business for me. Success often comes down to how hard you can be—not mean or angry—but willing to make and enforce hard decisions when that is what is required. A lot of people won't or can't do that.

Do you have an academic education?

I have a couple of years of liberal arts. I went to Northeastern University; it was called a co-op school. We went full time the first year and the next

---

1 Hod is a trough with a wooden pole handle, carried on the shoulder to bring brick and mortar to masons.
2 Back-ended means the payment schedule pushes the bulk of the payment toward the end of the job. Strung out means you are running the job without enough money to operate normally. This arrangement hurts the customer as much as the builder because decisions are made based on poor cash flow instead of what is best for the job.

four years we'd spend three months in school and three months working in the field. Three months in, three months out. I traveled a lot when I was out and worked construction. I was bored with college and just as I went back after three months out, I got a job offer from a company in Maryland, where I had worked as a laborer, about an opening as an assistant superintendent.

How long did you work for other companies and did it help in your career?

I worked for a number of companies. Did it help me? *Absolutely!* I advanced quickly from superintendent to project manager. A company in California sent me to Oregon to open a new division as vice president of construction, I was twenty-six. I learned the good and bad about business. I learned to trust my instincts about who I was dealing with, and the way I developed those instincts is by numbers. Numbers tell the whole story in construction and this is why you have to know your costs. If you don't know the price of labor, material, overhead, workmen's comp, and taxes, you don't know what a job costs and you're depending on subs to tell you what the price should be. That's not the way to do it. First you estimate the cost, then you buy that job.^ A good buyer knows the numbers of the trades and materials he is buying. Consequently, the bids he receives are no surprise. The end result should be putting the most qualified subs at the right price on your job. Then you have a win-win situation and you both make money.

I also learned that the low bid, in most cases, can be rejected because the sub forgot something or didn't consider the construction schedule. The tendency is to go with the low number but replacing that sub in the middle of the job—because their work suffers from their low bid—is costly in time, money, and the legal action that may follow. And I speak with the low bidder because they might have a tactic I hadn't considered and I want to know why they are low. Same holds true for higher bids. Typically they have a more inclusive scope-of-work and production schedule than required. On the other hand, they might just have too much fluff in the bid or run an inefficient operation.

Did you have long-term goals when you started your business?

Yes. I wanted to be a successful builder and retire early, to make a lot of money, to build nice projects. I had a general contracting company and

I moved into other businesses, so I was able to maintain some income. If I go through New Jersey today, and see the jobs I worked on as a kid, or tradesman, I'll say, "I built that house. Oh, and I built that Blockbuster and fifteen others." I identify with the jobs. If you're a schlock builder you don't take pride in what you produce, it's just another job. I left the building business before I met my goals. My divorce was the main reason.

What do you do if you lose direction in business?

I ask, *What's going wrong here?* I take quiet time to reevaluate. I resort to my basic construction philosophy that I learned from my father: production, budget, quality. You can't have tremendous production without sacrificing the budget and quality. But you can watch the budget so carefully that you sacrifice production. These three things have to work in harmony.

What big mistakes did you make in business?

Not passing on jobs when the margins were too low. I built a chain of restaurants, and the market was getting bad, so I bid one with 7 percent profit. Typically I ran 15 percent overhead and 10 percent or more profit. The reason I was able to make 7 percent work is that I took over from my project managers who were really under the gun, and we made the difference up in hard buying.[3] I did okay on that job, not like in the past, but okay. The next one we did I bid at 4 percent, and we didn't get it because somebody took it at cost. I called the guy and said, "Are you out of your mind?" He said, "Bill, I gotta keep the doors open." I got to a point where I said to myself, *I don't need to keep the doors open. If I'm doing this for exercise, it's too hard.* You bid 4 percent and have one blowup and lose 10 percent or more.

What do you wish you had done differently?

The easy answer is, I wouldn't have gotten into the business. [*Laughter.*] But I grew up in it and I *really* liked it. I liked the camaraderie of the men and women I worked with. I saw how hard my family worked and I saw how rewarding it can be. What I loved, when we got done, there was a monument to our effort that will outlast me. Coming up in the trades and the business, that was the easy part. The difficult part was managing money. I would tell

---

3   Hard buying, Bill's definition: "Negotiating the scope-of-work with subs to eliminate the fat they allow in their bid for contingencies, and in return the general contractor must perform so that the subcontractors won't need those contingencies. You also play subcontractors off each other, because there is a lot of competition for the work you are offering."

any youngster, "Learn math, accounting, overhead, and law, because these are the areas that will impact you."

What advice would you give to young tradesmen?

I'd say if you want to be a tradesman, start early, you'll make a good income and it will be hard physically. If you want to run the company, learn your trade, go to school—any kind of school—get a broad education. Study economics and math, it will help. And I would say, "Keep your eyes open wide to the world around you." That year and a half I spent on the road was the best education I ever had. I learned construction is a hard business and there are evil people who will gravitate to the lowest form of making a buck.

Do you know what question is missed most often in the California contractor's exam? "How do you determine profit and overhead?" If you ask nine out of ten people, "If you have a $100,000 job, and you need to make 25 percent profit and overhead, how much are you going to charge for the job?" Most will say "Twenty-five grand," which is not the answer. It's thirty-three.[4] At twenty-five, you might cover overhead, but you're not making profit. Compound that over a few million dollars, and you're losing a lot of money.

How did you learn about business?

Being exposed to trades for all those years I was growing up, I learned a good job from a bad job. I was in a number of businesses, framing and drywall/steel. Those were both fairly large companies. I had been general contracting when I was young, picking up jobs, often doing them on weekends. I learned estimating and hiring by working in other companies.

Do you have any failures that set you up for later success?

Sure. The biggest failure would be taking a job that was too cheap, even when I knew it was too cheap. I thought, somehow, I would make it work. I learned to walk away. It was painful if they wanted me to do it, but putting my money in a job is more painful. So I asked myself, *What hurts more?*

---

4   Bill's method for arriving at the final number: "To determine how you make a 25 percent profit, subtract 25 from 100, you get 75. Divide $100,000 by 75 percent to get your true profit and overhead of $33,000 [rounded]."

If you were to start again, what would you do differently?

I would have no-nonsense, numbers-oriented accountants and project managers. I would have an excellent attorney. I would run the company on the numbers. There's no room for gut feeling in this business, the dollars are way too big.

What didn't you like about being in business?

The pressure. A lot of it was self-inflicted. I felt dedicated to my employees, everybody gets paid, every week, whether I did or not. Sometimes my payday waited until retention was paid.

How did you decide what to focus on in business?

It was a combination of drift and opportunity: I'd drift around and see where there was an opportunity. When I started building restaurants, construction was booming, restaurants were the last bastion of real quality work and there weren't that many of us doing it. It's a different general contractor that builds a restaurant than builds a commercial building: different codes, trades, furniture, fixtures, and equipment. I was dealing with high-end trades—electricians, HVAC, plumbers—I really liked that.

When you were working in the trades and beginning to run your business, was there a conflict?

Not being on the job to do some of the high-end work was hard. I wanted to work with my tools, but I was going to the jobs making sure that they were running right. I never resolved that conflict.

How do you respond to this idea? If your goal is to be a tradesman work for someone else. If your goal is to establish and build a significant company put your tool belt aside and focus on business as soon as it is practical.

The age-old conflict is, when you put your toolbelt down, will the work suffer? Do you trust your guys enough? When the work doesn't meet your standard, are you going to let it slide or go into your pocket to make it right? If you're there all the time, you can head that off.

What is the most important thing to learn when starting a construction business?

Know your trade. The intangible thing, that some people have, and some don't, is how well do you deal with people. I don't know if you can develop people skills. You've got to learn to sell yourself. You've got to know your costs and know what to charge. I can't tell you one is more important than the other.

How did you learn to manage money?

If you can't get skinny yourself, if you don't have that ability, you're in trouble. I don't know how you learn it; it's a work ethic, I think. Every time I made money, I tried to stash it away. You have to be strict. You have to sacrifice when it comes to money, and if you can't do that, you're a schmuck, because you're not going to be able to pay somebody.

Did you actively mentor people?

Yes. All the time. It worked wonderfully on some and was a total failure with others. We did not do it formally, but if I thought someone had potential, I worked with them. I imparted my philosophy; production, budget, quality.

What would you tell a group of tradesmen about going into business?

Be ready for sacrifice. It's your other child. It's *very* time consuming, you have to make sure you have the time. I had one strict rule, I didn't bring a briefcase home. Thank God we didn't have cell phones!

If you had a method of reaching every builder and tradesmen in the U.S., what would you say?

Lead good people from behind; your job is to eliminate their obstacles. Also, I'd ask, "What can you teach me?"

What is great success in a construction business?

The greatest success is making a fair profit and having an organization that shares in your success.

How did you learn to sell?

Are you kidding, my whole family is from Brooklyn, I heard it my whole life! [*Laughter.*] On my travels, one of the jobs I had was selling Kirby vacuum cleaners door to door. But selling is more than a natural ability to talk, you need to know your product and your talking points. You need to know what you can deliver. Integrity is the final word on selling. My eyes are wide open, I'm looking right in their face and I'm talking straight from the shoulder.

Name an important investment that you made.

My kids. Also, I sponsored a Mexican cruise for purchasing agents once. It really paid off.

What made your best and worst customer?

They pay on time and a fair price. They are a repeat customer because they recognize our worth. One of the best companies I worked for was Carl's Jr. back in the '80s. When our check was always ready on the date it was due and they called to let us know. If there was a problem on the job site, they came out and asked, "How can we help?" They knew there was no point beating the GC down, that was not going to get it built faster.

The worst is slow pay. Busts your chops over every little change. Talks to your subs personally. "Don't ever come onto my job and direct my subs. You talk to me. I talk to them." My subs were directed to tell the customer to go through me or my superintendent, who was always on the job.

Did you turn down customers, and if so why?

Yes. As a sub—all the trades talk about slow payers—so they had a reputation and we would not bid for them. In residential jobs, it was the overbearing know-it-alls we avoided.

How would you respond to this quote by Richard Branson: "Clients do not come first. Employees come first. If you take care of your employees, they will take care of the clients."

They're both up there; clients and employees are your lifeblood.

What do you look for when hiring?

Work ethic. Their age and what they've accomplished. If they say, "Yeah, I can do that and I can't do that, or I'll try." The I'll try guys, don't make it for me. I've had my failures in hiring, obviously.

What do you and don't you expect from employees?

Dedication. I never told a superintendent or project manager how many hours they need to be on the job, my schedule told them that. I said, "If you can finish this job in forty hours a week, God bless yeah, but if you have to be there on Saturday and Sunday, you need to be, and you will be nicely compensated." I expect a very good job, done on time, and on budget. Production, budget, quality. I don't care if you're mean and grumpy, if you're giving me the product, God bless yeah. I get along with all kinds of people. I expect them to work as hard or harder than me, because I want them to take my job. What I don't expect is that they suck up to me. I just hate that.

When do you let people go, how do you do that?

I let them go for poor performance or causing conflict in the company. I told people when I hired them, "When it comes time—and there's always a time—you can count on two weeks from me." If they stole from me, that was different, they didn't get anything. I wasn't yelling or screaming. I'd just say, "It's time, you need to be out of here today." Otherwise they spread poison.

When did you let subs go?

Non-performance, not performing according to schedule. That was like stealing. That happened rarely. Also, if I was getting notices in from their suppliers that they weren't being paid, that was a problem.

What's a bad tradesman?

Bad habits. Shows up at nine thirty and leaves at three. If the plumber has solder dripping down everywhere, that's bad workmanship.

What books have been most important in your life?

Herb Cohen's *You Can Negotiate Anything*.[5] One of the best books I've ever read. He had simple principles and he believed in win-win negotiations. You can crush somebody in a negotiation, take every advantage you want, and it will come back and get yeah. He taught me to recognize the power you have and don't have, the power your opponent has, and how to even that out.

---

5 You Can Negotiate Anything: The World's Best Negotiator Tells You How to Get What You Want, Herb Cohen, 1982, A Bantam Book / Lyle Stuart, Inc.

What would you tell a young business owner about sales?

If you don't have the personality for it, get somebody that does. But select someone who really represents you and does not make promises you can't keep. People will tell you quickly, either by body language or talk, what turns them off and what turns them on. Some people just want to hear the facts and another person will say, "Hey, let's go out for sushi." I always did my own sales.

How did you learn to market?

I had a big sign out on every job. That's a free billboard. We didn't advertise in newspapers or magazines. My best marketing was my customers. What better marketing can you have then that? I had a book of photographs and comments from owners: "Delivered on time," "Zero extras." I had a handout for new clients and kept it updated. My marketing had a little more shine to it as I got bigger. When work slowed I called contacts and bid more.

When you had too much work, what did you do?

I didn't have that happen much. I was measured in my growth and when I knew I was getting a new job I would bring on a superintendent. I'd put him with my best superintendent, so they had a chance to break in and see the way we did things.

Why did you have so many different businesses?

I get bored. Me and a partner had a business where we bred mice and rats. Things were good in construction and I decided to diversify a little bit. I bought the business for fourteen thousand and sold it three years later for three hundred thousand. That wasn't net, we had invested money, but we each walked away with a nice check.

What do you love?

I love hand-tool work.[6]

If you were to lecture to a class of aspiring tradesmen what would you tell them?

Stick your nose into the industry, find what's a good job and what's a bad job. Then find the oldest guy, learn from him. Watch, talk, listen, ask questions. Learn the history of your trade, not just what's in front of you,

---

6   Using hand tools like planes, handsaws, and chisels; not using power tools.

but why we do what we do. If you can find a good foreman, they'd love to tell you about the trades. Listen.

What would you tell people about getting an education apart from their trade?

It doesn't matter what you get an education in, it will make your life happier. My real education was being on the road. I got an education in human nature. My world was then was the United States and swaths of Mexico and Canada. I loved it.

What is the best path to learning a trade now?

Go work for somebody for free—or dirt wages—they won't be able to turn you away. If you have a good work ethic, they'll start paying you. Tell them, "I'll do anything. I'll haul lumber. I'll carry brick and block."

When I was about ten my dad dropped me off in front of a house with these two old guys and told me to watch them all day. They were Italian masons, brothers, and they came to work in a black jacket and a white shirt with a black tie. They'd take the jacket off, tuck the tie in, and put on an apron. One guy was laying stone and the other had an elevated box with sand in it and he would be breaking stone to fit. Those joints were so good, even with stone, it was perfect.

Word Association

Communication: Absolutely the most important thing, in anything; relationships and employees. Absolutely critical to everything in life.

Fear: Hmmm, big job. Being low bid.

Company image: Oh, very important. Logo, integrity, quality of product.

Gratitude: Reciprocal. My gratitude is for their performance, their gratitude is for how I treat them.

Integrity: Dealing honestly with your subcontractors. Paying on time. Running a job like you'd want it to be run if you worked on it.

Job safety: Very important. I've been on jobs where guys died. It's dreadful. I was a laborer on a job when an electrician electrocuted himself. I was a superintendent on a job where a guy fell off a bathtub while hanging drywall and died. It's a dangerous business and accidents happen; work to eliminate them as best you can.

Overhead: Watch it like a hawk.

Profit: Increase it through efficiency and effective buying.

Sales: That's on the individual. You've got to have a personality to go out there and mingle and sell yourself.

Estimating: Sharpen your pencil, learn other people's trades. Keep studying.

Employees: Dedicate yourself to your employees. Take care of them, they're going to take care of you.

Cut-Offs

I knew framing companies in California that had three different companies under their wing and they'd say, "You bid low, you bid middle, you bid high." They'd give three different bids to each builder.

I always wrote a CPM[7] so we knew how long it would take to build a job.

I went to study with Mike Dunbar in New Hampshire to learn to make Windsor chairs. That was the most fascinating course I ever took. I learned the anatomy of a chair and that a Windsor is an engineering miracle. One of the most important things I learned was, you can't make money at it.

I never paid yearly bonuses because I couldn't afford to wait. For most people, the yearly bonus is disappointing and that's when people look for another job. I always paid my bonuses quickly.

I worked for a guy setting telephone poles. He said, "Billy, climb up on that ladder and measure how tall that pole is." I said, "George, why didn't you ask me when it was laying down?" He said, "I don't want to know how long it is, I want to know how tall it is!"

We've all met tradesmen who are hard asses. You might deal with them because they're giving you the product at a price you like. Part of your job is to deal with all kinds.

After I got rid of the company, I was doing woodworking and I made more money that way, I really did. It was wonderful. Little overhead, no office, it was simple.

I learned from my dad: "Good times don't last forever, and neither do bad times. But when you hit the bad times, you've got to be able to maintain your lifestyle without disrupting your family."

Low bids are valuable for the leverage they provide in negotiations with a more desirable contractor.

---

7   Critical Path Method (CPM) is a method of scheduling jobs.

Blueprints often look complicated beyond
understanding to customers.
To an experienced builder they rarely say enough.

Jim Locke

Michael McVey,
Remodeling/Restoration Contractor

builditwell@gmail.com
www.builditwell.net

Mike is an intense guy, engaged in working out how to hire well and do great work. He is forty-seven and has been in residential construction since 2004. He worked briefly in the trades as an employee. He began buying, fixing, and renting Victorian houses in Kansas City and moved to California in 2007 and received his general contractors license in 2008. A mutual friend who was a long-time builder, now retired, said that he recommends Michael "without hesitation."

> *I get more work than I can possibly handle with only a couple hundred bucks a month for online marketing ■ I loved seeing old buildings being taken care of ■ My mentors are authors ■ I love getting up at four a.m. and feeling like the whole world is present to me, and nothing else is going on ■ I retired from painting in 2010 because I badly underbid an old house paint job*

I was a teacher for a time. I have no formal training in construction. I got into it by buying a junker house across the street from our home in Kanas City. I went from having no houses and no construction experience, to owning three. The smallest was an 1890 Victorian and with the help of some neighbors, I developed an idea of how this house could go from a junk to a really appealing small home.

What drew you to building?

I have a master's degree in education. I taught English as a foreign language at an institute in Caracas, Venezuela from 1996 to 97. Then I had a job as writing teacher at two universities and one community college and I began teaching English as a foreign language in Chicago for the Hispanic community. It was satisfying work but a financial dead end. My teaching years ran From 1996 to 2004, when I decided to switch to construction. I got this idea of taking old things and fixing them up and when I saw the opportunity to buy these beautiful houses and fix them, I decided to do that. I also wanted independence. I learned electrical by reading a book by Rex Cauldwell[1] and plumbing from a book by Peter Hemp.[2] I read other trade books. *This Old House*[3] was inspiring and had useful hints. I did a lot of experimentation too, and there were some mistakes.

What is most difficult for you about being a general contractor?

Having people understand that I'm right sometimes. People are always thinking, "I don't wanna spend too much money; it only has to last for so long." I say, "No, we've got to build toward a future that we hope exists. It may not, but we should at least step out and say buildings are relatively permanent things and the work on them needs to be done well."

Has your academic education helped you as a builder?

It helps with communication. There are many educated people with disposable income in the Bay Area, and when they recognize that I bring thought and care to what I do, that helps me get jobs.

What do you do when you are overwhelmed in business?

Take a break and try to figure out what the most important actionable next step is and do that. Then the next, and the next.

When you began working in the trades, did you have business goals?

My long-term goal in Kansas City was to pay off some debt and decide what to do next. We moved to California in 2007. My wife got a job here, and I decided to keep doing what I was doing. I seek larger jobs now

1   Wiring a House: 5th edition, Rex Cauldwell, Taunton Press, 2014
2   Plumbing a House, Peter Hemp, Taunton Press, 1998
3   This Old House is a home-improvement television show, magazine, and website; WWW.THISOLDHOUSE.COM

because they don't feel as large and overwhelming as when I started. Back then I was less realistic about labor needs. I would churn out large projects in a time frame that was overly ambitious, not to mention exhausting. I work smarter now.

When you estimate, do you use a cost book?

No way! I think they are worthless. I estimate based upon experience. But when I'm asked to do something that I don't have experience with, well, I don't have a good approach to that. It's why I stick with work that is similar to what I know.

What advice have you given most to builders and tradesmen?

Be honest and realize that if you show people you have integrity and expertise, they will respond to that. If they don't, you don't need them as a client. I guarantee you, the minute you begin concealing information—by practicing "change order artistry,"[4] or being dishonest—that is the minute you will have trouble collecting money. Being honest and upfront, I don't have a moment of worry about collecting money.

Do you use contracts?

Contracts are important for larger jobs. I don't like the standard one for California that I use now. It is just legal boilerplate^. The protection from any contract feels precarious if there isn't clear and careful understanding between my client and myself on what clauses could, potentially, be activated by a job. For example, I lost money last year abating a small asbestos hazard. Under the terms of my contract, I could have billed them, but it caught my client off guard—we had not discussed contract details beforehand—so I decided it violated the spirit of trust and I took full responsibility for the work. A sense of honor can be more important than the legal fine print in terms of what I actually do in a situation.

In the past few years, what habit has most improved your life or your business?

Developing a meditation practice.

---

4   Michael is referring to builders who knowingly submit a low price for work, expecting to make the shortfall up in change orders to bring the final price up to or higher than what an accurate figure would have been to begin with.

What do you like and dislike about being in business?

I like that I don't have to deal with highly conceptualized and remote things; I'm dealing with practical and immediate issues on a job. The principle is honesty. The absolute rule is accurately representing what I do for the client. What I don't like, when it comes to the government—paying insurance and taxes and all that stuff—it's ridiculous because these forces try to get me to work differently, to make it all about get in, get out, and get paid.

How would you respond to this idea: If your goal is to be a tradesman, work for someone else. if your goal is to establish and build a significant company, put your tool belt aside and focus on business as soon as it is practical.

I agree with that. The challenge is to move into a position of running the business in an organic way.

What do you think are the most important things to learn when starting a construction business?

You have to know your trade. Anybody who thinks of starting in business and trusting people to perform seamlessly, not knowing anything about the trade, is going to have real problems. They don't have to be an expert in every trade, but they must understand the elements of each and understand how they fit together so they can hold people accountable. They must also understand that their business is a public entity and that state and federal governments see you that way, and if you don't have payroll checks and taxes dialed in properly, they will eat you for lunch.

What advice would you give a new contractor about money?

Put your money into what will produce the best work, not into what will impress people.

What is a great success as a general contractor?

To provide community benefits, client benefits, and personal benefits, and to cause as little harm as possible.

How did you learn to sell?

I did not learn to sell. I was so conflicted about how to identify myself as a contractor I could not come up with a business name and I didn't have business cards for six years. I sell by talking about the technical merits of the product. I am forthright: "You have a beautiful design, this price is for labor and material, I want to build it to last."

What makes your best and worst customer?

The best is someone who gives you the space to solve difficult problems without pushing for a solution before its time. The worst is somebody who thinks they know all the answers and wants to hire commodity labor. Many are young and naïve about the complexities of construction and think they can buy the service like they buy any other commodity.

How do you shape customers' expectations, and do you ever turn down a customer?

I tell them we make mistakes, these things happen on jobs, but we'll fix it. I don't dwell on it, but I make it clear that it is part of the process and we'll take care of it. Generally my price gets turned down before I have to say anything though. I had a customer that wanted me to build a "spite fence." I won't do that kind of job.

How do you respond to this quote? "Clients do not come first. Employees come first. If you take care of your employees, they will take care of the client."

I think it is true that if people exploit and abuse employees, they are ultimately going to have unhappy clients. That's the long view, and it's true, but it cannot be applied to every situation. You have to look at both interests as important. Still, it makes sense that taking care of employees means the clients will be well cared for.

What do you look for when hiring, and what don't you expect from employees?

The first thing is, do they enjoy this kind of work? I expect them to put in their best effort while they are working. I don't expect them to obsess over work after hours. I don't expect them to work weekends or evenings researching jobs, talking about jobs, or taking my phone calls. Unless it's absolutely necessary.

How do you let people go?

The three people I've fired, rather than laid off for lack of work: one threw tools in anger on scaffolding, he was fired on the spot; another was trying to get out of the pot business and into construction, but he smoked too much of his own supply; the third constantly turned my instructions into conversations about why I wanted something done.

What is a bad tradesman?

Somebody who has no creative intent and no vision besides doing what someone tells them to do. That's a defeated human being and not a tradesperson.

What books have been most important in your life?

The Bible is a compilation of books and it was influential in my growing up. I remember reading the Gospels as a child. I'm really into poetry and it has a big impact on my way of thinking. I also read Buddhist literature.

What would you tell a new business owner about marketing and sales?

If you're a small-volume contractor, like me, you will need to do it, and the best thing you can market is integrity. It takes a small marketing budget to overwhelm yourself with work if you're good at what you do. Construction is not a high-need marketing business. It is word of mouth, word of mouth, word of mouth, and reputation. It's a complex service—like being a dentist or doctor—and the people with the big billboards are probably not as good as the people that hardly market at all.

Have you gotten bad business advice?

Get in, get done, get paid, get out. The badness is in seeing work as purely transactional, and the relationships developed as disposable once the money has been earned.

When work slows, what do you do?

It hasn't slowed for a long time. Back in 2009, when the recession was on, I didn't have much work, so I subscribed to Home Advisor.[5] I communicate with old clients a bit more. I strengthen my connection with people I know want work done but have not agreed to anything yet. Digital marketing has been a mixed bag. I mostly hate the ethics of these companies, especially Yelp and Home Advisor. But they are a way to keep busy with small job requests and I've met some wonderful clients through them.

---

5   Home Advisor is a nationwide web-based service that helps homeowners find contractors (among other services) locally. WWW.HOMEADVISOR.COM

If you were to lecture to a class of aspiring tradesmen, what would you tell them?

That I understand many people who do this work do it in far from perfect situations, with far from perfect bosses and clients, and that they are doing the best they can with what they have. I would say to build and repair buildings for a world that needs them and will appreciate them indefinitely. I would say to build with the hope that what you build will serve its users for as long as possible.

What would you tell them about getting an education apart from their trade?

It is incredibly important! If for nothing else, then to go home at night and have a richer life. I don't know what that education involves, everybody's education is different, but people should seek a life of the mind.

What do you think the best path to learning a trade is?

Doing it. And, if you're lucky, having people help you along the way because it will save a lot of time. Ultimately, no matter how many TV shows and videos you watch, or how many books you read, you have to get out there and do it.

Word Association

Integrity: In a trade it means understanding that each trade is not about how to do the trade properly—it is not your personal invention—it's a pattern of how things work, proven by time, over and over, over a long period of time.

Job safety: I'm looking out for the welfare of everyone, everyone on the job and myself at all times.

Communication: Communication involves the whole body and the whole world, not just words.

Fear: I'm afraid of making a commitment I can't keep.

Company image: Trustworthy experts with high standards of craft and ethical business practices.

Gratitude: For life itself.

Marketing: It is creating a presence so that people come to you.

Selling: Is persuading people that they should hire you to do their work.

Cut-Offs

We can't sell perfection; we can sell excellence.

I have a pile of "useful idiot" tools. A useful idiot may be inferior, but it's used and abused precisely for something that nothing else can do. It is a badly designed, gimmicky, or poorly made tool. I don't throw them away. The corded tools form a pile on a shelf in my garage, and the hand tools rest in peace in a couple of bins.

Anyone in the trades must learn where certain tolerances are required. Crown molding has tight tolerances—especially stain-grade, which is tighter than paint-grade—framing not as tight. You need a feel for when precision matters.

I do not like managing things on a computer or phone. With all of the amazing computer power of Google, I use the search box in Gmail, and it doesn't work, so I am constantly finding job leads and customer communications buried in unsearchable emails. Now I am putting fewer things on the computer and more on paper, because it is so hard to access the information digitally.

If you can hire people whose
passion intersects with the job,
they won't require any supervision at all…
Their fire comes from within, not from without.

Stephen Covey

Steve Ferguson,
Cabinetmaker

Steve is a forty-three-year-old production cabinetmaker in Eugene, Oregon. He has lived in the house he grew up in his entire life and works in the shop his dad built when he was a kid.

> *If you're more interested in doing your trade, you're better off working for somebody else* ■ *The bigger the business, the less trade work you get to do* ■ *The problem with academic education is that they make you take so much stuff just to kill time* ■ *If you're interested in a trade, shop time is far more valuable than a college degree* ■ *I learned to manage money through hard knocks* ■ *A good customer pays on time, is decisive, as opposed to someone who doesn't know what they want, or can't visualize, or changes their mind a lot*

I work for myself because of the flexibility. I'm four hundred feet from my house. I walk home for lunch. We order stuff on Amazon, get it shipped here, and hardly have to go to town. I like the convenience of naming which fifteen hours a day I get to work. [*Laughter.*] My dad built this shop when my brother and I were eight and ten, so woodworking was a hobby that turned into a business. People started asking us to make stuff. When I was young, we were making stuff and selling it. I took the ends of two fingers off with a plane when I was thirteen and had skin grafts to fix it. We tended to do things that nobody else would do. We'd give it a go if it was made out of wood. For a while we made wooden barrels for a coffee grower in Hawaii.

I had some other jobs, off and on. I started off moving irrigation pipe and farming. We subbed for a cabinet installer. I've done other random things. I guess technically, though, the first job I had on my own was when my dad had the portable sawmill and he broke his back, and my brother and I ran the business. The advantage to cutting lumber is that you were the first person on the job and you always got paid. That was a pretty good business; it was just a whole lot of work and labor-intensive.

Then we went into construction. So we started with roofing and we were doing general contracting and we built spec houses. After that we were doing high-end custom finish work and subbed for a cabinet company doing installations here in town. I've had no formal training, but we had a cabinetmaker that we knew—he built the cabinets for my parent's house—and we watched while he did it, and then we kind of went from there. I decided to focus on the cabinetry; that was the area I enjoyed the most. I sold to a high-end builder here in town, but by competing with other cabinet shops there wasn't a profit margin. So I got hooked up with a designer in California. I was able to sell my cabinets for 30 or 40 percent more down there. That went on for seven or eight years. I used to like to do cabinetry, but not so much anymore. Well, actually, I still love building cabinets, but I don't like collecting the money. Yeah, people wanted the cabinets and didn't want to pay. [*laughs*]

I'm in manufacturing now, I manufacture display systems and I do custom computer programming for a cabinet manufacturer in Miami. I got into the Computer Numeric Control (CNC)^ industry when I bought a CNC machine. After I bought the equipment, I started working for the company as an employee, and got really involved in the software part of that business. I traveled all over the U.S. and Canada setting up CNC machines and training people in the software. Then I worked my way into this line of food manufacturing displays that I make now, starting with cutting out wooden rolling carts. I had been doing business with them over a period of time and they approached me about taking over their entire product line. When the cabinetry was going great guns, I wasn't interested. When building tanked and people were late paying, I thought I'd take a look at it again. I picked the option of customers who paid their bills.

I work mostly by myself. I have a guy that comes in part time. I do what I do because I love wood, and I enjoy the challenges, and I enjoy making really cool, pretty stuff. I did not have any long-term goals or ambitions—just to fill the gas tank without thinking about it. [*laughs*] I'm not interested in a business degree. I went through high school and that has been enough for me. I never did a business plan or marketing. Getting work was never an issue. We got work through word of mouth, and it seemed like whenever we would focus on one particular area, because of the obvious quality of our work, we had a ton of other work off of that. It's not a foolproof system. There were slow times. So it's a fight, but as far as long-term with the business, I just kind of pushed through.

In business, especially if you get employees, you start having issues with managing and figuring out their day and trying to stay ahead of them. You know, the more you get into the business—taxes, accounting, sales, all that stuff—it takes away a lot of the time you could be doing cool trade work. There's a lot of difference between doing the trade and doing all the paperwork and organizing your office. At this point, I am working with another small business, and I'm not involved at all in the sales; I manufacture, they sell. But it's a challenge when the sales department is a different company. There's nothing I can do to affect sales. It's an odd situation for me.

I learned to estimate by asking questions. When we started, I was asking what the going rate was and afterwards there was an analysis on how the job went, and whether or not we made any money at it. After that it was like, *Well, that one didn't work, [laughs] let's try something different.* On spec houses we figured cost and our time, and electrical and plumbing were the only two things we couldn't do ourselves. On the first one, we forgot to figure paint. It was pretty much trial and error.

I usually hire friends. I look for dependability. I've worked with enough people to know. The first guy I hired was actually with the company that I built most of the cabinets for around here. The other two people who worked for me were people that I went to church with, so I knew them.

Well, there are options for learning about business: jump into it and make a bunch of mistakes, learn from someone else, or take classes. Some people learn from a textbook. Some learn from experience. In business, you've got to have cash flow^. You have to set up your payment terms so that you know you can, through the course of the project, get enough money up front to pay your bills for the job. It's never going to work all the time, so cover yourself financially.[1]

I don't typically separate overhead and profit. When I started ... well, I guess I kind of did, because I figured cost of material and then time and doubled it and hope it all works. After you've done it for a while, you start to know how long it's going to take and you know your basic expenses for the shop per month, and that kind of stuff, and you can calculate it based on the number of weeks it will take to do the project and the material cost.

I would tell young people to pick something they enjoyed—don't do something you hate—and if they didn't know, go out and start trying things. If your job is putting in staples, be the best staple installer in the shop and pay attention. If they have the chance to swap around and give somebody a break and do five other things, then do it, because the more you know the better.

---

[1] When Steve says, "Cover yourself," he means you should make sure that the draw schedule allows for payments of enough money so that you are not using your cash to finance the job. You are a builder, not a bank, it is not up to you to carry a job financially.

Cut-Offs

When starting a business, if you have a customer base, people that you've worked with and have a relationship with, that helps.

Especially if someone was thinking about going to college to learn a specific trade, I'd tell them to go get a job in that trade first and find out if it's something they're going to enjoy.

If you have a trade and you go out and start your own business, you have no idea of the different hats you have to wear.

Whatever you do, buy quality tools, don't buy cheap stuff.

A successful tradesman provides a superior product and takes pride in his craftsmanship.

Business is not my main priority in life, so if it pays the bills, I'm good. I'm interested in a life apart from work.

The greater the outward show,
the greater he inward poverty.
J. Krishnamurti

Chris Clark,
Electrician

Chris is fifty, he is clean-cut and his answers are direct and clear. His business, Clark Electric, was started in 2001 in Jamaica Vermont. For ten years, while working as an electrician, Chris was a guitarist in local bands, and he continues to play regularly. His two brothers are also electricians. Chris is an electrical sub and good friend of Jim Fleming, another interviewee.

> *When I get overwhelmed, I pick my battles and focus on what's important ■ As I get older, my mind makes promises my body can't keep; accepting that is the most difficult thing ■ I love a good sense of humor ■ If I say something is stupid, people's egos get bruised; instead I say, "There might be a better way to do this" ■ When you're young and hungry you think, Okay, you're going to pay me to do this, I'll do it! ■ Stay away from people who grind you down ■ In my earlier jobs l learned thru trial by fire, they threw me into something and said, "Learn how to do this" ■ Man, there are some strange people in the world, and some great people too ■ You are paying for my experience, not my time ■ When I go to renew my master's electrical license every four years, there are not many young guys there*

I was living at home, just after high school, working at a sawmill. The job wasn't going anywhere, and my dad said, "How'd you like to be an electrician?" He had contacted a local electrician and I met him the next day. It was 1989 and I became an apprentice, a gofer, the bottom rung of the ladder.

To become a journeyman electrician, I had to be sponsored by a master who paid to send me to trade school two nights a week. Trade school was the textbook end of it, the hands-on training was the apprenticeship. I needed two years of schooling and 400 hours working in the field with a licensed electrician before I could take the journeymen's test and get my license. Another two years of school and another 400 hours and I took the test for my master's license. My journeyman's card and master's license are my diplomas. There were bumps in the road. I was laid off in 1991 during the recession—I mowed lawns—but I was still going to trade school. When the recession ended, I went back to work for an electrical contractor.

It was overwhelming in the beginning. I watched and learned all the parts and pieces, trying to get it right. The first year I was not allowed to do much; I drilled holes and pulled wires. Then I worked my way up to connecting wires. The most difficult are motors and boilers, intricate things that have a lot of moving parts. If you have a good teacher, they show you how to do it and make you feel comfortable.

What drew you to the trade?

It just came along, but as I got into it, I found it interesting. I was always comfortable with my trade and I still like the puzzle parts and solving problems. I like moving around, working in different places, and meeting new people. Like any job, after a while I got sick of it, that is why I moved from job to job. I always knew I wanted to have my own business though.

Any memorable mistakes as you were coming up in your trade?

Oh ya, thanks for bringing that up. (*Laughter.*) I was working at a mall and I mixed up the neutral and hot on one leg of a 240-volt outlet and I cooked a microwave and refrigerator. My boss had to buy new ones; he was not happy. But it stuck with me because, by messing up, I learned to pay attention and not do it again.

In the early '90s I was putting in under-cabinet lights and I took all the dishes and everything out of the cabinets. The woman came home and asked if I had mixed them up because they were kosher. I had. I was a kid from Vermont, I didn't know what kosher was. As far as my business, growing up with a Yankee father, he is a kind man, but I was taught not to take chances, which is limiting, so I never made major mistakes in business because I never got big.

What is most rewarding and most difficult about your work now?

The most rewarding is being confident in what I do; I'm not a deer in the headlights, like in the beginning. Now I know how things work and I like that and it's always rewarding to help people solve a problem. I've worked for multiple electricians over the years and did a lot of big and small commercial work. Now I do mostly small things, but I like working for businesses. A house is a stove, lights, outlets, all that, but a restaurant has different pieces of equipment and that's challenging. I like to move on to the next job too.

Dealing with difficult people is hard. There are a lot of people who are pushy, and I tell them, "We don't work, you should find someone else." Now that I'm established, I pick and choose who to work for. I have relationships with certain general contractors, I work with ten or fifteen of them. As we've gotten older, some have retired or died. I pick who to work for by their attitude, their good work, and if they have the same work vision that I do—to work together to give people a good product—and they're not backstabbing or shady. I don't work with people who yell and scream. I've done that, but as I've grown older, there is only so much of that I'll take. Everybody makes mistakes, and yelling doesn't make the job better and it stresses everyone out.

What advice have you given most to young tradesmen?

Usually it's about pacing yourself, not getting overwhelmed, and being present in the job you're doing. It is hard because we can all be scatterbrained. When I had apprentices, I always gave them a little more responsibility than I had. I have them figure things out, rather than me telling them. And I recommend learning anything that will enlighten you. I was an avid reader in my early twenties, I read everything, and it *really* helped my spelling and reading capability, and it opened my mind.

Talk about working with designers or architects.

The architect is not in the field, everything is on paper, in real time that often doesn't work. Most architects don't like to be questioned, so I'll say to the customer, "This switch behind the door is not going to work." They call the architect and hash it out. It's their decision, I've taken it as far as I can and that's all I can do. I work with a great architect once in a while; he says, "If you have a better way of doing this, Chris, we're going to do it that way."

He does not consider himself the overlord of the thing, he respects me for what I do, and that feels good.

What would you tell someone about learning a trade today?

The first thing: go into it knowing you want to deliver something worth putting your name on and to be proud of what you do because you do it well. To this day I say, "Someone will go into an electrical panel or a house and say, 'Chris Clark did that.'" I want that person to say, "He did a really, really good job."

If a guy wants to stay in Vermont, I'd say, "Go to a high school with a trade program or find a trade school." The average age of electricians in Vermont is fifty, carpenters it's fifty-six. If you start as an apprentice you might make twelve dollars an hour. That's why it is hard for someone who's thirty years old with a family to do it, it's why you have to dedicate yourself to a trade at a young age. I have a young guy who helps me—he's twenty-four—and I think he's interested in being an electrician, but the low starting pay and four years of schooling scares him.

I would tell them to stay away from negativity. I think of myself as floating on a river; when I run into someone who's a jerk, they are a rock in my river, I'm not going to keep ramming that rock, I'm going to bump it, go around, and leave them behind.

How would you describe a successful tradesman?

They have good clientele and work with good people—carpenters, plumbers, sheet rockers, insulators—a network of friends to call for help. It's not about money for me. I make good money, and it is a good trade, but that alone wouldn't bring happiness. Enjoying company with people on the job and talking about experiences in life: these are good things. Twenty years ago I wouldn't have answered the same way. I was starting a family and I had different goals, so I worked a lot of hours. Now I want to be happy and enjoy life and my kids. I've been around tradesmen who are all gung-ho, chasing that dollar and they'll often say, "I don't spend any time with my wife and kids and they are going off in different directions."

Tell me about a good investment you've made.

My first home and what came from it. I was twenty-five and my father said I should buy this rundown logger's camp. I remember two years into it being upset because he got me into debt—it was $48,000—and there was homeowner's insurance and electric bills and I wanted to be an electrician on the side and a rock star in the making. But I built it from nothing into a nice little house, and the journey to get there, as I look back, made it the right investment.

Also, I bought a 1941 Ford 9N tractor. It gets me outside and allows me to think about other things. It's the hum of the mower, it's kind of a Zen thing. I thought, *If I have a tractor, I should have a little field.* So I cleared some land and our neighbor put cows on it. To me, my property is an artist's pallet where I put my time when I'm not doing electrical work.

What about your best and worst customer makes them that?

The best ones know me and my work and they trust me. Good customers know life is imperfect and that things happen. I went through a divorce five years ago. I didn't work much because I was trying to recuperate; some people cut ties because it did not work for them.

The worst customers are pushy and aggressive, an alpha, male or female. And the ones who don't pay. I don't take jobs that I think will be chaotic. It could be the customer's personality or they think they know more than they do. Although, twenty years ago I had customers I thought would be bad, now they are some of my best customers. The president of a condo association called me to do their work in 2001. He would call me all the time: "Where are you? I need to be able to contact you any time and you need to be here when we need you." That's not one of my favorite things. On the phone I said to him, "Steve, I'm not the electrician for you." He said, "Please meet with me, I'd like to talk to you about this." I was ready to be done with it, but I met him and he apologized. I still do work for him and consider him a good friend.

How do you influence a new customer's expectations?

With new customers there are personality types; the lots-of-questions person, the quiet person, the quick-to-decide person, the person who mostly cares about money. Whoever it is, I spell the work out carefully. I say, "There is going to be a light here, switches here, outlets here." I give them a mental image of what it's going to be like.

What would you tell new business owners about marketing and sales?

Because we are in a rural area, it's mostly word of mouth. People see each other at a restaurant or gas station and ask, "Who's your carpenter? Who's your electrician?" But new guys should start off with some ads and having their truck lettered, to get themselves known. I learned to sell by watching people who were bad at it, I did not want to be that. I'd tell them to remember, you're selling yourself. However big or small the project, it's important to the customer. I don't make people feel dumb and I talk to them the way that I want to be talked to and they trust that I'm going to take care of them.

When you have too much work, how do you respond?

Not well. The stress gets really bad. I handle it by telling people that work is not going to happen the way I thought it was. I put in time on weekends to catch up. But with my experience, I know my balance and I ask for deadlines—the worst thing you can do is ask a Vermonter for a deadline—and I say, "You want someone in here on August first, but I can't get here until September."

What has most improved your business in the past few years?

Lack of stress and enjoying life. People pass away and it bothers me terribly and—I know it is a cliché—but life is so fragile. I can't imagine anyone on their deathbed saying, "I wish I'd worked ninety hours a week." I don't take things too seriously now. For me, it's family and friends. I have a nice group of friends, in and out of the construction industry, and it's a nice place to be, but it takes work.

As you opened your business, did you have a conflict between running the business and working in the field?

The most frustration is the constant paperwork. I do my own and after work today, I'm going home for a few hours of ordering material and making calls. When I make calls, every one of them has to be my favorite job. It can't be, "Yeah, I'll get to it. Whatever." It's important to them and they need to feel it is important to me. But it is taxing making calls at eight p.m. when my kids are hungry. When I'm working in the field, I have a goal, my mind is set, nothing is bothering me, and it is satisfying. I'd rather just work in the field.

Do you have business principles that you follow?

Yes. Don't rip anybody off. You can be a lot of things in the world, but don't ever be a thief. If people think the price is too high, I will tell them that Time & Material may fairer to them and to me. I believe in honesty.

Why don't you have employees?

I don't want the responsibility of finding them work. The reason to have employees is to get bigger or to make more money, and it can be an ego thing. That doesn't float my boat. I like being a one-man show, pulling help when I need it, and the freedom of that.

Why did you open your business and what did that transition looked like?

I was working for someone I didn't like. I should thank him for being a prick and motivating me to go into business. Around that time I bought the old camp and got married. I had worked for electricians for twelve years—I was a journeyman and had my hours to get my master's license—I had the knowledge I needed and in Vermont you don't need a license to do residential electrical work. Also, I wanted to be my own boss. Most electricians want big jobs, big money, which is great, but I noticed that people couldn't get one outlet fixed. I saw a hole that needed to be filled and thought, *I can do that*.

The first thing I did when I went into business was buy tools, a truck, and business cards. I started with five customers and it steamrolled and the phone kept ringing. I billed the work out and someone sent me money; that was a nice feeling. I've had bosses who did not do their paperwork for a long time and it's tough, weeks or months later, to send a bill and the customer says, "I don't remember you doing this work." So I learned, you gotta stay on top of the paperwork.

I learned to estimate using "cost per stop," a charge for each switch, outlet, light, etc. So that's how I estimate. I don't use cost books. If it is a restaurant, it's plug 'n' play, I'll run a wire from the panel to the location of the stove and hardwire it or they plug it in. If it's not straightforward I'll tell them it needs to be Time & Material because I've never done this item before and if I bid it, it is going to be very high.

I don't use contacts much, mostly I use email because I have a record of what was said. I do a lot of verbal agreements. If it is a big job or if they ask me for a contract, I will write it. I have a reputation for being honest and I'll say, "You can make this bathroom $600, which is basic outlets and lights, or $3000 will take it beyond the basic."

What do you like and dislike about owning your own business?

I like traveling from job to job and meeting people. There are some interesting characters out there. I love that, and I find humor in it. I don't like that when I disconnect the power for a bathroom renovation, I can't tell the contractor, "Build that wall right now so I can finish my work." No, I have to leave and fill in the hole of my eight-hour day and that's frustrating. Being on call twenty-four hours a day is a bad thing too.

How did you decide what you wanted to focus on in business?

In Vermont, the terrain tells you what to do. Most of my work here is houses. If I were in Brattleboro or Rutland, I would lean more towards commercial work.

What do you think of this idea: "If your goal is to be a tradesman, work for someone else. If your goal is to establish and build a significant company, put your toolbelt aside and focus on business as soon as it is practical."

Put your tool belt aside? No. No sir. I don't agree with that. I think you pull up your bootstraps, do a good job, be a tradesman. You ask it as if they are not compatible. I think you can balance the trade work with the business work.

What advice would you give a tradesmen or business owner about money?

Flash and substance. These guys with fancy cars and big trucks, all lettered up, in six years they're gone. That's flash. It's okay to play hard, but you can make a million dollars and spend it all. It doesn't mean shit how much you earn; it's how much you save. That's substance.

What would you tell a group of tradesmen to learn first about business?

If you are true to your job and you enjoy what you're doing, the money will come. If you put out positive energy, it will come back. If you're miserable, negative energy will find you. Have a vision of what you want the business to be. If you want to be the biggest electrician in Vermont, go for it. If you want to be a one-man show who helps the people in your village, be that person. Either way, enjoy what you are doing.

If you had a method of reaching every electrician in America, what would you say?

The common theme of this interview: be true to yourself and your customer.

What makes a contractor's business successful and what is a successful career?

A business that treats employees really well—the boss cares about them—the employees are happy and the business doesn't have a lot of turnover. A place where the goal is not just to make money, but to improve everyone's life. Where they pay everyone a little more and the business does not have to make all the money. My family will tell me if my career was a success. When my kids look back, they will tell me if I had a good career and if I was present in their lives.

Word Association

Integrity: Truth.

Communication: A two-way street and it's key to everything. Lack of clear communication leads to trouble. You can't be brutally honest with everybody—friends or business—you have to smooth things over sometimes.

Job safety: A priority.

Fear: Is a killer. Everyday fear of failure, of letting people down.

Company image: Honest.

Overhead: As little as possible.

Profit: As much as possible.

Marketing: Nonexistent, for me.

Sales: Personal. My image, of who I am.

Estimating/Bidding: Building a job. Going back, into my experience. Learning how to read the room, read the house. Anyone can wire a new house, it's the 1800s Victorian and knowing the bones of it.

Community: Very important. In my working community, I try to bring everybody up. In my town, I try to be as involved as I can be.

Quality: Try for it.

Cut-Offs

I enjoy it when someone tells me I can't do something. Tell me that I can't and I'm going to show you that I can. I like that.

I remember telling my wife at the time, "If you say, 'Would you fix that drawer when you get a chance?' It will never get done. But if you tell me, 'Fix that drawer now!' I'm on it."

Marketing doesn't apply to me. It applies to bigger companies, with a crew counting on them for work. I know electricians with nine guys, landscapers with twenty guys, that requires marketing to keep everyone working.

Avoid doing a job to impress other people—because you want to be rich and flashy—because that doesn't work.

I had a boss in the late '90s who was a mentor—he was picky as all get out—but he was really a good boss, with a good work ethic and he did *really* nice work. He had a way laying out a job that made the work clear. That's hard to learn.

Remember what I said about the lack of trades in Vermont? My work doesn't slow down. If I advertised, I'd have more people to say no to. At this point in my life, it is okay if it slows down. I have little debt and I've saved money, I'm not a hungry thirty-year-old anymore. A guy called me who had bought a hot tub for his wife for Christmas and he wanted it wired on New Year's Day. Twenty years ago I might have done it, but now I'm not going to make myself miserable just to get work.

We need to tell better stories of men and women who master a trade. We have to stop telling kids to blindly follow their passion and show them the opportunities that exist.

Mike Rowe

APPENDIX

NINE KEYS TO SUCCESS IN THE BUILDING BUSINESS[1]

Matt Risinger, from August 5th, 2018 blog entry.

1. ***Start the day early.*** Get things done without interruption. Respond to emails. Do your to-do list, beginning with what you need to accomplish the first two or three hours of the day. Throw in some exercise.
2. ***Time block the day.*** Set aside time for research, contacting clients and prospects, cold calling for new leads, meetings, and administrative tasks. Block a half hour each morning for emails, a half hour each afternoon for social media. Use time in the car for some (hands-free!) phone calls.
3. ***Keep the schedule flexible.*** Stay accessible. Be ready to respond to clients/trades at your job sites and make a trip to another job.
4. ***Build relationships.*** Know your clients' needs and dreams. Communicate constantly. Become their friend. Remember birthdays and anniversaries. Stay in touch after the house is done.
5. ***Pick up the phone.*** Nothing beats real physical connection. Let people hear the sound of your voice.
6. ***Work with the best.*** Only use subcontractors who are the best in their fields.
7. ***Stay healthy.*** Eat well, get some exercise and the sleep you need. (I've been doing CrossFit for several months and I feel great!)
8. ***Unwind with your family.*** Don't bring work home. Take regular family vacations. Put your phone down and be present at home. Respond to late texts in the morning.
9. **Build better. Be a lifelong student.** Take time weekly to learn more about your craft. Make every house you build better than the last and you'll be the top builder in your area before long.

---

1 With permission from Matt Risinger, from his August 5th, 2018 blog entry.

GROSS PROFIT vs MARKUP, David Lorber

The numbers that matter on an operating or financial statement are gross revenue (sales), direct expense (labor, material, subs), indirect expense (overhead), gross profit, and net profit. Each of these categories is made up of many line items, and each line item should be shown as a percentage of gross revenue on your financial statement so that you can easily see where you are losing money.

Say you have annual sales of $1,000,000 (gross revenue) and your direct expenses are $600,000, or 60 percent of revenue. $1,000,000 minus $600,000 = $400,000 gross profit or 40 percent. Now let's say that your indirect expenses are $300,000, or 30 percent. Which means you have spent $900,000 ($600K direct and $300K indirect), you are left with $100,000 net profit before taxes, or 10 percent. The point of this method is that you are thinking in terms of gross profit, not markup,[1] so that you can analyze the business without converting back and forth from markup.

---

[1] David's definition of markup: a percentage added to the hard costs (labor, material, and subs). If something costs $1000.00 and I mark it up 20 percent and charge the customer $1200.00 ($1000.00 x .20 = $1200.00) that is a 20 percent markup, but only 17 percent gross profit.

INSURANCE NOTES, David Lorber

The Oakland fires were some 28 years ago, so not everything I say about insurance work will apply now. Also, the claims I'm discussing are large, I know nothing about settling claims for roof damage or a leaky dishwasher. Small claims are an entirely different business.

1) We worked with people who were adequately insured. The insurance companies had written "deluxe policies" with "guaranteed replacement." They were obligated to pay for code upgrades and every expense necessary to reconstruct the home to its original condition, regardless of stated policy limits. These policies no longer exist, but the principle still holds; on a major loss, you must know the policy limits. If you are looking at insurance work on most tract houses built from the 1970s onward—sheetrock, carpet, paint-grade trim, etc.—you are wasting your time with insurance work, except on a house that has been extensively remodeled, with high-grade finishes and workmanship. Those may be worth going after.

2) Even with guaranteed replacement policies, settling these claims was an uphill battle. The key is to understand the principle of indemnification, which entitles people to get back what they had. That meant that if we were working on a house built in the 1920s, we got paid for lath and plaster, every layer of wallpaper, special trim, hardware, and so on. This was difficult work that required a great deal of knowledge of old houses and the discipline to itemize and price *everything*. Every insurance claim you wish to settle, and make a decent profit on, requires an extensively detailed estimate. I should add that I would, under no circumstances, spend time on an estimate unless the client is wholeheartedly committed to us doing the work.

The man who taught me about insurance work had two mottos: "We are not going to ask for a dime that the client is not entitled to, but we are not going to settle for a penny less," and "For every insurance claim that gets overpaid, there are nine-hundred-ninety-nine that are underpaid." It will take pressure on the insurance company from the contractor and the owner to get the claim settled properly.

3) That brings me to the Xactimate estimating system. It was new when the Oakland fires happened, but now it seems universal in the insurance industry and I believe that insurance adjusters know the prices in this program are unrealistic, although they are required to justify payouts based on the program.[1] My advice is to estimate every project the way you normally would, so you know what you need to sell the job for, then fit those numbers into the Xactimate format. I do not know the program and never will, but with the adjusters estimate, you can more or less follow their format.[2] Stay on good terms with the adjuster, but don't be afraid to say, "There is no way in hell I will do this for this price." They will often find a way to make up for the shortfall in other categories and this is why it is crucial the owner is backing you up.

4) Know the insurance carriers. In my experience, most are terrible, but I have had great experience with Chubb and some others who pay a fair price as long as you have things well documented, including well-written bids from your subs. Wealthier clients tend to use premium carriers and you should know which those are. Generally we turn down insurance work, but we have clients who want us to do their work and we want to serve them, in these cases we do insurance work. We have done well on claims where the owners were with us. In many cases, my clients know they would get crappy work from construction companies specializing in insurance work, so they hire us and make up any shortfall.[3]

---

1 An email from David: "Recently, I ran into a young man I've known for years who is working as an adjuster for Allstate Insurance. He remarked, 'I hope you are not using Xactimate.' He complained that he could find no one to do the work for the prices in the Xactimate program."
2 Generally insurance adjusters do their own estimates and give it to the GC, expecting/asking/hoping that they will work for those numbers.
3 The reason "clients know they will get crappy work" is because many insurance companies pay unrealistically low prices. The reason contractors agree to work at these prices is because they don't understand their basic costs or how to estimate, and therefore they don't know that there is not enough money in the job to do anything but quick and dirty work.

5) Insurance companies require a line item cost estimate for every job, and the customer sees that estimate. But because those prices are unrealistic—in many cases costs are manipulated to work around Xactumate's too-low pricing—the GC's contract must stipulate that the job includes all of the items provided for in the scope-of-work and that nothing can be removed from it. The reason is that some line item prices will be low [using the insurance companies' Xactimate pricing] and some will be inflated by the adjuster and contractor to make up for the low prices. Therefore, explain to the client that the prices in the line item estimate mean essentially nothing, otherwise they may decide that the tile price is too high and have their brother-in-law do it, or, finding the price to paint a door low, ask that you paint every door in their house at that price.

CREATE A HOMETOWN SPLINTER GROUP, David Gerstel[1]

YOUR BEST OPPORTUNITY FOR BUSINESS EDUCATION MIGHT BE IN YOUR HOMETOWN

- Ask a few trustworthy fellow builders if they would like to get together for dinner and share ideas about construction and business management.
- Let the group grow as members spontaneously invite other builders to the gatherings.
- When necessary, put a bit more structure in place.
- Establish one officer—a Keeper of the List—who will maintain a list of the contact information of all members.
- Hold an annual Board of Non-Directors meeting to select topics for the year's gathering.
- At the meetings, select a years' worth of topics and a person to lead each of the gatherings.
- Otherwise, resist bureaucratization.
- Host your meetings in attractive spaces.
- Don't allow architects or other designers (and probably not even subs) into your group.
- Encourage the code: No member ever takes advantage of what is learned in the group to ace another member out of a job.
- Don't charge dues.

---

1   With permission from David Gerstel, from an article written for *JLC*, March 2019.

THE JOURNAL OF LIGHT CONSTRUCTION (JLC), Mike Reitz

Mike is the founder, and for eighteen years the editor of *The Journal of Light Construction* (*JLC*). In April, 2020, while editing yet another interview where the person mentioned how important *JLC* and *Fine Homebuilding* were to their careers, I emailed Mike to let him know. He responded with the following:

First email:
It is a curious cosmic coincidence—of which, there are none—that while I was pondering the idea for what would eventually become *The Journal of Light Construction* in Newark Vermont, just down the road, in Lunenburg Vermont, there was another guy—whose name I no longer remember and whose history has been expunged from the annals of Taunton Press—who was pondering the same thing and ended up calling his "classroom" *Fine Homebuilding*.

Second email:
I had a letter years ago, postmarked Houston Texas, from a woman on behalf of herself and her husband, both of whom were Vietnamese refugees. They weren't able to escape on the last helicopters out of Saigon but via the circuitous ways of black-market smuggling, and they finally arrived in the United States, three years later, broke, and homeless. Things didn't improve. Simple survival was a daily struggle. Her husband followed the lead of Mexican day-laborers and when he was lucky, he ended up doing construction scut work in the booming residential subdivisions around Houston. He came home one day with a tattered copy of *JLC* (*New England Builder* back then) someone had left at a break site, which he asked his wife to read to him. A few more "found" copies and his skills and their financial prospects improved enough to get them a place with a mailbox and a subscription to *JLC*. It also became his guide to reading and writing English.

Some fifteen years on, she was writing to say thank you. Using *JLC* as their guide they had gone out on their own, built their own construction business and flourished, to the point where they were able to locate and bring "lost" members of their extended families into the business and put their kids thru college. It was their guidebook to a blessed life which had once seemed unimaginable.

I think I was about fifteen when I decided teaching was the professional career I wanted. But within a few years it became clear that wasn't in the cards for a guy with my attitude, skewed perceptions, and uncredentialed abilities. And "teaching," in its popular pedagogical form of experts dumping "knowledge" into the heads of vacuous students, wasn't going to be an option for a bumbling construction novitiate like me. Like all the parts which make up a completed house, the materials and know-how were out there somewhere, and needed to be rounded up—and shared. I did the best I could for eighteen years and it worked out for some of our readers. Twenty years after I sold it, that "house" still stands. So yeah, I'm happy, and thanks for letting me know about the folks you are interviewing.

PROCESS OF LEARNING TO ESTIMATE, Sal Alfano

I started out as a stick estimator[1] and counted every piece of material and every labor hour that went into a project. Even a small project, like a deck, could take several hours to prepare. In the beginning it made sense because I was working for friends, I wasn't competing against other contractors, and I was trying to provide a good price to the homeowner. I would have to do a stick-by-stick material takeoff for the project anyway, so I wasn't risking much by doing all that counting.

Some of that came from my training as a project lead for Circus Studios. One of the standard practices was to have the lead carpenter or foreman on a given project do the material takeoff. A lot of companies had someone in the office do that or they ordered materials based on square-foot calculations, but our idea was that by the time the foreman was done making the list of materials for the project, he would have spent several hours poring over the plans and would know the building inside out. When I left Circus in 1979, I was already in the habit of doing a close material takeoff.

My projects were all custom designs and a whole house estimate could take anywhere from twenty to forty hours to complete. Eventually I created a unit-cost system^, but the advantage of having done all of those stick-by-stick estimates was that I had historical data on what it cost to build a variety of projects. That was incredibly valuable, especially when it came to estimating labor. Unit pricing would allow me to measure the square footage of floor area in a room or the entire floor of a house, for example, and plug in a cost per square foot that covered material and labor. For subs, like plumbing or electrical, I would count fixtures, and I had historical pricing that I could plug in. It still took time, but it was faster than stick by stick, and it did not sacrifice accuracy.

---

1   A stick estimate breaks the work into its smallest parts and prices each as line item^ (within reason, not counting nails or linear feet of caulk), in contrast to one that is done using square/linear foot or assemble pricing.

The real change came with estimating software. In 1987 I was doing estimates on Excel spreadsheets (Excel was called Multiplan back then) and that helped—a lot of people still use Excel—but these estimates required debugging to make them reliable, so I set out to find software dedicated to estimating. At the time, I had just started writing a regular business column for a trade magazine. I proposed to the editor that I review the available estimating software. It would serve his readers, and it would get me sample copies of the software. There wasn't much on the market, but my search coincided with the release of Precision Estimating by Timberline. It was miles ahead of everything else, and after writing the review I ended up using it in my business. It took time to learn and to set up the database, but it streamlined the estimating process. It was my introduction to what Timberline called "assemblies," which are formulas that use simple inputs, like the length and width of a room, to assemble a complete bill of materials with labor attached. It was my unit-price system on steroids.

Even so, I used an exhaustive estimating checklist to ensure that I didn't forget anything. Like all software, Precision Estimating was literal, and its accuracy depended on the accuracy and completeness of the input. I still pored over plans and used standard procedures—like using colored pencils to keep track of what I had and had not estimated—and this was part of my meticulous approach. When something unusual came up, I still had to estimate it manually.

THE PERFECT WALL, Sal Alfano

According to current building science, the "perfect wall"[1] controls water, air, vapor, and heat in layers, all of which are applied on the outboard side of the structure. Cladding keeps bulk water out of the building, but it should be applied with an air space behind it to allow for drainage and drying, a so-called "rain screen." Next comes the "thermal layer"—insulation, which can be rigid foam, rock wool, fiberglass, or other materials—and behind that an impermeable layer that keeps outside air and vapor out of the building and inside air and vapor inside the building. The configuration works in heating and cooling climates because the location of the insulation keeps moisture from condensing on the impermeable layer. And there is always a chance of moisture getting into the wall because "perfect" is easier to accomplish on paper than in the real world. But the perfect wall allows for the wall to dry.

---

1   A term coined in an article by Joseph Lsitburek in 2010, called The Perfect Wall: WWW.BUILDINGSCIENCE.COM/DOCUMENTS/INSIGHTS/BSI-001-THE-PERFECT-WALL
    This is an excellent video on the perfect wall by Joe Lsitburek: https://www.youtube.com/watch?v=E_ngmbANeOg

IT'S A MYTH THAT THE LOW BID ALWAYS WINS, Sal Alfano

The term 'bid' assumes every one bidding meets a set of professional criteria and that there is a comprehensive set of plans and specs so that everybody is pricing the same work. But residential 'bidding' is often loosey-goosey with each bidder providing a unique solution to the problem. The homeowner, who doesn't understand what they are buying, is faced with a series of singular designs with little detail and often the only thing to base a decision on is low price.

But I know hundreds of remodeling contractors whose prices are not the lowest in their market, who manage to win in competitive bid situations. Not every time, of course, but often enough and some at the high end of the price range. They are able to do it because they focus on projects that will be profitable, they know their ideal customer, and instead of following every lead, they screen them to find those whose motivation, schedule, and budget most closely resemble past successful projects. They learn to say , "No"—in a nice way—and turn down projects that don't fit them. So by the time they've decided to bid a job, they've increased their odds of winning it. They also build trust with the homeowner, helping them to feel comfortable about their purchasing decision. Most contractors don't have a clue how to do that. Remodelers who provide a good experience, before, during, and after the project, are worth more than those who only provide the physical stuff of building. Some homeowners value that service, and some don't, remodelers who win bids without being the low bidder work with those who value what they provide.

The greatest day in your life and mine is when we take total responsibility for our attitudes. That's the day we truly grow up.

John C. Maxwell

ANONYMOUS

Some people are self-conscious about discussing their finances. Therefore I have included a few quotes here, giving only the region of the country in which they work.

- We're at $92 an hour. It should be more. The lead guys cost me around $55 an hour. West Coast
- We currently charge $65 per hour. A mentor taught me that if the customer can see it at Lowes or Home Depot, you can't mark it up much. Those things I mark up 15 percent, other things are a 40 percent markup. New England
- I charge $65 an hour for my time and $52 to $55 for my guys plus a 12 percent markup, which covers overhead and profit. I pay $32 and $34 per hour. West Coast
- I charge $50 per hour with no markup. West Coast
- Our field labor billing rate is $60 across the board—it's easier to use the average than trying to predict what the skill mix will be on a particular project—and we mark up all hard costs (labor hours x $60, materials, subs) by 1.5 for a 33 percent gross profit (GP). It yields a budgeted profit of about 10 percent, which turns into an actual net profit of 5 to 8 percent.
- I used to have a flat rate for all of my employees, from apprentice to my best carpenter, but customers always asked for my best guy—he is getting the most money of course—but I was charging an average rate, so I was losing money. Now I add 85 percent to each trade's hourly rate—apprentice, $18–20, carpenter, $20–25, and so on—that 85 percent figure derives from the hourly rate, overhead, and 10 percent for profit. We also have a constant 15 percent added to material and subs. In theory we should have a 10 percent profit on labor and a 15 percent profit on subs and materials. In reality we end up eating some

sub and material cost. If all goes as planned, we end up with 10 to 15 percent profit at the end of a job. New England

- We start an apprentice at $19 an hour. A lead carpenter is going to be in the high thirties to mid-forties. We have five lead carpenters, one of whom is the production manager, he gets an extra three dollars an hour. We charge an average of $60 per hour plus a markup of 55 percent (charging $93 per hour). New England
- 55 percent times any item gives us a markup of 34–35 percent gross margin. There's a couple percent points slippage, so we end up over the course of the year, for variety of reasons, with a gross margin of 32–34 percent. Of that somewhere between 5 and 7 percent is net profit. New England
- I also play hard to get. It makes people want to work with us more and it is how I weed out customers. If I miss an appointment and the customer doesn't get upset, it shows they are flexible and understanding. It's terrible, but my theory is that if we appear to be uninterested or not desperate, people are more likely to want to work with us. New England
- Right now I pay my crew between $22 and $34 per hour. What I charge varies. My minimum—on a big job, when there are loads of subs and materials—is in the high $50s. If it's a dinky job, I charge in the $90s. New England

TERMS & DEFINITIONS

Apprentice, Journeyman, Master. These classifications originated in European medieval trade guilds. Each trade (carpenter, plumber, etc.) recognized three ranks of workers. Although not common in America, there are trades in which some version of this system is still in use.

Apprentice is trained in a classroom and on the job in order to become eligible to take the journeyman's examination.

Journeyman is skilled in the trade and successfully completed the apprenticeship qualifications, earning their license through supervised experience, classroom work, and having passed an examination. Journeymen are considered competent and authorized to work in their field as fully qualified employees but may not own a company.

Master or Master Craftsman has mastery in their trade and may own a business and employ apprentices and journeymen.

BIA, Building Industry Association Remodelers Council, is affiliated with the National Association of Home Builders. The BIA represents and promotes the home building industry in order to benefit and serve its members and the community.

Bid, competitive bid, often called simply **bidding**, is a process in which general contractors, trades, or specialty firms are asked to submit proposals stating what they would charge to construct a project based on the job documents, which may consist of specs for a single item or a hundred pages of detail. These documents serve as the sole source of information, thus (in theory) ensuring that each bidder's estimate is developed using the same information. The client then chooses among the bidders, and the parties sign a contract.[1] While nearly every job requires an estimate, only some are put out for competitive bid.

Boilerplate is the text in a contract that covers most situations without need for revision and is generally used without modification from contract to contract.

Building Energy Bottom Lines Network (BLN), is a business development program that uses the peer-to-peer coaching model and is open only to NESEA^ members. BLN is designed to help member businesses build stronger organizations through triple-bottom-line (TBL) practice, a way of thinking and operating that assigns equal weight to "People, Planet, and Profits." Regional peer group networks meet several times a year with support from an experienced facilitator in order to help each other build organizational ability.

Business Networks, based in Eugene, Oregon, is a social networking organization that provides intensive business training for contractors and other small business owners through group workshops in order to further each others' business education.

Building science is the analysis of physical phenomena affecting buildings, for example, the study of indoor thermal, acoustic, and light environments, air quality, and resource use, including energy and building material use. During the design process, building science is used to improve and optimize building performance.

Buying a job means collecting bids for material and subs and negotiating the best price and quality, along with an agreement to work within the schedule provided.

Cash flow is the movement of money in and out of a business; income brings it in, payments send it out. see *EOB*, Money, pp. 238-250

---

1   This is the simple version. Depending on the size of the job, there are many variations on how work is contracted. See "Ways Jobs Are Contracted" in the estimating section of *The Elements of Building*.

Certified Public Accountant (CPA) is an accountant who has passed a series of exams administered by the American Institute of CPAs and is licensed by the state in which he works; all CPAs are accountants, not all accountants are CPAs.

Change orders (CO) detail and record job modifications made during construction, and they legally alter the construction contract when signed by all parties.

Computer numerical control (CNC) is the automated control of machining equipment (drills, boring tools, lathes) by means of a computer. A CNC machine follows programmed instructions to alter a blank piece of material (metal, plastic, wood, ceramic, or composite) according to precise specifications and without a manual operator.

Computer-aided design (CAD) uses computers to aid in the creation, modification, analysis, of a design. CAD software is used to increase the productivity of the designer.

Construction indexes are classification systems used to organize construction data, including specifications, estimates, and schedules. Indexes are divided into headings, subheadings, and line items, and arranged sequentially by number, in the order that the work is performed

Construction Specifications Institute's (CSI) Master Format (MF) is a standard construction index for commercial building projects in the U.S. and Canada, with its primary purpose to organize specifications and cost information.

Contract is a signed document, enforceable by law, between named parties—owner, general contractor, and subcontractors—creating obligations and detailing the rights, responsibilities, and relationship of the parties. The word **contract** is sometimes used more broadly to include all job documents.

Cost plus a fix fee means the contractor adds his agreed-to overhead and profit figures to the actual cost of construction—labor, subs, materials, setup, permits, fees, and so on—and that is what the client pays. see *EOB*, Types & Parts of Estimates, p. 202

Design/build, when one company designs and builds a project, as opposed to one company doing the design and another building it.

Employee Stock Ownership Plan (ESOP) in which a company's capital stock is bought by its employees and the company's ownership transfers to them.

ENERGY STAR is a program run by the U.S. Environmental Protection Agency and U.S. Department of Energy that promotes energy efficiency. The program provides information on the energy consumption of products and devices using standardized methods.

Fine Homebuilding is a monthly residential trade magazine.

Fixed-price (FP) or fixed-bid contracts, also called flat fee, lump-sum, or stipulated-sum, provide for a fixed amount of money to do the work—arrived at through a competitive bid or a negotiated contract—with the fixed price being adjusted up or down through the use of change orders.

General Contractor (GC), a company that has the primary contract on a project and is charged with getting the work done as detailed on the plans and specifications. GC's generally have employees working on the job along with subcontracting trades such as electrical, plumbing, and masonry.

Heating, ventilation, and air conditioning, (HVAC), is the technology of indoor environmental control. Its goal is to provide thermal comfort and acceptable indoor air quality. HVAC system design is a subdiscipline of mechanical engineering, based on the principles of thermodynamics, fluid mechanics and heat transfer.

Indemnification, the act or process of indemnifying, preserving, or securing against loss, damage, or penalty (as with insurance). The reimbursement of loss, damage, or penalty.

Job costing (also **job report, job cost**) is developed through your accounting system and tracks income and cost by job category (excavation, framing, etc.) and line items (site clearing, grading, 2x6s, nails, sheathing, etc.), providing an accurate breakdown of actual—from the field—labor, material, and sub costs for each task. When these categories and line items are compared with the original estimate, you'll know how accurate the original was, and with this information you can adjust the estimating database to improve future estimates. The more accurate your job costing system, the more accurate your estimates will be.

Journal of Light Construction (JLC) is a monthly residential trade magazine. *JLC* began as *New England Builder*.

Labor burden is the cost—above an employee's salary—that a company pays for each person on their payroll. These costs include benefits a company must or chooses to pay, such as payroll taxes (state/federal taxes, unemployment, and Social Security are a few examples), pension costs, health insurance, dental insurance, vacation, sick leave, and any other benefits provided by a company.

Leadership in Energy and Environmental Design (LEED) is a green building certification program used worldwide. Developed by the nonprofit U.S. Green Building Council (USGBC), it includes a set of rating systems for the design, construction, operation, and maintenance of green buildings, homes, and neighborhoods, which aims to help building owners and operators be environmentally responsible and use resources efficiently. www.usgbc.org

Line item estimates break work into its smallest parts, naming and pricing each item (within reason; not counting nails or linear feet of caulk).

National Association of Home Builders, NAHB represents the largest network of craftsmen, innovators, and problem solvers dedicated to building and enriching communities. www.nahb.org

National Association of the Remodeling Industry, NARI is the medium for business development, a platform for advocacy, and the principal source for industry intelligence. www.nari.org

Northeast Sustainable Energy Association, NESEA is a nonprofit organization that motivates people to learn about and ask for the adoption of sustainable energy processes and sources. NESEA connects ideas about whole system thinking and integrated design to people who can assimilate these ideas in the economy. https://nesea.org/

Preconstruction services or **Preconstruction phase** is the time allowed to plan a project before construction begins and includes the overall planning, coordination, and control of a project, from inception to completion. Its aim is to produce a functionally and financially viable project, and accurate estimates are vital in that process.

Production building, the construction of many similar homes on large tracts of land that have been subdivided into lots. It is often referred to with derision as tract housing or cookie-cutter housing.

Punch list is a list of minor touchup and repair items required to complete a project. The lists are developed as the project nears completion and the final punch list is often completed after the space is occupied. Many builders will say that completing the final punch list is the most difficult part of a job.

Retainage or retained funds is a percentage, generally from 2 to 20 percent, of the total contract amount retained or withheld from each construction draw as it is paid by the client. Retainage is paid when the job is completely finished. In EOB, See pp. 277-8 for notes on retainage in residential construction.

Scope-of-work (scope) or **project scope** provides a broad summary of the work with the specifications and blueprints providing the details. The terms scope-of-work and specifications are sometimes used interchangeably.

Splinter Group was a builder's organization formed in the early 1980s in the San Francisco Bay Area, which did organically what is now referred to as peer-to-peer learning. Deva Rajan, Steve Nicholls, and David Gerstel were involved in establishing and maintaining the group.

Specifications (specs) are the written requirements giving depth and detail to the materials, products, procedures, systems, and services required to build a project. On small projects, specs are generally included in the contract. On larger ones, they are found on the blueprints or in a separate text document. Specs for residential work are produced by tradesmen, subcontractors, builders, design-build or design firms, and engineers.

Speculative home building (spec building) involves buying land and building homes in advance of having them sold, gambling that there will be demand for the finished product.

The American Institute of Architects (AIA) is an organization for architects in the United States offering education, government advocacy, community redevelopment, and public outreach.

Time & Material (T&M) contracts, also called **labor & material contracts**—as opposed to fixed-price^ contracts—are contracts where the builder adds overhead, profit, and labor burden^ to the tradesmen's hourly rate and a predetermined percentage to the cost of material and subs, and the client is charged for everything required to complete the project.

Unit cost breaks a job into parts—linear foot, square foot, square yard, per square (roofing), cubic yard (excavation), assemblies, or each (a 2x4 or a bathtub, for example)—and assigns a cost to each item.

Value engineering is the process by which the contractor, engineer, and designer offer cost-saving suggestions and construction alternatives as the project develops, in an effort to reduce construction costs and to build as efficiently as possible.

Window buck is a square or rectangular box, usually made out of metal, that is installed within a concrete foundation or block wall into which a window is installed.

www.ingramcontent.com/pod-product-compliance
Lightning Source LLC
Chambersburg PA
CBHW020415010526
44118CB00010B/267